THE ROOTS *of* DEMOCRACY

TWAYNE'S
AMERICAN THOUGHT
AND CULTURE SERIES

Lewis Perry, General Editor

THE ROOTS *of* DEMOCRACY

American Thought and Culture, 1760–1800

ROBERT E. SHALHOPE

Twayne Publishers • *Boston*
A Division of G. K. Hall & Co.

Copyright 1990 by Robert E. Shalhope.
All rights reserved.
Published by Twayne Publishers
A division of G. K. Hall & Co.
70 Lincoln Street, Boston, Massachusetts 02111

Copyediting supervised by Barbara Sutton.
Book design by Janet Z. Reynolds.
Book production by Gabrielle B. McDonald.
Typeset in Janson by Compset, Inc., Beverly, Massachusetts.

Printed on permanent/durable acid-free paper
and bound in the United States of America.

Library of Congress Cataloging-in-Publication Data

Shalhope, Robert E., 1941–
    The roots of democracy : American thought and culture, 1760–1800 /
  Robert E. Shalhope.
        p.   cm. — (Twayne's American thought and culture series)
    Bibliography: p.
    Includes index.
    ISBN 0-8057-9051-9 (alk. paper).—ISBN 0-8057-9056-X (pbk. : alk. paper)
    1. Political science—United States—History—18th century.   2. Political
culture—United States—History—18th century.   3. United States—
Civilization—To 1783.   4. United States—Civilization—1783–1865.   I. Title.
II. Series.
JA84.U5S49   1990
973—dc20   89-15455
                                                                              CIP

To Adelaide

Contents

About the Author

Robert E. Shalhope received his B.A. from DePauw University and his M.A. and Ph.D. degrees from the University of Missouri. Since receiving his Ph.D., Shalhope has taught at the University of Oklahoma, where he is professor of history. A specialist in the political culture of Revolutionary and early national American society, Shalhope is the author of *John Taylor of Caroline: Pastoral Republican*, 1980; "Toward a Republican Synthesis: The Emergence of an Understanding of Republicanism in American Historiography" (*William and Mary Quarterly*, 1972); "Thomas Jefferson's Republicanism and Antebellum Southern Thought" (*Journal of Southern History*, 1976); "Republicanism and Early American Historiography" (*William and Mary Quarterly*, 1982); "The Ideological Origins of the Second Amendment" (*Journal of American History*, 1982); and "The Armed Citizen in the Early Republic" (*Law and Contemporary Problems*, 1986). Shalhope and his wife, Emma, currently reside in Cambridge, Massachusetts, where he is a fellow at the Charles Warren Center for Studies in American History, Harvard University.

Foreword

The American Thought and Culture Series surveys intellectual and cultural history from America's colonial origins to the present. The time is auspicious for such an extensive survey because scholars have carried out so much pathbreaking work in this field in recent years. The volumes in the series reflect that scholarship, as well as valuable earlier studies. The authors also present the results of their own research and offer original interpretations. The goal is to bring together books that are readable and well informed and that stand on their own as introductions to significant periods in American thought and culture. There is no attempt to establish a single interpretation of all of America's past; the diversity, conflict, and change that are features of the American experience would frustrate any such attempt. The authors can, however, explore issues of critical importance in each period while identifying those of recurrent or lasting importance.

As these volumes appear, the culture and the intellectual life of the United States are subjects of heated debate. While prominent figures summon citizens back to an endangered "common culture," some critics dismiss the very idea of culture—let alone American culture—as elitist and arbitrary. The questions asked in these volumes have direct relevance to that debate, which concerns history but too often proceeds in historical ignorance. How did leading intellectuals view their relation to America, and how did their countrymen regard them? Did they participate in international movements? What were the links and tensions between high culture and popular culture? While discussing influential works, creative individuals, and major institutions, the authors of the books in this series place intellectual and cultural history in the larger context of American society.

In this volume on the late eighteenth century Robert Shalhope surveys events and conflicts of long-lasting consequence. He shows how colonists who thought they were building a culture comparable to England's found themselves caught up in revolution and how revolutionaries who cherished visions of republican stability were unable to stifle tendencies leading toward a democratic culture. In addition to political thought, he analyzes developments in law, religion, art, literature, and education, and he asks how the cultural changes of a revolutionary era affected women, Indians, artisans, and slaves. Readers will find this book an accessible guide to a key period in the development of American culture.

Lewis Perry

Preface

American society underwent a tremendous transformation in cultural and intellectual life between 1760 and the 1840s. That transformation has variously been described as the opening of American society, the shift from Enlightenment rationalism to romantic democracy, or the democratization of the American mind. While scholars agree that the years 1760 to 1800 comprise the fertile seedbed within which the forces that formed America into a modern democracy took shape, nevertheless this critical era has been the source of tremendous interpretative disagreement among them.

Over the past several decades historians have attempted to explain American thought and culture during the Revolutionary and early national years principally through the perspectives of classical republicanism or liberalism. Advocates of the former view have insisted that Americans adhered to a secularized form of the traditional values of Puritanism. Their watchword was virtue, or the willingness of the individual to subordinate private interests for the good of the community. Thus, American republicanism meant maintaining public and private virtue, social solidarity, and vigilance against the corrupting effects of power and the scramble for wealth. Adherents of the second interpretation, that of liberalism, have maintained that Americans in this era manifested aggressive individualism, optimistic materialism, and pragmatic interest group politics. For them John Locke's liberal concept of possessive individualism, not Machiavelli's republican advocacy of civic humanism, best explains American thought and behavior during the years 1760–1800.

This disagreement among historians threatens to cloud our understanding of the formative years of our nation's past. Certainly Americans living in these years never felt themselves confronted by two sharply contrasting modes of thought—liberalism or republicanism—or that they had some obligation to choose between Locke's modern ideas and Machiavelli's more traditional ones. Such modes of thought are the creation of recent scholars, and when historians insist upon forcing individuals or groups from the past into a particular intellectual mold, they distort our ability to reconstruct that past in a way that would be recognizable to people of the time who actually experienced it. Americans living in the late eighteenth century could, quite unself-consciously, believe simultaneously in the promotion of their own individual socioeconomic and political prospects, as well as in the distinct possibility that their liberty might be endangered by corrupt forces of power within their governments. By this time classical republican traditions and modern social, economic, and political behavior had blended so thoroughly and so imperceptibly that efforts by historians to force historical participants into one or another static frame of mind simply create a historical anachronism.

Historians dealing with American culture and thought in the last half of the eighteenth century have not yet created a conceptual framework that enables them to convey the complex blending of traditional and modern attitudes and behavioral patterns that characterize the era. Here the anthropologist's conception of a "marginal" or "liminal" state of transition provides useful insights. Individuals and groups find themselves separated from the fixed cultural standfasts of an earlier time, but they have not yet created new ones appropriate to their rapidly changing environment. Some cling desperately to outmoded customs of the past, while others graft new modes of thought and behavior to traditional assumptions in ways that seem to translate their experiences into meaningful cultural patterns. The result is a time of extreme flux and uncertainty—a struggle for predominance between competing cultural forces.

This is what occurred within America between 1760 and 1800, a time when many Americans began to draw away from the cultural norms that had defined their earlier society—hierarchically structured, gentry dominated, and committed to the ideal of organic unity under the leadership of gentlemen. By midcentury, however, these aristocratic hierarchies, never able to sink roots deeply into the New World environment, began to disintegrate under the pressure of long-developing demographic, economic, and ideological forces. Rather than halting such developments, the Revolution and republicanism intensified them. Republicanism's emphasis upon equality encouraged ordinary, obscure men to challenge all manifestations of authority and eminence within society. As a result distinctions of all sorts that had been accepted as a matter of course prior to the Revolution came under severe attack. In addition the burgeoning economic opportunities fostered by the Revolution transformed social mobility from a carefully measured upward movement that might be approved by staid republicans into a mad scramble. Thousands of Americans previously habituated to a humble status in life became caught up in the exhilarating possibilities of material advancement and refused to brook any interference with their opportunities for personal gain. Rather than instilling a regard for moderation, communal good order, and deference to natural authority, republicanism seemed to be breeding a utilitarian, materialistic individualism. Paradoxically, then, republicanism itself spawned the behavior that historians recognize as liberal, and few individuals living at the time could or would have distinguished between two separate schools of thought.

The turmoil of the Revolutionary years created a crisis of confidence in an ordered, hierarchical society that gave rise to widespread demands for fundamental changes in law, politics, religion, and the social order itself. From the time of the Revolution through the ascendancy of Thomas Jefferson to the presidency in 1801, an indigenous cultural movement arose within American society that joined those mistrustful of power with vast numbers of traditionally powerless people in a common attempt to break down the cultural hegemony of a genteel elite. The latter, clinging fiercely to earlier cultural values, resisted with all its might. Out of this tension between supporters and opponents of hierarchy arose a complex cultural phenomenon that historians are just beginning to decipher: a vast number of people on a wide variety of fronts—social, political, educational, religious, economic—began to challenge the eminence of a gentlemanly few. Some did this quite as a matter of course in their day-to-day acitivities; others deliberately spoke, wrote, or otherwise actively organized against the power of mediating elites, against social distinctions of every sort, against any obligation that did not result from purely voluntary consent. Here were the roots of the American democratic spirit that would transform American society throughout the nineteenth century.

This book is an interpretative synthesis; it attempts to integrate the work of many scholars in such a manner as to provide clarity and meaning to American thought and culture in the years 1760–1800. It assumes that the study of culture explores primarily systems of meaning. That is, the analysis of culture is the examination of widely shared modes of assessing and responding to the world—integral worldviews—that give meaning to the lives of those who share such perceptions. It further assumes that cultural assumptions cannot be analyzed as if they existed in a vacuum. Therefore this study makes every attempt not only to explicate cultural assumtions but to examine as closely as possible their history, the society in which they flourished, and the individual or group needs that they satisfied or failed to satisfy.

Acknowledgments

I owe a great deal to institutions and individuals; without their help this book would have been far more difficult and much less pleasurable to write. I am grateful to the Research Council of the University of Oklahoma and to the National Endowment for the Humanities for summer fellowships that afforded me free time to write. In addition, a sabbatical leave provided by the University of Oklahoma helped immeasureably. Lewis Perry read several drafts of my work and his trenchant comments aided considerably in sharpening my thoughts. Athenaide Dallet's careful editorial efforts helped to clarify my ideas and to tighten their presentation. I thank them both. I would also like to express my appreciation to James T. Kloppenberg. I benefitted greatly from his perceptive reading of the manuscript. As always my colleague David Levy gave generously of his time, talent and wit to improve the quality of my work. He is a true scholar and I thank him for his help and his friendship. I am also thankful to Martha Penisten for her good cheer and incredible talents as a typist-editor. My deepest debt is to my wife, Emma. I am grateful to her for reading the manuscript and sharing her thoughts with me on long walks during a beautiful autumn on the Vineyard. Most of all I am thankful for her abiding love.

Chronology

1763 Close of the French and Indian War.

1764 Sugar and Currency acts passed.

1765 Stamp Act passed; urban rioting breaks out. Baptists revolt against the gentry in Virginia.

1766 Land riots erupt along the Hudson River in New York. Religious strife tears at Concord, Massachusetts.

1767 Townshend Duties passed.

1770 John Trumbull delivers his commencement address, "An Essay on the Uses and Advantages of the Fine Arts." William Billings publishes his *The New-England Psalm-Singer*. The Green Mountain Boys appear on the New Hampshire Grants. The Regulators emerge in North Carolina.

1771 Benjamin West unveils his *Death of General Wolfe*. Hugh Henry Brackenridge and Philip Freneau deliver at the Princeton commencement "A Poem on the Rising Glory of America."

1773 East India Tea Act passed. Phillis Wheatley publishes *Poems on Various Subjects, Religious and Moral*.

1774 James Burgh publishes *Political Disquisitions*.

1775 Coercive Acts passed. Fighting breaks out at Lexington and Concord.

1776 Second Continental Congress calls for the formation of new governments in the various colonies. Declaration of Independence. Tom

Paine publishes *Common Sense*. John Adams publishes *Thoughts on Government*. "The People the Best Governors" published. Adam Smith publishes *Inquiry into the Nature and Causes of the Wealth of Nations*. John Trumbull publishes *M'Fingal*.

1778   William Billings publishes *The Singing Master's Assistant*. Andrew Law publishes *Select Harmony*.

1779   Thomas Jefferson presents his bill for the "More General Discussion of Knowledge" to the Virginia Assembly.

1780   American Academy of Arts and Sciences formed in Boston.

1781   Articles of Confederation ratified.

1782   Second edition of John Trumbull's *M'Fingal* appears. Harvard Medical School founded.

1783   Peace of Paris formally ends the Revolutionary War.

1784   William Thompson affair erupts in Charleston, South Carolina.

1785   Timothy Dwight publishes his epic poem, *The Conquest of Canaan*. The American Company of players returns to New York City.

1786   *Columbian Magazine* begins publication. David Humphreys publishes his epic, *Poem, on the Happiness of America: Addressed to the Citizens of the United States*. John Trumbull unveils his *The Death of General Warren at the Battle of Bunker Hill 17, June, 1775*. Benjamin Austin publishes his "Observations on the Pernicious Practices of the Law." Shays' Rebellion breaks out in western Massachusetts. The Connecticut Wits publish *The Anarchiad*. Peale's Museum opens in Philadelphia.

1787   Matthew Carey begins publication of *American Museum*. Royall Tyler's *The Contrast* opens at the John Street Theater in New York City. Joel Barlow publishes his epic poem *Vision of Columbus*. The College of Physicians of Philadelphia opens. The Constitution is drafted at the Philadelphia convention. *The Federalist* essays begin to appear. Anti-Federalist opposition to the Constitution emerges.

1788   Noah Webster publishes his essay "On the Education of Youth in America." Jonathan Jackson publishes his *Thoughts upon the Political Situation*.

1790   Secretary of the Treasury Alexander Hamilton offers the first of his series of reports on fiscal policy to Congress.

1791   Tom Paine publishes *The Rights of Man*. George Logan publishes *Letters Addressed to the Yeomanry of the United States*.

1792   Joel Barlow's *Advice to the Privileged Orders in the Several States of Europe* appears. Hugh Henry Brackenridge publishes *Modern Chivalry*.

1793   Democratic-Republican societies begin to appear. Nathaniel Chipman publishes his *Dissertation on the Act Adopting the Common and Statue Law of England*. William Bradford publishes his *An Enquiry into How Far the Punishment of Death Is Necessary in Philadelphia*.

1794   John Taylor of Caroline publishes *An Enquiry into the Principles and Tendency of Certain Public Measures*. The Whiskey Rebellion breaks out in western Pennsylvania. William Findley publishes *A Review of the Revenue System adopted by the First Congress under the Federal Constitution*.

1795   Jay's Treaty ratified.

1798   Charles Brockden Brown publishes *Wieland; or, The Transformation*. William Dunlap's play, *Andre*, opens in New York City. The Alien and Sedition Laws are passed. Thomas Cooper publishes *Political Arithmetic*. William Lyon publishes the magazine, *Scourge of Aristocracy*, while in jail in Vermont.

1799   Charles Brockden Brown publishes *Arthus Mervyn; or, Memoirs of the Year 1793* and *Edgar Huntley; or, Memoirs of a Sleep-Walker*. Fries Rebellion breaks out in eastern Pennsylvania. Joseph Priestley publishes *Letters to the Inhabitants of Northumberland*.

1800   Thomas Jefferson is elected president.

one

The Old Order in America

By the close of the French and Indian War (1756–63), Britain's North American colonies had, in many ways, taken on the appearance of the home culture. This was particularly true in the more mature areas of each colony where, after several generations, a recognizable, reasonably stable elite had emerged that strove mightily to reproduce English society in the provinces. Depending upon their particular locales, colonial elites attempted to recreate English country life or the metropolitan atmosphere of London.

The English Model

The traditional English culture so admired by the American gentry rested on a patronage society of personal influence and dependent relationships that sustained a carefully ordered hierarchical world. This society consisted of a pyramidal structure of subtly arranged degrees or ranks running from the king, royal officials, and nobles at the pinnacle to bound laborers at the base. Society was held together by vertical lines of interest that connected men and women who had a precise, almost intuitive knowledge of their relationships to those directly above and below them. A social nexus based on trust, or friendship, bonded the patron-client links in the vertical chains of society. Only those at or near the top of the social order had more than a vague awareness of any connection with others of their station. Consequently the sole horizontal cleavage in the old order separated the gentry from commoners. "Gentlemen"—a sociological as much as an economic cachet—incorporated not only the nobility and the gentry but clergymen, physicians, and

1

barristers. It did not, however, always include the dissenting minister, the schoolmaster, the apothecary, or the solicitor; overseas merchants, but not inland traders, gained access to privileged status, as did amateur authors, painters, musicians, and sculptors. Professional artists had little, if any, claim to gentility.

Each place in the social hierarchy carried with it certain unquestioned obligations and responsibilities to ranks above and below. A myriad of visible signs proclaimed status. Speech, deportment, manners, and dress revealed station in society, as clearly as did liveried equipage, the size and splendor of the home, and the quantity and quality of food consumed by the household. The nobility displayed distinctive badges and honors of place, the gentry exhibited coats of arms, and those of the middle ranks, lower orders, and the laboring poor wore clothing appropriate to their position. Charity schoolchildren had "clothes of the coarsest kind, and of the plainest form, and thus are sufficiently distinguished from children of the better rank, and they ought to be so distinguished."[1] Stylized behavior bespoke a formalized social consciousness.

In such a culture the patronage and personal authority wielded by those of property and standing counted for everything. Their influence pervaded English society and affected governmental appointments, judicial positions, military commissions, land grants, and commercial contracts. The lines of interest and dependency that emanated from personal influence connected social relations in many ways: masters and servants, creditors and debtors, fathers and children, as well as landowners and tenants. Advancement within the hierarchy resulted not from hard work and thrift but from gaining the favor or friendship of some individual of authority and position. Eminence exerted its greatest influence over the political life of the nation; here the vertical lines of patronage and friendship most clearly converged to create a highly personal structure of politics characterized by the private machinations of powerful men and their followers rather than by cohesive political parties. England's political world in the eighteenth century mirrored the ascriptive society of which it was an integral part.

An American Gentry

By mid-eighteenth century the British gentlemen's emphasis on order and hierarchy had permeated American attitudes as well. Even William Livingston's *Independent Reflector*, the bête-noir of privilege in New York, assumed the importance of recognizing *just* distinctions:

The great Variety of Powers, Characters and Conditions, so obvious in Human Life, is an illustrious Proof of the benignity and Wisdom of the Supreme Governor of the

Universe. From this vast Diversity naturally result Superiority and Pre-eminence in some, and Dependence and subjection in others. To this *natural* Difference of Character, Society has introduced the additional Distinction of a political Disparity, by conferring on various of its Members, a Variety of Honours and Privileges in a gradual Subordination from the chief Magistrate, to the least dignified of his Subjects. Hence we owe a becoming Regard to those who are advanced by the Wisdom of the Common Wealth, in Proportion to their Elevation, unless they forfeit it by their Demirit.[2]

If such attitudes characterized the social beliefs of a colonial radical, they comprised unquestioned truths in the minds of the rich and successful members of the American gentry and penetrated far deeper into colonial culture. When Rev. Devereaux Jarratt recalled his childhood in Virginia in the 1730s and 1740s, he emphasized the simple nature of his family's existence. Raised by industrious, plain, pious people who believed that the family's food and raiment should reflect their modest life, Jarratt recollected that his parents never allowed tea or coffee in their house. Only the "richer sort" should enjoy such luxurious items. Jarratt recalled that "to such people I had no access. We were accustomed to look upon, what were called gentle folks, as beings of a superior order." "For my part," he added, "I was quite shy of them, and kept off at a humble distance. A periwig, in those days, was a distinguishing badge of gentle folk—and when I saw a man riding the road, near our house, with a wig on, it would so alarm my fears, and give me such a disagreeable feeling, that, I dare say, I would run off, as for my life." For an experience to have left so indelible an imprint upon Jarratt's mind after some fifty years, social distinctions must have existed as felt realities, not social pretensions. Indeed Jarratt exclaimed that "such ideas of the difference between gentle and simple, were I believe, universal among all of my rank and age."[3]

The emergence of a native American gentry that saw colonial society divided into "gentle" and "simple" folk spawned a distinctive pattern of social attitudes that set families of wealth, eminence, and authority off from the rest of their countrymen. Two interrelated conceptions—organicism and the chain of being—underlay the worldview of the elite. Organicism drew an analogy between society and the human body; both comprised complex, interrelated unities composed of indispensable though distinct parts. The chain of being conceived of the whole universe as organized by God into hierarchical orders of subtly arranged ranks of beings, each with a specific function and allotment of virtue. The images associated with these two conceptions combined to form a powerful shaping influence on the way in which the gentry perceived their society. Out of these beliefs emerged a system of values preeminently based on order.

Viewing their society as an organic whole, distinct from and greater than the sum of its individual parts, the gentry stressed the harmony and unity of the people. The family, the church, the community, and the political state

3

bound individuals together and linked them to the natural world of which they were an integral part. The good society the gentry envisioned consisted of a cohesive social order in which each individual knew his or her proper sphere, moved contentedly within it, observed and respected social distinctions, performed the social functions allotted to that station diligently and faithfully, and practiced the individual values of thrift, humility, moderation, and deference. Above all else individuals must willingly subordinate private interests to the larger communal good.

To achieve such cohesion, the people required a proper model. In the mind of the elite, the gentleman performed this vital role. Greatness of soul characterized his attitude toward public honors and offices; the public's greatest good stood foremost among his concerns. Societies should foster and respect those gentlemen in their midst, for they alone had the natural capacity and the leisure to be fully virtuous. Their virtue would permeate the entire community and thus ensure harmony, order, and well-being.

Such beliefs fostered a presumption of superiority that formed the quintessence of gentility in the American colonies. Assuming themselves worthy of their social eminence, wealth, and political influence, the genteel class exuded an easy confidence that the perpetuation of their exalted station from generation to generation remained essential to the well-being of their society. They felt no anxiety about their social identities. Instead they assumed that ordinary folk would naturally respect and follow them simply by virtue of the fact that they had what commoners did not: character, education, rational minds. Respect for these virtues was the vital element that bound society together.

Convinced of their natural superiority, members of the gentry addressed themselves in their letters, speeches, newspaper articles, and political pamphlets solely to the rational and enlightened portion of the populace.[4] Gentle folk would bring commoners along by means of the subtle lines of personal and social authority—"friendship"—that tied the society together. The perception that intellectual activities involved only a small fraternity or "republic of letters" affected the literary style of the gentry. Obscure historical citations, extensive Latin quotations, and classical references of all kinds characterized their literary efforts. These aristocrats, reveling in polite erudition, filled their speeches and essays with citations from Plutarch, Aristotle, Plato, Montesquieu, Pufendorf, and Rousseau. Their frequent resort to a highly personal form of invective designed to impugn an opponent's reputation as a gentleman and their constant use of satire depended on an intelligent audience capable of discerning proper standards of behavior.

Gentlemen attempted to persuade other gentlemen and used a particular form of rhetoric to achieve that end. The emergence of their distinctive rhetorical style reflected their attempt to set "gentle" people off from "simple" folk. Asserting the natural hierarchy of the chain of being, they revealed through their language a sense of distance from ordinary individuals as well as a superiority to them, The conversations of the elite referred reverently to rationality, merit, virtue, and the common good and led naturally to invidious contrasts between the "better sort" and the "common people," "inferior orders," or the "rabble." Such terms betrayed a certain social arrogance and, from time to time, outright contempt for those who lacked gentility. "When I mention the public," John Randolph declared in 1774, "I mean to include only the rational part of it. The ignorant vulgar are as unfit to judge of the modes, as they are unable to manage the reins of government."[5] While few others were as candid as Randolph, fewer still would bear any encroachments upon their prerogatives. Consequently their attitude toward ordinary men and women depended entirely upon the behavior of the latter. If compliant, common folk were regarded as sober, humble individuals of solid common sense, if tumultuous or uncooperative, they became an "unthinking rabble," ruled by passion rather than reason.

The American gentry, then, like their British counterparts, assumed authority to be the natural appendage of affluence and superiority. They anticipated being called to govern at all levels of colonial society. By and large, particularly in the more settled areas, this was indeed the case. Town fathers or local patriarchs maintained control of affairs in small communities, while individuals distinguished by family, wealth, education, and a bearing that exacted the obeisance of others assumed power at the provincial level. The gentry accepted their prominence and power as their just due. Their confidence emanated from their ease with power and authority, whether exercised by themselves or by others. From childhood, the genteel looked upon authority as benign and supportive of, rather than hostile to, their personal needs and interests. This sense of security provided them with the self-assurance to defer to authorities placed over them while at the same time retaining the freedom to govern those below.

The easy assurance the gentry felt toward authority stemmed in large part from their deep regard for institutions. As men intimately involved in the institutions of central importance in their society, they knew from personal experience that these were not abstractions to be feared but rather known realities essential to the good order of the community. In addition, the various institutions of their society offered the means by which the gentry exercised the authority necessary to reinforce their sense of eminence and superiority.

The ease with which so many of the genteel folk assumed this sense of superiority resulted from extensive involvement in the commercial, political, agricultural, and social affairs of the larger world. The flourishing Atlantic trade brought large concentrations of new wealth to the colonies and involved a good many of the gentry in affairs that often extended beyond their local community to the provincial level or even to distant parts of the British Empire, and thus many of the gentry assumed a cosmopolitanism. Numerous merchants became intent upon expanding their overseas trade and obtaining the flexibility to operate in a marketing climate free of restraints on entrepreneurial activity. As a result their economic decisions increasingly responded to the dictates of the invisible laws of an international marketplace rather than traditional communal needs. Such an open espousal of the world of international trade and capitalist relations made these gentry appear to be "modernizers," and yet they remained profoundly conservative in their social philosophy.

Like the increasingly orderly, affluent, and predictable middle and upper classes in Europe, genteel Americans took as their own the moderate Enlightenment of Britain in the first half of the eighteenth century.[6] Most of the American gentry encountered the Enlightenment more as a mood or a style than a fixed set of intellectual principles. They admired the order, moderation, and compromise of English society; the balance of forces seen in the Newtonian cosmos seemingly had been recapitulated in British institutions. The Glorious Revolution of 1688 had achieved a miraculous equilibrium: government had been framed to fit man's mixed nature—a precarious balance between passion and reason, public spirit and the lust for power—just as the orbits of the planets were controlled by mutual attraction and repulsion. The primary purpose of the British constitution became the protection of liberty, which included control not only of one's person but one's property as well. The ideas of the moderate Enlightenment appealed to an Anglo-American world of comfort, prosperity, and success rather than one inhabited by the frustrated, resentful, or unsuccessful.

Toward an Anglicized Culture

Just as the elite in America absorbed the thought patterns of the English gentility, so too did its members attempt to recreate European cultural standards. In many ways eighteenth-century America underwent a process of Anglicization: the rich became richer, their style of life more lavish, and their influence over economic and social affairs more pervasive. Moneyed families built handsome neoclassical townhouses, filled them with the costliest and most beautiful furnishings in the latest English mode, and complemented them with lavish formal gardens. They acquired country estates, self-consciously adopted the most recent English style in literature and clothing, dabbled in letters, formed social clubs, and even left the traditional religion of their family for the church of England. They imported expensive carriages, dressed their servants in livery, raised their children for the genteel life, and attempted to create family dynasties by calculated intermarriages among themselves.

The English government, too, encouraged Anglicization. Its officials discussed plans for an American bishopric, as well as schemes to sire a provincial nobility. In addition, the Anglo-French wars brought colonists into close contact with the mother culture through substantial military contracts and the presence of professional soldiers. In response to the increasing importance of colonial markets and trade, the British posted many more officials in the American provinces. Consequently royal governors, customs officials, naval officers, and high-ranking army personnel offered the refined tastes that upper-class colonists so desired. Their wives and daughters served as fashion plates for the provincial ladies, who, along with their husbands, struggled to create an outpost of English culture in the New World.

Genuine aristocrats, however, were rare. Only in New York did a true rentier class emerge. For the most part provincial leaders elsewhere were urban merchants, comfortable farmers, or slaveholding planters: a bourgeoisie enjoying an ample rather than a magnificent style of life.[7] The sober, self-reliant merchant and his attractive, competent spouse who sat for a John Singleton Copley portrait remained a far cry from the arrogant British officers and their languid ladies painted by Gainsborough. The spacious and elegant mansions of Philadelphia, the handsome townhouses of New York and Boston, and the commodious yet simply designed rural estates of Virginia bore no similarity to the palaces of British grandees.

No matter how Anglicized various segments of American society may have become, they were never Anglicized enough to satisfy the aspirations of the majority of the elite. By midcentury many individuals attempted to depart from their solid bourgeois origins and, as they moved, to shut off opportunities for others to follow. Some argued for the creation of an American aristocracy, a titled nobility that could provide the social stability and order necessary to create a true English society in the colonies. Others sought to control the sources of capital, credit, British commercial connections, and political influence that were rapidly becoming the keys to real success and opportunity. In nearly every province wealthy members of the elite controlled the upper houses of colonial assemblies, where they wielded power to gain extensive land grants for themselves as well as other lucrative favors from the government.

In the end, though, the gentry's greatest hope for a thorough Anglicization of their society lay with the extension of the monarchical culture of the home country to America. In England, in return for the king's protection of their personal safety and his preservation of their essential rights, the people pledged their fealty to the monarch. The emotional fabric of the protection-allegiance relationship, however, subordinated this mutual obligation to the familial images of tender father and affectionate children. For his part the king went far beyond his contractual obligations to defend his people against foreign invasions and to administer justice in his courts. His province included the entire well-being of his people—their food, their health, and their families. In return, the people yielded their allegiance, not out of interest or duty but out of the gratitude and love a child feels for its benevolent parent.

The social order that sustained this monarchical culture replicated the interdependent relationship between king and people downward through all levels of society until royal influence permeated even the lowest orders in the nation and the most distant points of the empire. Dependence defined this hierarchical relationship between superiors and inferiors. Such a relationship far exceeded deference, which characterized the respect owed by any and all persons to those of superior rank, with total strangers enjoying the same deferential treatment as familiar persons. By contrast, dependence defined a relationship between two particular individuals, not between groups or ranks of people. Dependence involved an award, a favor—office, land, a contract— granted by one person to another that created a mutually recognized debt or bond. Such a debt made the recipient materially dependent upon the patron; loss of favor meant loss of wealth and position. The bonds of dependency thus went far beyond simple respect for rank and eminence; they imposed a duty of unquestioning submission to the will of the benefactor.

Monarchical government did extend throughout the American colonies, where it drew its strength primarily from the cultural consciousness and consciences of the people. The forms and language of monarchy were so pervasive in the colonial atmosphere that they were a natural part of everyday life. Colonists celebrated royal birthdays and coronation anniversaries and constantly declared their loyalty and allegiance to the crown. The phrase "God save the King" echoed and reechoed throughout all ranks of colonists. As a result a moral force emerged that enabled the crown to rule in America with only minimal control of the courts and without the force of arms. Colonists respected regal authority day in and day out less out of fear of royal power than from both a genuine affection and an untroubled faith in the legitimacy of the king and his officials to govern.

Such faith grew out of a belief in a protection-allegiance covenant between the king and his people that pervaded the colonies in the language and practices of government at all levels. Governors' speeches, the public addresses of the legislatures, and petitions to the colonial assemblies articulated the familial relationship between a benevolent king and his loyal, dutiful subjects. Magnificence, too, played a role in the colonies. When debating governors' salaries, colonial legislators freely expressed their belief that governors must be able to sustain the "dignity" of their position. The governor's office represented regal power and required a measure of support commensurate with such an exalted station. The governor's salary must be ample not for his personal use but for the sake of the people whom he protected. Visible symbols of status and magnificence reinforced the bond between superiors extending their power and protection and inferiors who returned their loyalty and submission. In addition, royal governors constantly reminded colonial assemblies of the king's protection and favor. They claimed moral authority to govern from their position as representatives of the solicitous care the king felt for his people. On the other hand, those asking the assemblies for favors couched their petitions in the language of humble supplicants appealing for aid from their superiors.

A Different Society

The forms of monarchical culture permeated every level of government and society in the colonies: the presumption of a hierarchical social and political structure, the magnificence of office, the extension of protection by superiors to inferiors, and the latter's grateful submission in return for the rewards of this friendship. Yet the protection-allegiance formula did not exist in quite the same way in the colonies as it did in England. Indeed it took on subtle nuances of meaning for the colonists, who emphasized far more than did citizens of the mother country the ruler's obligation to protect the people and their rights. With this emphasis, the protection covenant itself offered a clear justification for resistance by the subject: if rulers failed to protect them, the ruled had every right to defend themselves.

That argument found its boldest articulation in the lower houses of the colonial assemblies, where a stress on the contractual nature of the covenant emerged from a colonial consciousness that expressed loyalty to the king while sanctioning unremitting opposition to his officials. In the assemblies, the popular side of provincial culture revealed itself. Legislators constantly stressed their defense of the rights of the people. The "people" came to symbolize popular rights, while the "king" represented allegiance and submission. However, the people were never set against the king; even in the wildest flights of political rhetoric, popular rights never stood in opposition to the principles of monarchy. On the contrary, opposition leaders in the assemblies upheld the king's primary role as protector of the people's rights. When they opposed royal government in the colonies, they did it as loyal subjects; they simply assumed the responsibility for upholding the king's promise to protect his people whenever they felt royal officials were misusing their prerogatives. Consequently the popular opponents of royal officials within the legislatures assumed the right—as protectors of the king's covenant with the people—to be forceful, contentious, and suspicious. Central to the actions of the colonial legislators were a deep suspicion of power and a fear of oppression. The accepted political wisdom of the day warned colonists that self-interest governed all human nature. A belief in the insatiable avarice of men in power and authority fed the assertive and litigious nature of legislators and fueled their half-century-long controversy with royal governors and other crown officials. In their minds, those with political authority would eventually abuse that power to serve their own selfish ends. Legislators therefore must hold officials strictly within colonial charters or provincial laws so as to protect the people's rights from encroachment by avaricious royal appointees.

This emphasis on the people's rights rather than their obligations sprang from a social structure quite different from the one that supported a monarchical culture in England, for, try as they might to Anglicize their society, the American elite could never enjoy complete success. A hierarchical order was not as strongly rooted or as rigidly structured in the colonies as it was in England. In America no doors were firmly closed. Men of recently acquired means aspired to the ruling oligarchy; middle-class merchants struggled to become gentry; farmers, shopkeepers, and artisans became assertive in the politics of the church as well as the state. Far more precariously grounded in a volatile economy than their English counterparts, American "aristocrats" were, as a result, much more bourgeois in nature. Forced to scramble for wealth, status, and signs of eminence, the American gentry always seemed more venal than the English squirearchy. The relative security and stability of the English hierarchy, with its titled nobility and rigid orders, eluded the American gentleman.

The personal influence that supported the vertical lines of dependency in England never became firmly entrenched in American culture. Militia companies elected their officers; congregations hired their ministers; and an unusually broad constituency elected a wide range of political officials. Relatively few landed tenants existed in the American colonies, and vast numbers of yeoman farmers asserted an extraordinary degree of political awareness and independence. Religious and ethnic groups multiplied throughout the colonies, and the outward thrust of thousands of migrants into wilderness areas shattered traditional communal bonds as well as lines of interest or patronage. Aggressive competition between individuals and groups, far exceeding that found in Europe, fed feelings of suspicion and jealousy. Consequently a wide range of privileges or monopolies—military contracts, licenses for taverns or ordinaries, mill sites—that made sense in the hierarchically structured patronage societies of Europe aroused suspicion and mistrust in America. Indeed such manifestations of influence, because of the frail nature of patronage or friendship in the colonies, appeared all the more arbitrary and unfair and thereby became increasingly vulnerable to challenges by numerous competitors.

Although each colony produced a ruling elite to whom ordinary folk normally deferred, this was not sufficent to support a monarchical culture. Deference did not mean dependence. Royal governors did everything in their power to surround themselves with dependent clients and to extend their influence throughout the colonial legislatures, but their efforts met with little success because English ministers retained the most important appointed positions within their own purview in order to create personal webs of dependency quite separate from those of the governor. Thus precious few positions remained to be filled by the governor. He could tie a small group of influential individuals to him—his council, major military officers, and justices of the superior courts—but these men had little if anything to offer to individuals in their own communities. The governor's lines of authority thus ended with those immediately around him. Since so many offices were elected rather than appointed, officials facing frequent elections became dependent on their constituents rather than the governor, and the political climate in the colonies further severed connections with the royal government by dooming the governor's toadies at the polls. Royal governors lacked the vertical lines of dependency essential to create an English-style society in America.

By and large, the same proved true for the native American elite. As the eighteenth century progressed, the distance between rich and poor in America increased, and the "aristocracy" expanded; whole new groups of wealthy merchants or great planters came into being. These powerful and wealthy men became the justices of the peace and the colonels of the militia in their local communities, with any number of small favors to dispense: they might license a tavern, ferry, or mill, grant small loans for minor undertakings, assist others with legal technicalities, provide occasional work for artisans or sons of neighbors. They might also confer social blessings or chastisements upon their neighbors: a tip of the hat to a tradesman, a dinner invitation to a lesser merchant, attendance at the funeral of a loyal servant, or a visit to the bedside of an artisan's sick child. But none of these gestures seemed sufficient to establish a network of dependency. The freehold system and the increasingly competitive nature of colonial society inhibited the creation of such dependent relationships. Contractual relations rather than bonds of dependency characterized most relationships in the colonies, even including tenancy. The forms and language of monarchical culture permeated the American colonies, but they rested on a deferential rather than a dependent culture.

Tensions Arise

Even deference lacked the pervasiveness and servility in America that so characterized it in Europe. The social and economic tensions that affected various segments of provincial society were manifest in the fitful and unreliable subordination owed by inferiors to superiors. Nowhere did this prove more true than in the urban areas of the northern colonies.

By the end of the French and Indian War in 1763 New York, Boston, and Philadelphia had become bustling commercial centers able to compete with such British provincial port cities as Bristol and Glasgow. They had populations of between 13,000 and 15,000 each and found themselves becoming increasingly involved in a coldly rational market world. This world opened whole new avenues to wealth and material comforts for some but also brought confusing change for many others. The vagaries of such a market economy produced erratic fluctuations in the demand for goods and services, created periodic unemployment on an unprecedented scale, changed traditional work patterns, generated serious economic disorders, and brought about a massive redistribution of wealth in which sumptuous wealth existed side by side with abject poverty.

Such bewildering changes left most urban dwellers searching to make sense of their lives. As they struggled to adjust, many individuals—simple folk as well as genteel—began to behave in ways that legitimated private profit seeking. However, while the day-to-day activities of most urban inhabitants had changed in the face of their altered economic enviroment, their habits of mind were more stubborn. Lacking a new ideology to make sense of their new world, most people clung to the old ideology of the traditional corporate society, although in practice, competition rapidly displaced consensus.

These circumstances belied the harmony envisioned by the corporate traditions that still prevailed in the minds of most urban inhabitants and led some to speak out in frustration. A Bostonian, "Phileleutheros," drew an organic link between grinding poverty and sumptuous wealth. He exclaimed to that city's workers: "From your Labour and Industry arises all that can be called Riches, and by your Hands it must be defended: Gentry, Clergy, Lawyers, and military Officers, do all support their Grandeur by your Sweat, and at your Hazard." And yet the burdens of taxation and the hardships of war "fall signally upon the middle and inferiour Ranks of Mankind." In 1765 a New Yorker expressed similar feelings when he noted that "some individuals, . . . by the Smiles of Providence, or some other Means, are enabled to roll in their four wheel'd Carriages, and can support the expense of good Houses, rich Furniture, and Luxurious Living. But is it equitable that 99 rather 999, would suffer for the Extravagance or Grandeur of one? Especially when it is considered that Men frequently owe their Wealth to the impoverishment of their Neighbors?"[8]

Such observations not only questioned the ideas of deference and hierarchy but implied that the whole concept of a common good fostered by the disinterested services of those at the top was simply a mask to protect the personal interests of an economic elite. Defining their lives in terms of a moral economy based on the fair wage and the just price, an economy where it was "unnatural" for any person to profit from the necessities of others, ordinary colonists faced an economic environment controlled by a cash nexus in which free competition and the laws of supply and demand took precedence over all other considerations. Worse, economic changes wrought disturbing social transformations. The emergence of a regionally or even internationally oriented merchant class, tied together through lines of marriage or mutual interest, gave rise to a sensibility and a mode of behavior entirely alien to the traditional attitudes of those accustomed to a local subsistence economy. In this way the strains becoming manifest in urban areas reflected a larger cultural conflict spreading throughout the American colonies: the clash of values resulting from a confrontation between traditional, local attitudes and modern, cosmopolitan ones.

Signs of cultural tension abounded throughout New England in the 1760s. The population of many towns had grown too large and too widely scattered to achieve an easy consensus on issues of importance to the community.[9] As a result "outlivers" petitioned the selectmen of the original town for permission to withdraw from the community in order to form their own towns. The town fathers opposed these petitions and accused the petitioners of being poor folks attempting to avoid taxes, or religious dissenters desiring a minister more sympathetic to their beliefs, or simply being people with an unreasonable obsession for "independency." Such accusations were not without substance. Outlivers did in large part resent the growing social hierarchy, formal religion, and political elitism of the old town centers. More often than not they were subsistence farmers suspicious of the increasing commercialization of the original towns and desirous of a unifying religious experience and political leaders more closely identified with their needs and desires. Above all, however, they felt that their communal homogeneity had been violated, that their deepest traditions were endangered by an emerging social hierarchy in the old town center. They wanted to recreate the original piety, unity, and homogeneity of their village through the establishment of an intensely local authority in their new town. One group expressed this desire, however inadvertently, in exclaiming, "We desire to be a free people of ourselves."[10]

The desire to be a "free people" resulted in large part from outlivers' fear and suspicion of the commercial activities they witnessed in the old town centers. Town leaders seemed to embody a threatening new ethic guided not by order, social stability, and discipline but by economic expansion, mobility, and a worldly materialism. As participants in a larger provincial community—perhaps even a greater Atlantic community—prosperous elements in the older towns patterned their lives after the English gentry rather than the Bible, parental wisdom, or communal values. For many outlivers, then, the old town centers meant elegant homes, extravagant living, and self-interested social and economic behavior. Something perceived as corruption was threatening traditional values. Corruption meant commercialism, competitive materialistic strivings, and dependency; it manifested itself in preoccupations with stylish carriages, periwigs, and social distinctions. Most of all, it meant more and more men assuming the title of "gentleman" and becoming integrated into a hierarchical system of government responsive to royal authority rather than to local control.

In response to these threats to traditional communal values and local control, the newly created towns stressed consensus and homogeneity in their religious and political affairs and worked mightily to prevent interference from higher authorities. They sought to achieve the piety, unity, and autonomy that alone could ensure the safety and the perpetuation of their values and traditions. No provincial hierarchy culminating in the figure of the king should intrude upon their world. Locally validated elites or hierarchies emerged within each village, but the impulse to level society by valuing membership within the local community above all else impelled local leaders to be responsive to the community and its values. Elites became acceptable and gained legitimacy only insofar as they emerged from within the community itself and remained loyal to its values. Such locally validated elites served primarily to protect local customs and traditions from the encroachments of larger outside interests and allegiances. Above all, inhabitants of these communities wanted to be left alone in their relative equality, with the means to prosper and the right to shape their own moral and political worlds.

The same localistic impulses that characterized the behavior of outlivers within New England permeated religious revivals that spread throughout the mainland colonies at midcentury. The most powerful of these resulted in serious breaches of the old order by Separate Congregationalists in Connecticut and Massachusetts and Baptists in Virginia. In both areas the elevation of a vital faith as the single standard of judging human qualities leveled all social pretensions and posed a potential threat to the political order as well.

The revivals that swept through New England from the 1740s onward convinced great numbers of people that a sudden miraculous outpouring of God's grace was among them. None who received the "new light" of God's love could doubt this. They could no longer believe that God worked only through such earthly intermediaries as kings and bishops, a learned clergy, or an elite social order. Instead God communicated directly through His chosen few regardless of their rank or learning; He brought grace directly to the common people and called for ordinary men and women to be His new ministers. "The common people," exclaimed Isaac Backus, "claim as good a right to judge and act for themselves in matters of religion as civil rulers or the learned clergy."[11]

While the pietism of New Lights may have brought them an inner peace, it also brought them into conflict with unconverted ministers and eventually with civil magistrates as well. In the eyes of the newly saved, the church had wandered from the true path; it had fallen under the control of ministers deaf and blind to God's grace. However, the emergence over the years of ministerial associations that usurped control from autonomous congregations meant that New Light congregations could not remove an unconverted pastor. Driven by the dictates of their pietism, many such congregations left their pastor and formed Separate Congregational churches under the guidance of their own lay preachers. Such actions brought them into conflict with secular authorities who stubbornly denied them status as a new denomination and forced them to pay taxes in support of the orthodox Congregational church. New Light consciences would not allow them to pay such taxes, and so state authorities forcibly confiscated the property of Separates and often dragged men and women off to jail.

The Separatist movement greatly disturbed members of the established order. Lay exhorting elicited particular fear and hatred because it threatened the dominance of the educated clergy over religious discourse. Worse, it accorded equality to all people in religious affairs, granted legitimacy to the oral culture of the simple folk—their spontaneous outbursts contrasted shockingly with the gentry's literary culture—gave ordinary people the idea that they, rather than the established clergy, were responsible for their own souls, and disrupted the hierarchy by granting members of the lower orders privileges generally reserved only to an educated elite. The open forums of Separate churches allowed common folk to gain a sense of moral equality with those toward whom the traditional order had always taught them to defer. This lay at the base of the brutal suppression of Separates at the hands of the established authorities. To tolerate the Separates as bona-fide dissenters and either grant exemption from taxes or the right to tax themselves to support their own churches would have been unthinkable. To allow them the freedom to proselytize would be to give free reign to attacks upon the established system. What was permitted the few Baptists, Quakers, and Anglicans within New England would have proved disastrous if granted to the thousands of Separate Congregationalists. Therefore the standing order harassed Separates unmercifully. Local authorities declared Separate meetings illegal and arrested, fined, and jailed their ministers and lay exhorters for disturbing the peace. When Separates refused to attend the regular Sabbath worship of established churches, they suffered fines and public disgrace in the stocks. Students at Harvard and Yale who attended Separate meetings or espoused radical New Light doctrines faced expulsion. Judges lost their seats on the bench, and legislators could be removed if they became too sympathetic to Separates. By 1765 civil authorities in Connecticut and Massachusetts had taken their toll: over a hundred Separate congregations had been reduced to just sixteen struggling groups.

Although the power of the magistrates managed to eliminate most Separate congregations, it could not destroy New Light spirit and ideas. After the revivals, a great many New Englanders became far less sympathetic with the call for moderation, compromise, deference, and order in the name of the public good. In addition, the revivals revitalized the localistic impulse of thousands of New Englanders. The actions of Separates paralleled those of outlivers; they withdrew in order to form a unified moral order under leaders who were an integral part of the community and spoke for its interests. The Separates intended to revitalize their religion and to remove it from a corrupting subjection to higher authorities. They withdrew from the established order to create a communal society, to oppose an authoritarian hierarchy. The Christian liberties they demanded did not mean license, though, for Separates remained socially and politically conservative. And yet the political potential of localism coursed just below the surface of the New Light protest against the established order.

The evangelical reorientation of popular values and modes of behavior in New England had emerged in Virginia in the 1740s under New Light Presbyterians.[12] By the mid-1760s, though, religious dissent had become a major force under Separate Baptist preachers and came to be viewed as a social revolt against established authority by most of the Virginia gentry. The social structure of Virginia was composed of a squirearchy of rank and precedence existing within a traditional environment of friendly neighborliness. The scattered and diffuse population found cohesion in local centers of communal activity and communication: the Anglican parish church, the county court, the local militia. The gentry dominated these centers, where common folk had the rank structure of their society visibly acted out for them at each church service, court day, and militia muster. At these occasions, as well as at horse races, cockfights, and the gaming tables at local taverns, the gentry's authority diffused itself throughout society. Conviviality may have characterized these occasions, but underlying such pleasantries was the knowledge that to be accepted in such a society, one must defer to the authority of the gentry.

Only the gentry in Virginia had access to the larger literary world and the printed word by which higher authority communicated itself throughout the entire colony. This linked them to the chain of authority running from local parishes to the county, the colonial assembly, the governor's council, and eventually to England. For this reason, the gentry, as upholders of the traditional standing order, deplored the emergence of so many itinerants within their midst. This pejorative epithet captured the gentry's perception of authority and society: every member of the community must be under a spiritual or secular guardian who required an appropriate authorization to perform his role. Such authorization came formally from the Anglican church, the colonial assembly, or the county court; it emanated from the gentry through their informal domination of the social institutions of the colony and the deference exacted from the lower orders. Itinerant preaching—the very essence of the Baptist movement—encouraged unlearned farmers or mechanics, moved by some "gift" of the Spirit, to expound upon the Scriptures. This affronted the very hierarchy upon which Virginia society rested: licensed ministers only—integral elements within the established gentry—were to interpret the Bible and to expound upon social behavior. Itinerancy posited a new center of authority, the saved individual, and rested on an entirely new set of social values than the ones supporting the gentry establishment.

For this reason the Baptist "revolt" in Virginia penetrated deep into the colony's culture and the eminence and authority of the Virginia gentry itself. The evangelical movement challenged the life-style and behavior of the gentry and presented a radically different perception of community. In place of the aggressive world of convivial excesses, the Baptists offered a warm brotherhood of God-humbled men, a communal society, a deep emotional fellowship of comparative equality. Baptists cried out against gambling, drinking and horse racing, urging instead the "spread of seriousness," the internalization of rigid Protestant Christian values that promised an orderly moral community. The source of this order would be the redeemed individual, not the external hierarchy of the established social order.

The Baptists did not attempt to wrest political control from the gentry, nor did they wish to level or to redistribute economic wealth. Their mission was to redefine moral behavior and the basis of human relationships. They supported a radically new social order whose members were drawn together by bonds of mutual trust and love. In an intimate face-to-face society held together by bonds of deference within an ordered hierarchy, such a redrawing of social lines of responsibility was a powerful challenge to the standing order. The Baptist movement's initiation of a cultural disjuncture between the gentry and the lower orders, previously held together by convivial, neighborly deference, posed an enormous threat to the gentry, who responded with ridicule and contempt. Gentlemen whipped itinerants, led antievangelical riots, and had Baptist preachers jailed for disturbing the peace and for disorderly conduct. Behind these exaggerated responses to the itinerants lay doubts and fears of a movement that to the gentry seemed both unintelligible and menacing.

The Separates of New England and the Baptists of Virginia, by sowing the seeds of an intensely localistic moral order, created a shock that reverberated throughout the gentry establishment. These hierarchies understood that local rejection of religious authority carried a terrible potential for the rejection of an overarching political hierarchy as well, one that was facing threats from more than simply religious dissent.

Intense localistic feelings among many simple folk were also stirred by a parallel concern regarding the supply of land in the colonies. By the 1760s many New Englanders had become convinced that unclaimed land was in short supply. As their sons remained in eastern townships, land was divided into increasingly small parcels. At some point, it could be divided no more, and these sons would slip into tenancy. Western lands within these colonies were filling with those sons who chose to migrate. Hostile Indian tribes and

British authorities, however, prevented settlement beyond provincial boundaries. Increasingly, then, it seemed as if social opportunity—the privilege of remaining a yeoman—was falling under the control of members of the colonial elite who already held large amounts of land or could use their influence to gain control over vast proprietary tracts. Many farmers feared lest the day might come when they would be forced to go, hat in hand, to ask permission to rent lands from such "lords of the manor."[13]

These social tensions fueled a bitter struggle in Connecticut throughout the 1760s. There the Susquehanna Company's claim to land in northern Pennsylvania created serious divisions. Those desirous of emigrating felt that conservative members of the Connecticut Assembly blocked the company's efforts to gain clear title to the land in order to keep land values high in Connecticut and to force down the value of labor. Gradually the Susquehanna matter became embroiled with other issues, and when the conservatives tried to reduce the number of legislators in the lower house in order to maintain their majority, a New Light minister challenged them in print. His piece in the *Connecticut Gazette* shocked the hierarchy by urging voters to elect men "firmly attached to both your civil and religious interests." Government, still under the will of God, ought to be administered by regenerate men; it should be the servant of the people rather than their master. Annual elections should result in rotation in office rather than perpetual power for an elite. Only this would make rulers "tender all your rights and privileges."[14] This controversy became so vicious that one combatant exclaimed candidly that "gentlemen, who love to monopolize wealth and power, think it best for lands to remain in a few hands and that the common people should be their tenants."[15] In the midst of such a furor, resistance to social authority mounted.

Given its tradition of covenanted communities, such an integration of localism and the demand for an adequate supply of land was to be expected in New England. An intense localism emerged in other colonies as well, where increasing numbers expressed concern over the future of social opportunity and became ever more skeptical of the pretensions of provincial elites. Scattered through the colonies, this unrest represented the embryonic stages of an as yet inchoate political impulse supporting at varying times and places religious liberty, local autonomy, and access to land but always opposing centralized "aristocratic" power.

Resistance Breaks Out

Throughout the 1760s the demands of plain folk for social opportunity—the ability to take up land and to prosper—led to conflicts with evolving hierarchies. Such confrontations fueled unrest to a greater or lesser degree depending upon conditions within the separate colonies. In some instances, physical violence resulted. The more severe eruptions included the Regulator movement in North Carolina, land riots in New York, and the emergence of the Green Mountain Boys on the New Hampshire Grants (Vermont).[16]

The Regulator movement that culminated in riots in Hillsboro, North Carolina, in October 1770 resulted from years of frustration on the part of small backcountry farmers and planters. Over the previous three decades, migrants—small farmers, tenants, and mechanics—had moved southward out of Pennsylvania, Maryland, and Virginia, regions of diminishing land and rising prices, seeking cheap land in western North Carolina. Although these immigrants came from diverse religious and ethnic backgrounds, all shared the desire to take up land and to improve their lot in life. Success meant the ability to raise small crops for a local market and perhaps to emulate the more prominent planters among them—the local gentry—who controlled the socioeconomic and political life of their locale.

Chances appeared good in the early decades of settlement. By the mid-1760s, though, conditions began to change. Towns arose in the piedmont area, and with them came an infusion of merchants and lawyers with minimal connections to the soil, few links with the locale, and ambitions that conflicted with those of the local planters. Merchandising, previously handled by small operations run by local planters, fell to new merchants linked to the larger Atlantic community through Scottish mercantile firms or commercial connections in North Carolina seaports. These men promoted a shift away from a subsistence economy by providing a readily accessible market for surplus wheat and tobacco. Opportunities abounded, labor became scarce, and planters turned to the use of slaves, which resulted in an inequitable distribution of income and changes in the patterns of indebtedness. Previous to the arrival of the new merchants, neighbor had loaned money to neighbor on good faith. Indebtedness now involved legal suits for collection and forced many planters and farmers—unacquainted with the pattern of a cash crop economy—to sell their lands and to move away.

The appearance of large-scale mercantile firms greatly altered social and political patterns as well. In the earliest years of settlement, the planters who monopolized political power had a great deal in common. Few had any training in law or in any of the other professions. Some had a modicum of formal education, but none had attended college. They placed a high value on kinship ties, a close web of neighborhood acquaintances, and, above all, land and landownership. Many owned taverns, mills, stores, or mines, but these enterprises remained secondary to the land. Planting and land speculation constituted the socially legitimate means to wealth, and since inhabitants chose their political leaders from among the most successful planters, landed wealth was the most important prerequisite for gaining political authority. This constituted the essential element in their traditional world of politics: locally legitimated elites—men who had risen gradually within the community according to time-honored standards of behavior—should hold political power. Within such an environment, rising planters expected economic success to bring social status and, in turn, political power.

But the changes taking place in the piedmont short-circuited the latter expectation and led to the Regulation movement. Rapid commercialization brought professionally trained lawyers to the region, and backcountry planters were soon complaining that the presence of so many lawyers increased the number, complexity, and cost of suits. They accused attorneys of changing the county courts, once the bastion of planter strength, into a preserve for lawyers. Legalistic terminology and the manipulation of esoteric laws in the interest of the commercial community seemed to be replacing common sense and neighborly goodwill. Worse, attorneys rapidly displaced the established planters as the key political figures in the area. Most of these attorneys had been educated at Harvard, Yale, or Princeton and had read law in the offices of prominent lawyers in eastern North Carolina or in other colonies. They used their eastern connections and professional skills to rise rapidly in the political structure of the backcountry, where they promoted a set of cultural values entirely different from those already established. Landed wealth and local status no longer guaranteed prestige and political power. Lawyers imposed new standards—academic training, sophisticated professional and cultural modes of life, and widespread provincial contacts and influence—which the local planters had little chance of meeting. In addition, those attorneys could, through their influence with the royal governor, hold important positions without gaining the acceptance of local residents. In fact, the goodwill of resident freeholders became irrelevant to men like Edward Fanning, a Yale-educated attorney popular with Governor William Tryon and the most powerful—and most hated—man in Orange County by 1765. The rapidity with which Fanning and others like him came to positions of political prominence greatly antagonized the local planters—men accustomed to gradual advancement with the approbation of their neighbors.

The concentration of power in the hands of a courthouse ring did not offend most local residents; they were accustomed to that. But the new makeup of that ring certainly did distress them. Previously planters attached to the traditions and values of the local community held political authority and wielded it in the interests of that community. Now merchants and lawyers who were part of a colony-wide network governed in the interests of seemingly alien values and on behalf of men who had nothing but disdain for local farmers and planters. As entry into politics became more and more difficult for local planters, suspicions grew that the local population was being exploited for the benefit of outsiders. Social and economic opportunity now fell under the control of a provincial hierarchy. Hermand Husband, leader of the Regulation in Orange County, saw the world in just such conspiratorial terms. He felt that "individuals in Power and who has [*sic*] Money" meant to engross the remaining vacant lands in the area to themselves and to employ legal legerdemain to challenge the titles of those already holding land in the area.[17]

In the Hillsboro riots, Regulators attacked the homes and offices of lawyers, as well as the business establishments of prominent merchants. The Regulators—wedded to local unity and autonomy—had grown increasingly concerned over the loss of social opportunity, ever more hostile to the political control of a colony-wide elite and their centralized state. While the Regulators lost their struggle with the royal governor, the localist sentiments that prompted their revolt continued to simmer throughout the backcountry of North Carolina.

As in North Carolina, agrarian disturbances smoldered along the eastern shore of the Hudson throughout the 1750s and finally flared up in the Great Rebellion of 1766. The central problem there emerged from the fact that Massachusetts claimed the territory east of the Hudson, and land-hungry Yankees had moved into the area by the hundreds. Massachusetts speculators, who had purchased Indian titles in the region, sold deeds to farmers migrating there. These settlers came into conflict with the great New York landlords, who claimed the same land as part of their estates. Sporadic conflicts broke out until 1757, when the Board of Trade interceded in favor of the New York claim.

The British decision that the region belonged to New York did not halt the steady influx of New Englanders. Determined to maintain local control of their affairs, these people instituted township systems, elected their own officials, and remained fixed in their intent to stake their futures on possession of these lands, though their only legal titles stemmed from Indian deeds. The fact that the titles held by the lords of the manors were often cloudy complicated matters, as did their engrossment of far more land than even their legitimate titles covered. Consequently wherever Massachusetts immigrants could find the slightest fault in a landlord's title, they proceeded to settle and to make improvements upon the land. Due to the vastness of the region, these people went about establishing farms and townships largely unmolested for nearly a decade. The closest New York authority was the sheriff in Albany, so nearby officials generally held Massachusetts commissions. With the passage of time, the settlers became convinced that, as actual residents rather than absentee lords, their claims to the land would be upheld by British authorities. Such was not the case.

In the mid-1760s the New York manor owners instituted ejectment suits and began to engross the land that settlers had occupied and improved for years. Seeing no chance for their cause within the New York legal system, farmers took up arms and banded together to defend their land. They stubbornly refused to become tenants on the lands in question. Simultaneously tenant uprisings broke out on the Cortland Manor to protest the overbearing behavior of the landlord. The tenant rebellion merged with the antiproprietary struggle into a massive insurgency. Responding to the power and influence of the landed gentry, the British army intervened and crushed the rebellion.

The suppression of the riots in the summer of 1766 ended any slim chance that the settlers had to acquire title to their lands. Whatever vestiges of hope remained after the end of the riots dissolved with the complete failure of Indian claims. The squatters now faced a difficult choice: to remain on the lands as tenants of the lordly patentees or abandon their farms and move away. As New Englanders fiercely determined to retain a freehold system within a society under local control rather than subservient to an alien hierarchy, most of these people moved on. The triumph of the landlords, by closing off the unoccupied portions of the Housatonic Valley in New York to settlement on favorable terms, diverted the ever-increasing flow of New England emigration farther north. A great many New Englanders followed the Housatonic and Connecticut rivers into the New Hampshire Grants, where the struggle along the Hudson would be reenacted; this time, however, with different results.

The troubles that arose on the Grants stemmed from the same source as those in the Hudson Valley: vague or overlapping land grants. In this case both New York and New Hampshire claimed the area lying between them. The governor of each colony made extensive grants within the region, but most of the overlapping grants lay west of the Green Mountains. Consequently the initial conflict arose in and around Bennington, which had been settled by a group of New England Separate Congregationalists holding New Hampshire grants.

Having gained a decision from the Board of Trade that the entire area west of the Connecticut River belonged to New York, authorities from that colony sent surveyors out to run lines for massive grants made in areas already settled and improved by New Hampshire claimants. The chief beneficiaries of these grants included prominent New York land speculators James Duane and John Tabor Kempe. If settlers holding New Hampshire grants desired to stay on their land, they could purchase titles from the new grantors, but such titles included the payment of annual quitrents.

At the same time that these New York grants were being made, peddlers roamed about western Connecticut and Massachusetts selling New Hampshire land grants at incredibly low prices, bringing in streams of New England settlers. Hundreds of poor, land-hungry individuals moved to the disputed region and established their pitches on small acreages under the impression that they had purchased legitimate titles supported by a representative of the English government, Governor Wentworth. Once on the Grants they organized themselves into townships, elected selectmen, held town meetings, and remained determined to establish traditional New England customs.

During this time, the Bennington Separates took the position that jurisdictional authority had passed to New York but that this did not invalidate land titles that had been obtained in a legitimate manner from the governor of New Hampshire. New York authorities did not share this view, and a confrontation took place when New York surveyors arrived in Bennington in October 1769 to run lines for the New York patentees. The survey party encountered several town leaders who asked them to withdraw. This request gained a good deal of authority from the presence of a large group of armed men standing a short distance away. The New York commission withdrew. Both sides, however, were anxious to have the issue decided in court, and the New York authorities brought ejectment suits against a number of individuals holding New Hampshire titles. The Bennington leaders, certain of the legitimacy of their case and anxious to proceed according to the law, looked forward to this judgment in order to validate their claims and to calm the entire affair.

It was at this point that Ethan Allen came upon the scene. Allen, an aggressive petty entrepreneur with a reputation in western Connecticut towns as something of a troublemaker, had been in and out of the Grants for several years and had been diligently buying up New Hampshire titles from Connecticut speculators. As the tension between New York and New Hampshire authorities increased, nonresident proprietors of New Hampshire townships met in various Connecticut towns to organize meetings to protect their investments. One such gathering chose Allen to hire an attorney to defend the New Hampshire claims and to proceed to Portsmouth, New Hampshire, to procure the necessary documentation to support the case.

The test case came to trial on 28 June 1770 before Judges Robert R. Livingston and George Duncan Ludwig. Attorney General John Tabor Kempe and prosecuting attorney James Duane served as counsel to the plaintiff. Allen described the opposing sides:

The plaintiffs appearing in great state and magnificence, which, together with their junto of land thieves [Livingston, Kempe, and Duane held thousands of acres in the disputed area], made a brilliant appearance; but the defendant appearing but in ordinary fashion, having been greatly fatigued by hard labor wrought on the disputed premises, and their cash much exhausted, made a very disproportionate figure at court.[18]

The court disallowed the New Hampshire patents on the grounds that New Hampshire never had jurisdiction over the land in question and that Governor Wentworth never had the authority to grant it. With this ruling, the

Bennington Separates, Ethan Allen, and hundreds of poor settlers had to get new grants from New York at a prohibitive cost or defend their property. They chose the latter course.

Shortly after the successful prosecution in June, New York authorities ordered the Albany sheriff and his representatives to serve eviction notices, as well as writs of possession. By that time the towns in the area had organized militia groups under the unofficial colonelcy of Ethan Allen. These bands of mounted men roamed the area west of the Green Mountains terrorizing settlers holding New York patents, burning houses, and destroying mills. Whenever they could get their hands on New York officials, Allen and his captains held unofficial trials. Perched upon benches they called "judgment seats," leaders of the Green Mountain Boys, as Allen's group had come to be known, passed sentence on these unfortunate Yorkers; usually a number of lashes from the "beech seal" well laid on. Allen and the Green Mountain Boys, poor individuals who had come to the Grants in search of economic opportunities denied them in the older colonies, had great fun mocking New York gentlemen by parodying the pomp and circumstance of the New York courts.

Gradually an alliance emerged west of the Green Mountains between Allen's Green Mountain Boys and the more cautious and conservative Separate leadership in Bennington. The organizational structure of the towns in the region always remained under the control of the Bennington group; but Allen and his captains controlled the armed bands. Both sides had a great deal at stake. The Bennington group held large tracts of valuable land already under cultivation, Allen controlled vast areas of virgin wilderness with a tremendous economic potential, and hundreds of settlers wanted to maintain clear title to their own small plots of land. The Green Mountain Boys successfully kept New York authorities out of the region and made good these land claims with the nervous approbation of the Bennington Separates.

In many ways, the struggle on the Grants epitomized the strains characteristic of agrarian disturbances by the mid-eighteenth century. Above all else, control of land meant control of the economic future of people living in an agrarian society, while an equitable access to land constituted the vital prerequisite for political and social opportunity for the ordinary citizen. The triumph of the settlers on the Grants over their New York opponents represented a victory for men desirous of attaining access to the means to prosper within an environment of relative equality. It also constitued a triumph for localists in their effort to fend off control by a hierarchy composed of cosmopolitan gentlemen. This victory did not, however, come totally free of anxiety and stress. The alliance between Bennington Separates and Green Mountain Boys joined two very different sorts of localists. Allen and his captains represented a new breed of entrepreneur: aggressive, individualistic, acquisitive men distrustful and envious of the gentry. In their minds, gentlemanly elites always monopolized the primary means of gaining wealth: land-ownership and land speculation. Allen and his followers had no respect for the gentlemen of New York and very little for those of Bennington. The Bennington Separates professed a devotion to a pious, corporate community of order and stability. Thus the localist impulse on the Grants sprang from traditional communal values combined with individualistic and materialistic ones in quite an uneasy balance.

Hierarchy against Localism

The social struggles appearing in the colonies revealed cracks in the established social order. Throughout the colonies for various reasons, many simple folk came to doubt the efficacy of social deference in practice if not in theory. Their challenges to authority existed as separate manifestations of a silent struggle taking place throughout the American colonies between two cultural forces: the process of Anglicization at the hands of cosmopolitan elites attempting to establish social hierarchy in America was being resisted by an as yet amorphous, fragmented impulse to retain autonomy and control in scattered, disparate, local communities.

The localistic impulse assumed a variety of forms: religious congregationalism; the secession of hundreds of outlivers in order to be a "free people"; the opposition of Connecticut and Massachusetts Separates to the state's tax collectors; struggles over land titles along the Hudson; Baptist dissent from the Virginia squirearchy; the Regulation in North Carolina; and the "judgment seats" of the Green Mountain Boys on the New Hampshire Grants. These events were all characterized by the urge to make local leadership, whether religious or political, respond to the needs and values of the local community. The great bulk of Americans rejected as immoral a cosmopolitan elite integrally linked with governmental officials and institutions resulting in a centralized hierarchy that engrossed social and political power and authority. These beliefs gained strength from the conditions of everyday life throughout the colonies. Most people still lived far removed from the sophistication of market commerce and true gentlemen; they remained remote from the real weight of authority, whether practiced by ministerial consociations, royally appointed sheriffs, or even tax collectors and land registrars. In most areas a locally validated elite shielded local customs from such outside interference. Localistic feelings asked that such isolation be allowed to continue. With the passage of time, however, such desires became increasingly political, and yet, although emanating from the very conditions of American life, they remained inchoate. They were too visceral, too instinctive, and their outward manifestations too occasional, scattered, and ephemeral to assume the force of a generalized social or political ideology.

Such was not the case with the colonial elites supporting an Anglicized society. These articulate gentlemen, supported by the authority of two hundred years of European thought, confidently espoused an organic society based on order and hierarchy. Appalled at localistic mentalities, these men know the assumption of authority by the rich and the well born to be the precondition of a viable state. They placed their full faith in hierarchy and thus supported the integration of elites into a carefully ordered set of institutions stretching eventually to the crown itself.

Yet try as they might to impose an unquestioning deferential respect for their social eminence and a dependence on the political authority they represented, these gentlemen faced continual frustration. An aristocratic order could never sink deep roots in America; the hierarchical principle of legitimacy on which it depended did not correspond with the experiences of the great bulk of Americans. Consequently hierarchy remained a painfully artificial creation. If the localist impulse represented an environment without an ideology, hierarchy became a fully articulated ideology without a secure foundation within the environment.[19]

The monarchical culture that appeared to permeate American society rested on an insecure base. This became starkly apparent when the British began to legislate for the colonies in the decade following the close of the French and Indian War. That legislation not only brought on a revolution that separated America from Great Britain but greatly increased the tension between advocates of hierarchy and supporters of localism.

two

Revolutionary Republicanism

Following the successful completion of the French and Indian War, Great Britain attempted to reorganize its empire in order to rationalize its structure and increase royal authority within the colonies. British authorities imposed a series of measures on the American colonists that initiated a decade of arbitrary and erratic colonial administration eventually culminating in the armed confrontations of 19 April 1775 at Lexington and Concord.

The British began by issuing the Proclamation Line of 1763. Intended to shut off white settlement west of a crudely drawn line along the Appalachians and to restrict trade with the Indians, this measure resulted in chaos and outrage among settlers, land speculators, and traders and proved impossible to enforce. In 1764 the Currency Act drastically curtailed the use of paper currency, which had become essential within the colonial economies, creating serious concern among the American commercial community and alarming many others to the serious threat posed by remote and arbitrary power. That same year Parliament initiated measures to gain revenue from the American provinces without consulting provincial assemblies. The Sugar Act imposed duties on many foreign products imported into the colonies, tightened customs regulations and enforcement procedures, and lowered the six pence per gallon duty on foreign molasses imported into the colonies to three pence. In 1766 this duty became one pence on all imported molasses, whether from foreign sources or from other British colonies. In this way the British altered the essential structure of the empire from a regulatory one to a revenue-producing one; a radical change from the mercantilistic principles that had governed the old colonial system for nearly a century.

To make matters worse, the Stamp Act (1765) imposed a direct tax on nearly every piece of public paper used in the colonies—newspapers, almanacs, wills, deeds, customs forms. It caused a storm of violent protests. Officials' homes were destroyed, stamp distributors were tarred and feathered, and British imports were boycotted. The following year Parliament repealed the act but affirmed in the Declaratory Act its authority to legislate for the colonies in all matters. Then, in an attempt to pass "external" taxes (ostensibly to regulate trade) rather than "internal" ones (which the colonists had opposed because they were designed to raise revenue), Parliament, under Chancellor of the Exchequer Charles Townshend, imposed duties (1767) on glass, lead, tea, paint, paper, and other items imported into the colonies. The revenue gained from the Townshend Duties would be used to pay colonial officials, thereby removing them from the influence of the colonial legislatures that formerly paid their salaries. In essence, the British intended to subvert the power and independence of colonial assemblies and to underwrite this effort with colonial tax money. American opposition mounted, and more economic boycotts exerted pressure upon the British.

By this time the British had moved troops that had been stationed along the frontier to coastal cities where, according to the Quartering Act of 1765, they were to be housed and supplied by the colonists themselves. The presence of the two regiments of British regulars stationed in Boston, rather than ensuring law and order, however, led to agitation and confrontation, resulting in the Boston Massacre (1770). Soon Parliament again retreated by withdrawing the Townshend Duties except for a symbolic tax on tea, and both sides enjoyed several years of calm. In 1773, however, the Tea Act, allowing the British East India Tea Company the right to sell its duties tea directly to American customers, undercut much of the local mercantile community and aroused tensions anew. On the night of 16 December 1773 participants in the Boston Tea Party threw the hated tea into the harbor. Their act of outright defiance outraged Parliament and resulted in the passage of a series of Coercive Acts (1774); laws that closed the port of Boston, reorganized the Massachusetts government by reducing the power of its popular assembly while enlarging that of the royal governor, allowed royal officials to be tried in England for capital crimes, and called for troops to be quartered in private homes at the owner's expense. These acts led directly to the summoning of a Continental Congress and the fateful confrontations in April 1775 at Lexington and Concord.

The Gentry Threatened

The actions taken by the British Parliament in the 1760s had the most immediate impact on the commercial and political power of the American gentry. Merchants and large planters found themselves in a direct conflict of interests with the English commercial community. The latter, intent upon protecting its ability to exploit the economic opportunities of the New World, enlisted the aid of Parliament in an effort that seemed heedless of colonial interests. The colonial gentry became equally aggressive in defending themselves. Having grown acutely aware of their personal and group interests and accustomed to having their own way, members of these elites were grimly determined to retain control over the economic lives of their respective colonies.

The strains that emerged in the 1760s between British and colonial commercial groups resulted from a quarter-century of fundamental transformations that saw the colonies become integrated into the Atlantic economy. British capital and British economic decisions increasingly came to influence colonial economies. With the passage of time, actions taken by the British commercial and political communities seemed to endanger American interests. Worse, the British government seemed callous to the entreaties of the colonists. This certainly appeared to be the case with structural changes instituted by British trading houses that threatened to transform trade relations in the colonial cities. More and more British mercantile firms attempted to bypass established colonial merchants by promoting vendue or auction sales. These common methods of disposing of damaged goods became major wholesale outlets. New colonial merchants, intent upon exploiting the economic opportunities of rapidly expanding urban areas, sprang up. These men imported large quantities of goods directly for the specific purpose of auctioning them off at a fraction of the profits normally gained by the established houses. British firms exploited this technique by establishing their own agents in various American cities. The complaints of the traditional American merchant houses fell on deaf ears; British exporters cared little who sold their goods so long as they continued to reap enormous profits.

The suspicion that Parliament favored British commercial interests over American ones gained credence with the passage of the Currency Act of 1764. Colonial leaders had long considered the emission of paper currency to be a local method of meeting local economic troubles, an important means of retaining control over their economic lives. British constraints on colonial currency systems threatened that autonomy.

The merchants' acceptance of the tactic of nonimportation of British goods in 1765 and again in 1768 resulted in large part from their desperate efforts to protect themselves against British competition. Nonimportation carried with it a host of tangible and immediate short-term gains for established provincial merchants. It allowed them to retrench and to reduce their unsold inventories at higher profits while temporarily eliminating the new traders who depended on the quick turnover of smaller stocks of goods. By 1770 economic conditions had eased, and many merchants, having disposed of their backlog of goods, agitated to abandon nonimportation. This brought charges of self-interest against the merchants by those opposing British authority on ideological grounds. Nonetheless, the repeal of all the Townshend Duties except the one on tea brought a resumption of trade.

Yet by the time of the Tea Act in 1773, American commercial centers were once again facing a substantial depression, exacerbated, in the eyes of the established merchants, by the same grievances that had troubled them for the last several decades: massive dumping of goods by the large British houses, and an even more widespread proliferation of small competitors, and vendue and auction sales. In large part, this downturn in the local economy helps to explain the angry reaction of provincial merchants to the Tea Act. When the East India Tea Company decided to sell its tea directly to specific American agents, many colonists objected not to the opportunity to buy cheap tea but to the fact that to buy the tea meant acceptance of Parliament's right to tax the colonists. For American merchants, though, the Tea Act represented yet another example of British exporters, with the support of Parliament, seeking unfair profits by going outside established trade patterns. The British imperial system seemed bent on helping British commercial interests and harming American ones. Thus, many prominent American merchants played leading roles in opposing the British actions of the 1760s and 1770s.

Just as Parliament's actions after 1763 threatened the economic interests of the colonial elites, so too did they challenge their political authority. In fact, British legislation endangered a century-long "quest for power" orchestrated by the provincial elites, a quest to achieve political legitimacy.[1] This drive for power was actually a struggle for political identity, an effort to fulfill the political ambitions of the newly emerging provincial elites. Indeed there was a close relationship within each colony between the emergence of social and economic elites and demands made by provincial assemblies to augment their status and authority.

By 1763 the colonial elites had by and large attained their goal: the colonial assemblies held political preeminence. They achieved this, after years of arduous struggle with recalcitrant royal or proprietary authorities, by gradually coming to dominate vital governmental powers. Like the House of Commons, which they so assiduously imitated, the assemblies had made themselves the sole authority over colonial finances by gaining control over all aspects of raising and distributing public revenue. Next, blunting efforts to grant permanent salaries to royal officials, they had voted these salaries on a yearly basis and even tried to regulate them by statute. In addition, they had freed themselves to an extraordinary degree from executive authority and even went beyond the House of Commons by sharing in executive affairs. The provincial assemblies had become bastions of provincial autonomy and authority. By the 1760s each colony had an impressive group of native political leaders experienced in governmental infighting, jealous of their prerogatives, and ready to defend the prestige and authority of their assemblies against any challenge.

Britain's effort to reorganize its empire after 1763 posed just such a challenge. Parliament's attempts to raise a revenue in the colonies between 1764 and 1766 represented a direct attack upon the colonial assemblies' exclusive power to tax, and the Townshend Duties subverted legislative control over royal officials by freeing them from financial ties to the provincial assemblies. The colonial elites, already uneasy over their ability to maintain control over their own provinces as a result of the various internal outbursts questioning their authority, could not afford to relinquish power to Parliament. To surrender these prerogatives meant to forfeit the hard-won gains of a century of political struggle, to give up any pretense of true political authority, to undermine gentry control over their own colonies, and to acquiesce in a subordinate status to Parliament rather than to maintain their stance as miniature Houses of Commons. Any one of these was intolerable; together they forced colonial legislators to take the lead in opposing Parliament after 1763.

This became a formidable task, for by adopting a new method of administration, Parliament transformed political life in the colonies. Previous to 1763 royal governors received instructions, which they transmitted to the colonial assemblies to be enacted into law. Parliamentary legislation arriving in the colonies after the close of the French and Indian War, however, carried with it the force of law. Royal officials no longer had to wait upon legislative action by colonial assemblies in order to enforce the parliamentary legislation. In a single stroke, Parliament had seriously weakened the colonial assemblies as an effective defense against imperial authority. Only by rallying the public to massive civil disobedience could the gentry hope to thwart the effort of Parliament to legislate for them.

To mobilize such resistance demanded a broad appeal through a diverse range of public communications—newspaper essays, pamphlets, broadsides, mass meetings held on city streets, at county courts, and rural crossroads. In their search for wider public support, the gentry found it necessary to alter their form of public address. Previously in their writings, these men had addressed themselves solely to fellow gentlemen. As they realized that they needed help from simple folk if they were to thwart the designs of Parliament, they began to address themselves to a much wider and more popular audience. At this point, such gentlemen found themselves in a delicate situation: they must solicit the support of ordinary citizens without at the same time encouraging such people to play an energetic role in shaping the political and social life of the community. This proved to be an impossible task. To gain the support of the common citizen, the gentry resorted to a popular mode of address that could not help but prompt ordinary people to view themselves as full participants in the life of the state.

The resultant deepening of the audience for political discourse helps to explain the incredible popularity of Thomas Paine's *Common Sense* (1776), as well as the inflated language employed by pamphleteers as revolutionary fervor increased. *Common Sense* had no pretense of the learned treatise, lawyer's brief, or philosophical discourse about it. Instead it constituted an outright attack on monarchy written in a blunt, straightforward manner. Paine deliberately eliminated the traditional elitist apparatus of satire and literary allusions; he addressed himself to the people in plain, direct language. His images—practical, coarse, even obscene at times—drew upon the common, everyday world of the unlearned; the only literary source his readers needed to know was the Bible. The style intensified the pamphlet's power, widened its readership tremendously, and introduced an entirely new kind of public literature.

This literature, created in response to the greatly expanded dimensions of its audience, became increasingly emotional as well as hyperbolic. When Joseph Warren spoke in 1775 about the Boston Massacre, for example, he exclaimed: "Take heed, ye orphan babes, lest, whilst your streaming eyes are fixed upon the ghostly corpse, *your feet slide on the stones bespattered with your father's blood.*"[2] Warren used such lurid images to persuade an audience he perceived as both diffuse and vulgar to stand up against the British. This desire led increasingly to a breakdown of the stylized rules of gentlemanly rhetoric and its replacement with direct, common expressions filled with emotional extravagance. The gentry now declared that the new imperial policy threatened to strip yeomen of their freeholds, artisans of their personal property, and all people of their freedom, to be replaced by a tyrannical social order serving corrupt royal officials and their greedy minions. British actions threatened to enslave all Americans.

Colonial Tensions

The popularization of gentry rhetoric coincided with the deepening of a number of strains within the colonies, which greatly complicated the manner in which different Americans perceived concepts such as tyranny, corruption, slavery, and despotism. This was particularly true in the northern cities where stress between the plain folk and the gentility intensified.[3] The former, still drawing the greatest meaning and indentity in their lives from family, church, and community, desired equity within a society in which they could maintain their modest livelihoods. They became politically active only to conserve their corporate view of community or to keep open the doors of opportunity. As trust in their social superiors waned, they began to take an active part in the political lives of their towns and political factionalism grew apace.

Problems had begun in Boston as early as 1760 when a group of conservative merchants and lawyers, led by the wealthy Thomas Hutchinson and identified in the popular press as the "Junto," attempted to alter Boston's system of government by dismantling the town meeting. These individuals, long indignant at being forced to attend town meetings where the laboring people greatly outnumbered them, intended to institute a form of government in which wealthy men would gain control through the appointive powers of a council. This became all the more important to them as the gulf between those at the top and bottom rungs of Boston society enlarged. Members of the Junto—wealthy, Anglican, interrelated by blood and marriage—became increasingly disdainful of the common people, whom they considered too ignorant, turbulent, and passionate to wield political power, particularly when that power intruded upon the prerogatives of the Junto itself.

Once it became clear that Hutchinson planned to undermine the authority of the town meeting, he became the target of popular opposition led by James Otis. Actually Otis served two groups affected by the hard times: merchants dependent upon circumventing British trade regulations and common people suffering from a depressed economy. He could offer palpable gains for the merchants by providing a strong enough resistance in the General Assembly to thwart the royal governor's concerted efforts to enforce commercial regulations. All he could offer the common people was a vitriolic attack upon Hutchinson and the Junto as grasping, self-serving elitists who disdained their inferiors while amassing great profits at their expense. Consequently a bitter popular-prerogative fight raged in Boston for several years before the passage of the Sugar and Stamp acts.

This political struggle led to the emergence of separate conceptions of government and society, as well as bitter suspicion and mistrust between the competing groups. The popular party consisted of a wide range of individuals—small merchants, lawyers, ship captains, Congregational clergy, as well as artisans, seamen, and laborers—committed to the town meeting as the foundation of Boston's political system. They supported the political participation of all property holders and sympathized with the needs of the propertyless, at least to the extent of allowing them to voice their opinions in the town meeting. In many ways, the popular opposition represented the efforts of local people and their leaders to protect social opportunities from usurpation by a prerogative party tied to royal authorities. Consequently its rhetoric reverberated with anger and frustration toward the wealthy, Anglican elite. For their part, the Junto expressed contempt for the laboring people and hatred and suspicion of their leaders. In the minds of Hutchinson and the others, "reform" meant cutting back on the powers of the town meetings, making more positions appointive rather than elective, muzzling the freedom of the press, and defusing the passionately anti-Anglican prejudices that permeated the popular party. For the conservative clergymen, lawyers, merchants, and royal appointees led by Thomas Hutchinson, the popular party stood for chaos and disorder and threatened a hierarchically structured organic society.

Clearly Boston was no longer an organic community of mutually interdependent parts. The years of economic change and turmoil had fragmented the town and left it riddled with uncertainty and internal strife. The court party, modern in its eagerness to participate in an international market economy and to incorporate the economic practices of a new capitalist age, remained traditional in its political views. Its members, still clinging to the ideals of organic hierarchy, continued to preach to the plain folk of the city that eminent, wealthy gentlemen alone were capable of governing in the interest of the entire community. They constantly stressed the traditional themes of public good, harmony, public virtue, and community. But after decades of increased hardship that saw the disparity between wealth and poverty grow increasingly wide, many of Boston's plain citizens began to suspect that some groups in the city had been promoting their own interests rather than those of the community. Members of the popular party used the same time-honored words and phrases to symbolize their call for a return to a "Christian Sparta"—a simple, austere, egalitarian society based upon mutual social and moral obligations rather than market calculations. But while leaders of the popular party drew their social and economic ideals from a nostalgic past, they were modern in their promotion of a participatory style of politics. For them, true economic justice and equity could not be left in the hands of the politicians of the court party "who grind the faces of the poor without remorse, eat the bread of oppression without fear, and wax fat upon the spoils of the people."[4]

These feelings seethed until the passage of the Stamp Act, when the pent-up tensions of a people impoverished by the postwar depression and enduring an extremely high local tax burden exploded in rage against the prerogative party and its support of the new British colonial policy. Led by Ebenezer MacIntosh, a poor cordwainer, crowds of angry Bostonians destroyed the brick office constructed by Andrew Oliver, the wealthy Junto member chosen as stamp distributor. That same night the mob started a bonfire in front of Oliver's luxurious home. When Thomas Hutchinson tried to quiet them, the people tore apart Oliver's stable house as well as his coach and chaise. Later in the evening when Hutchinson appeared with the sheriff, the people pelted them with stones and broke into Oliver's house, where they smashed windows, mirrors, elegant furniture, and a well-stocked wine cellar and then tore up his beautiful formal gardens. This destruction of the visible symbols of eminence and status did not satisfy the people; less than two weeks later they attacked the magnificent homes of the deputy register of the Vice-Admiralty Court and the comptroller of the customs. At last they turned their fury upon Thomas Hutchinson himself. The crowd caught him and his family at the dinner table in their luxurious mansion. It drove off the family and then demolished everything of value within the house until it remained an empty shell. The authorities stood by helpless in the face of the crowd's fury. Neither MacIntosh nor his followers received any punishment.

The unrest that surfaced in New York City took a different turn. Instead of the emphasis upon communal harmony and a selfless devotion to the public welfare emphasized by the plain folk in Boston, New York workers stressed individual self-interest. The popular *New York-Gazette* exclaimed that "*self interest* is the grand Principle of all Human Actions," and therefore it was "unreasonable and vain to expect Service from a Man who must act contrary [to] his own Interests to perform it. The publick Happiness is then in the most perfect State, when each Individual acts the most agreeably to his own Interest." Such an argument served both the popular party in New York vis-à-vis its prerogative foes as well as colonial leaders in their opposition to the oppression of new English measures. "Freeman" declared that "no Creatures suck the Teats of their Dams longer than they can draw Milk from thence . . . nor will any Country continue their subjection to another only because their Great-Grandmothers were acquainted."[5] Popular politicians in New York increasingly reduced matters to a simple calculation of personal interest.

While urban areas seethed with friction between the prerogative and popular parties, elsewhere throughout New England religious tension remained predominant. The struggle between Separatists and established authorities had died down, but divisions remained between Old Lights and New Lights. In Concord, Massachusetts, for example, strains within the established church severely tested the town's integrity in the 1760s.[6] Contention centered on Dr. Joseph Lee, the town's largest landholder and one of its wealthiest citizens. Even with such social position, however, Lee could not gain the political stature within the town that he so ardently desired. The majority of voters in Concord, a New Light town, refused to elect Lee, a prominent leader within the Old Light West Church, to the prestigious position of selectman or representative to the General Court. In 1766, with the collapse of the West Church, Lee remained outside not only the town's political structure but its religious framework as well. He needed acceptance within the town church.

Given the New Light structure of the church, this proved difficult. To be accepted into the church, Lee had to undergo searching questions from the elect, rich and poor alike. Only when a full consensus of the members emerged could an applicant be received into the church. This did not happen, and Lee's rebuff led to bitter recriminations between Old Lights and New Lights. As the bitterness of the religious quarrel increased with time, it permeated the political life of the town as well. Lee eventually attacked the pastor of the Concord church in a vitriolic newspaper article while at the same time announcing his candidacy for a seat in the provincial assembly to replace a staunch New Light leader within the town. Party spirit became violent, and on election day 1771 the crowd of prospective voters grew to such proportions that the election had to be held in the meetinghouse. Tension became so strong that a secret ballot was taken. Lee's opponent emerged the victor with approximately two-thirds of the ballots in his favor. Religious division lay at the core of the political fight, and former West Church members, sullen and vindictive toward the church that rejected their beliefs and yet compelled them to pay for its minister, now had all the more reason to be angry. As a result Lee's followers from the old West Church refused to join with the Concord majority at the communion table.

Factional lines remained tautly drawn. While the majority could not purge the dissenters from their town, it could deny them legitimacy within its communal life. Lee and his supporters, excluded from the church and denied political office, retained the power to be disruptive. Exercising this power at every opportunity, they badgered the beleaguered majority at town meetings and constantly questioned the authority of its leaders. At the same time a dissident group of outlivers from the northern section of the town attended town meetings to agitate for their secession. Torn by such constant strife, the citizens of Concord became involved in bitter, competitive politics that belied their professed communal values of order, peace, harmony, and public virtue. Concord was a strife-ridden town swiftly losing its moral center. Its inhabitants, whether consciously or not, sought regeneration for themselves and their town.

Religious tension, at the heart of Concord's unease, tore even more violently at society within Virginia. There, throughout the 1760s and 1770s, the gentry publicly whipped Baptists for their impudence and regularly imprisoned evangelical ministers for disturbing the peace. Both the Baptists and their antagonists responded to what they perceived to be mounting social disorder; both sides expressed concern over drinking, gambling, and other aggressive forms of behavior that disrupted all ranks of society and disturbed plain and genteel Virginians alike.

The Baptists responded to the absence of institutional restraints characteristic of rural Virginia society with calls for confessions, remorse, and expiation through the conversion experience.[7] Defining the social chaos surrounding their lives as sin, the Baptists set out to counter such evil by means of an emotional communal movement "under preaching." Once saved, converted individuals practiced a radical new life-style emphasizing "works" validated by their new community of brothers and sisters. This internalization of strict Protestant Christian values and norms led to the zealous censure of drunkenness, gambling, physical aggression, and other behavior that created a sinful environment. Baptists sought an orderly, moral community, a more secure system of social control centered in the people themselves rather than in a gentry-controlled social hierarchy. Regenerate men and women could no longer subordinate themselves to the sins and humbly defer to the sinners of the Virginia squirearchy.

The gentry, though thoroughly alienated and frustrated by the Baptist resistance to their dominance, responded to similar anxieties. They too were disturbed by increasing signs within their society of mounting social disorder. What Baptists denounced as sin—drinking, racing, gambling, and other social displays of competitive, aggressive behavior—more and more members of the gentry perceived negatively as luxury. What once seemed to validate the gentry's power now appeared to many to be destructive of it and community order as well. A social crisis began to build within the ruling gentry that heightened the reaction of its members to both the Baptist revolt from within and to the new colonial legislation being imposed upon them from outside by the British.

By the 1760s many within Virginia's elite were becoming increasingly anxious over their power within the province.[8] Upstarts seemed to be eroding their influence, even within the House of Burgesses. The increasing cost of elections, as well as the spread of corruption in the growing competition for votes, especially among "those who have neither natural nor acquired parts to recommend them," particularly disturbed genteel minds. Throughout the last years of the 1760s and the early ones of the 1770s, alarm over such threats to the electoral system as bribery and the solicitation of votes filled Virginia newspapers. Freeholders were urged to "strike at the Root of this growing Evil; be influenced by Merit alone," and to shun "obscure and inferior men" at the polls. One pamphleteer considered the demagoguery resulting from overweening ambition a "daemon lately come among us to disturb the peace and harmony, which had so long subsisted in this place." Robert Munford's popular play, *The Candidates* (1770), revealed the anxieties produced by an electoral system where "coxcombs and jockies" could defeat "men of learning." Selfless virtue prevailed in Munford's satire, but the play exposed the deep anxieties of an elite fearful lest irresponsible, ignorant, and ambitious men lead Virginia's freeholders away from the natural and benevolent guidance of its established gentry.[9]

By the mid-1770s many planters were openly concerned over the state of the gentry itself. Becoming obsessed with virtue, corruption, and luxury, these individuals feared that the true source of the disorders threatening their position lay in "our Pride, our Luxury, and Idleness." Many prominent families found themselves on the verge of bankruptcy, and while they might blame Scottish factors or corruption within the British imperial system for the sense of impending ruin that engulfed them, the disquieting fear always lurked in the back of their minds that they had only themselves to blame. Gentlemen spent beyond their means in order to maintain an aristocratic lifestyle. Landon Carter voiced the fears of those beginning to perceive the destructive nature of gambling and drinking when he despondently observed that too many of the gentry's heirs "play away and play it all away." When another planter exclaimed that the social crisis within the colony had been "produced by the wantonness of the Gentlemen," he revealed the social stress being felt by many within the squirearchy.[10]

Despite the obvious contrast between the life-styles and cultural beliefs of the gentry and their evangelical adversaries, both groups shared a need for emotional relief from the burdens of anxiety and guilt. They experienced a common need for the regeneration of their community. Like the inhabitants of Concord, Virginians entered the turmoil of the 1760s and 1770s without a strong moral center; they searched for order and revitalized meaning in their lives.

At the same time that religious tensions created anxieties for many Americans, socioeconomic and demographic forces altered colonial society in fundamental ways that affected the manner in which those caught up in them perceived themselves and the world about them.[11] Throughout the eighteenth century the American colonies experienced a constant process of change. Population doubled every twenty-five years, population density greatly intensified, arable land became ever more scarce, and migration away from established areas increased. In areas of high population density, concentrations of wealth in a few hands resulted from the mounting pressures on the land supply as well as from increases in the level of commercialization. This created greater social differentiation and social polarization. Individuals faced the choice of migrating, remaining near their native locale and attempting to become more deeply involved in the market economy, or staying and accepting a much lower standard of living than their fathers had experienced. A small percentage maintained their positions as gentlemen in established areas, while others scrambled frantically to improve their status in new areas or by commercial success in older ones. Most remained in familiar surroundings and sustained a relative decline in status.

As a result of these economic and demographic changes, two separate phenomena took place simultaneously within the colonies: the destabilizing effects of rapid change in areas opening to opportunity either on fresh lands or in new commercial ventures in older established areas and the frustrations created by a closing or increasingly Anglicized society of declining opportunity, increased social stratification, and a pronounced tendency toward political elitism. Deep frustrations and anxieties resulted from each experience—whether the fear of not succeeding in an opening society or the anxiety of being shut out in a closing one.[12]

In areas experiencing an opening of society, a growing number of men began to accept increasingly modern beliefs. In newly opened regions like the New Hampshire Grants or areas experiencing increased commercialization such as the northern cities, a pattern of behavior gradually emerged consisting of aggressively individualistic, optimistically materialistic, acquisitive actions on the part of many citizens. Releasing the individual from societal restraints meant that the contrasts between free and unfree, independent and dependent, became stark alternatives. Having a fixed place within a traditional hierarchy was very different from being dependent or dreading dependence in a society of independent individualism. Those caught up in such a new environment became peculiarly sensitive to any threat to their personal freedom, real or imagined. Liberty became vitally important in such a competitive milieu.

Colonists living within a closing society clung desperately to traditional images of community. Facing the deep frustration of constricting opportunities resulting from overcrowding, a shortage of land, and increasing social stratification, these people longed for the harmony and equity of an earlier day. Sensitized to threats of tyranny and oppression by their own loss of social and economic opportunities, they too cherished liberty. Liberty to them, however, did not mean maximizing the free choice and responsibilities of the individual. Rather it meant the continued existence of a traditional communal society, a moral economy, and the ability to transmit the birthright of political freedom to children to whom they could bequeath little if anything else. These colonists remained ever alert to any government actions that meant increased subordination on their part.

Parliamentary legislation attempting to impose a more rigid dependency upon the colonies coincided with the intensification of tensions affecting many Americans. Prerogative and popular parties struggled within urban areas, religious disputes divided villages, Baptists and planters agonized over sin and corruption, and aggressive individuals worried about succeeding within an open economic environment while many others faced the frustration of constricting opportunities. Americans, anxious over strains within their society and angered by British actions, searched for solutions to their troubled circumstances.

An American Theory of Politics

While many colonists expressed their disapproval of British actions by supporting economic boycotts, participating in street riots, or voicing approval of legislative protests, the creation of an articulate response in the form of pamphlet literature, broadsides, and newspaper essays fell to the provincial gentry. These literate gentlemen attempted to fashion a rational discourse convincing enough to change British administrative policy. In the process they created something quite different: a rationale for revolution and regeneration. Their efforts from 1763 to 1776 represented the gradual clarification and unification of a forceful image of the colonies and their place in the world that hitherto had existed as inchoate fragments of thought or perception.

In their effort to present a cogent defense against the actions of Parliament, the gentry drew upon a wide variety of sources.[13] They drew upon classical authors such as Cicero, Sallust, and Tacitus, who wrote during periods of fundamental challenge to the Roman republic or in the midst of the decay of moral and political virtues accompanying its decline. These authors contrasted the venality, cynicism, and oppressive corruption of their own era with the virtuous simplicity, patriotic character, and love of liberty characteristic of the earlier, glorious days of the republic. The provincial authors recognized compelling similarities to their own situation—simple, honest, virtuous provinces threatened by the corruption and tyranny overtaking a once honorable mother country and its venerable constitution. Classical analogies, though, served to illustrate rather than to shape the thought of colonial gentlemen, who employed classical citations in an ornamental manner to give added weight to their arguments.

They also employed traditions drawn from the English common law, primarily through the writings of Sir Edward Coke and later Blackstone's *Commentaries*. Again, like classical allusions, common law references, embodying principles of justice, equity, and rights, served to illustrate a particular interpretation of history that shed light on present events. The British constitution, long the hope of liberty in the Western world, had been corrupted by the machinations of avaricious ministers and their placemen.

Enlightenment rationalism played a more central role in the thought of colonial authors. Pamphlets, broadsides, newspaper essays, and legislative orations continually cited Locke regarding natural rights, as well as the social contract between a people and their government, and Montesquieu to explicate British liberty and the institutional arrangements necessary for its achievement. They drew upon Voltaire for the oppression of the church, Beccaria relative to the reformation of criminal law, and Burlamaqui, Grotius, Pufendorf, and Vattel regarding the proper principles of civil government, as well as the laws of nature and of nations. Here, too, however, the gentry's use of such authors reflected an often superficial or confused knowledge of these European intellectuals. Conservatives and radicals alike cited Locke, Montesquieu, and Rousseau to support their arguments. They combined such men as Bolingbroke and Hume with radical reformers if it suited their purpose and treated such peripheral figures as Burlamaqui on a par with Locke. Enlightenment thought pervaded colonial literature, but, like classical and common law ideas, it seemed more ornamental than determinative of colonial beliefs.

John Locke (1632–1704), however, stood as a major exception. His thought permeated the culture of the colonies by the 1760s. This was particularly true of his ideas regarding the social contract articulated in *Two Treatises on Government* (1690). He claimed that men, living in a state of nature, contracted to form governments in order to protect their natural rights of life, liberty, and property. If government broke that contract, if it threatened the natural rights that were its sole purpose to protect—for example, by taking a person's property without consent—then the people had every right to reassess their action in creating that government. This might, as a last resort, lead to rebellion. While Locke admitted that rebellion was a dangerous undertaking, its opposite, slavery for the people, was far worse.

The belief that the people retained the right to rebel against unlawful or oppressive authorities became entrenched in the consciousness of articulate and inarticulate colonists alike. Writers in the *New York Journal* in 1768 drew nearly verbatim upon Locke when they declared: "Good Laws and good Rulers will always be obey'd and respected." "Mobs and Tumults never happen but thru' Oppression and a scandalous Abuse of Power." Such observations became, in the hands of colonial authors, prima facie accusations of misconduct on the part of authorities rather than the people. Whenever the people became aroused, a New York writer claimed in 1770, it always indicated "a certain Sign of Maladministration."[14]

The petitions of colonial assemblies also exuded a Lockean spirit. While continuing to cast their pleas within the traditional structure of the protection-allegiance covenant, legislators employed basic Lockean principles to reformulate this ancient covenant to fit their needs. In the hands of aroused colonists, Locke's contractual ideas emphasized the king's obligation to respect popular rights if he were to continue to receive the allegiance of the people. Thus Locke did not offer fresh ideas but instead helped Americans refocus old ones in order to articulate their changing moral posture. Lockean principles and ideas regarding the social contract could be employed to highlight the resistant rather than the submissive side of traditional principles. For many colonists, then, Locke helped smooth the way from submission to resistance without a radical departure from a traditional ideology. His ideas became the essential and familiar conduit for changed colonial perceptions. His ideas were, however, susceptible to varying interpretations, depending on the circumstances of those who employed them.

While Lockean principles underlay the colonial perception of the relationship between rulers and the ruled, other writers—men who themselves incorporated Locke's fundamental ideas into their work—provided the colonial gentry with a theory of politics that simultaneously explained why the British behaved as they did in the post-1763 era and provided the ideological basis for an American response. These writers—eighteenth-century transmitters of the radical social and political thought of the English Civil War and Commonwealth era—offered Americans a cohesive set of concepts that fused classical thought, common law theories, and Enlightenment ideas into a coherent whole and provided clarity and direction to the colonial opposition.

Colonial pamphleteers drew their sharpest perception of contemporary politics in the mother country from English "country" theorists and politicians who opposed Robert Walpole, prime minister of George I and George II. The theorists most influential in America were the extreme libertarians John Trenchard and Thomas Gordon, authors of the widely read *Cato's Let-*

ters (1720), a bitter attack on early eighteenth-century English society and politics. Other writers contributing to *Cato's* passionate indictment of British culture found a receptive audience in America; most prominent among them were the liberal Anglican bishop, Benjamin Hoadley; the leader of the opposition to Walpole in Parliament, Robert Viscount Molesworth, whose *Account of Denmark* (1694) provided a detailed explication of how absolutism could assume control over a free state; the conservative politician and philosopher, Henry St. John Viscount Bolingbroke, who viciously attacked Walpole in his *Craftsman* (1726–36); and the Scottish philosopher Frances Hutcheson.

The writing of these men emerged from a deep hostility toward social, economic, and political forces transforming English society after the Glorious Revolution of 1688. The appearance of the Bank of England, giant mercantile firms, and stock markets, as well as the increasing commercialization of agriculture, the growing influence of new moneyed men, and an ever-increasing public debt seemed to endanger traditional values. Eighteenth-century country opponents of court politics perceived their society as falling prey to vice, luxury, and materialistic, commercial values. Behind their perspective lay a political critique: excessive governmental power had spawned the decadence and decay rapidly carrying the nation toward the fate of the ancient Roman Republic.

In midcentury men like Richard Baron and Thomas Hollis worked indefatigably to keep alive commonwealth ideas by widely disseminating the works of Trenchard, Gordon, and others. It was, however, a new generation of English authors who renewed and expanded the principles of their predecessors and applied them to the Anglo-American tensions of the 1760s and 1770s. Richard Price, Joseph Priestley, and John Cartwright became leading advocates of religious and political reform in this period. In addition, James Burgh's three-volume *Political Discourses* (1774)—a virtual grab bag of quotations from nearly every earlier opposition author—became a source for countless American authors.

It was not that opposition writers provided original theoretical insights to the American colonists; they did not. Their central concepts—natural rights, the contractual basis of government and society, and the unique, liberty-protecting nature of England's constitution that mixed the social orders of monarchy, aristocracy, and democracy—were virtually indistinguishable from mainstream political ideas advanced since the late seventeenth century. If the primary elements of thought remained commonplace, however, the stress placed on them and the manner in which they were employed by these opposition writers was decisive. Where supporters of the Hanoverians spoke with pride of the existing constitutional and political arrangements, opposition writers expressed alarm and dismay. For them government was, by its essential nature, threatening to individual liberty and happiness. In their minds, the stability praised by orthodox political theorists rested on a methodical subversion of Parliament by the executive. If allowed to proceed, such usurpations of power by the executive would destroy the liberty-preserving nature of the constitution itself. Opposition writers summarized the means by which the executive undermined the integrity and independence of Parliament—professional armies, placemen, excise plots, and funded national debts—under a single rubric, "corruption." For them, the degeneration of social and political life they saw about them resulted from one central cause: the self-seeking drive for power by corrupt ministers under the executive. Such ministries, epitomized by Robert Walpole, consciously fostered "*luxury* and *extravagance*, the certain forerunners of *indigence, dependence*, and *servility*."[15] After achieving power, these officials fattened on the corruption they had spawned. Their actions were predictable: burdensome taxes, massive public debts, and the creation of a standing army whose ostensible purpose was to protect the people but whose real function was to dominate them.

Such ideas gained little following within English society, but became popular and influential in the American colonies. There the imposition of new colonial legislation in the post-1763 years raised troubling questions, questions for which English radical and opposition writers seemed to provide reasonable and relevant answers. Thus a comprehensive theory of politics emerged within the American colonies that made sense of the bewildering changes of the mid-eighteenth century for many diverse sorts of Americans.

This theory of politics focused on the role of power—defined as the control or domination of some men over others—within American lives. For them power lurked behind every political event; it became omnipresent in public affairs and always aggressively expanded beyond its proper limits. It was this aggressiveness that so troubled provincial writers because in their minds justice, equity, and liberty always fell victim to the inordinate demands of power. They perceived the public world separated into two innately antagonistic spheres: power and liberty. The first, constantly and brutally assertive, must always be opposed, while the second, delicate, innocent, and passive, required a ceaselessly vigilant defense.

From this basic insight colonial authors drew a central conclusion: the preservation of liberty relied entirely on the moral strength and vigilance of the people. Only they could maintain effective restraints on those who wielded power. For generations Americans had felt secure in their liberties; protected by the English constitution. After 1763, however, they became increasingly alarmed. As evidence mounted in their minds that an independent Parliament—the primary safeguard for the maintenance of constitutional liberty—was being undermined by the demoralizing influences of the crown, colonists increasingly looked to *Cato's Letters* and *The Craftsman* for explanations. These periodicals flayed the official corruption that preyed upon the degeneracy of the era. Colonial editors published the most extreme of these jeremiads, and printers reissued the books and essays in their entirety. In addition, they repeatedly reprinted James Burgh's *Britain's Remembrance: or The Danger Not Over* (London, 1746). No other pamphlet of the age more bitterly excoriated the degeneracy of a government allowed to impose an outrageous oppression upon a people wallowing in venality and deceit.

Such fears led many colonists to perceive an unmistakable pattern to the British actions subsequent to the Stamp Act. Britain was succumbing to the all-too-familiar tendencies seen throughout history for nations to degenerate with age, to fall prey to the corruptions of power. Viewed in this manner, the actions taken by the British represented not only misguided behavior but a deliberately planned attack on liberty in England that was spreading its poison to the American colonies. What else could be the meaning of the unconstitutional taxes, the invasion of placemen, the deliberate weakening of the colonial judiciary, plural officeholding, the undermining of the prerogatives of the provincial assemblies, and the presence of a standing army? If allowed to remain unchecked, such a plot could destroy the English constitution and with it all the protection for individual liberties. Such reasoning led colonial leaders to declare their independence from Great Britain on 4 July 1776.

American Republicanism

In the minds of many colonists, the lamp of liberty still burned brightly only in the American provinces, and not to defend it would be treason to themselves and to posterity. The belief that they faced a ministerial conspiracy against liberty transformed the meaning of colonial resistance in their minds from a constitutional quarrel over the power of Parliament to govern them to a world regenerative creed.

A belief in the regenerative quality of their resistance meant that for many Americans the Revolution became more than simply a political revolt; it represented the creation of a fresh world, a republican world.[16] Consequently republicanism stood for more than the substitution of an elective system for a monarchy; it infused the political break with England with a moral fervor and an idealistic depth linked inextricably to the essential character of American society. Their familiarity with the classics continually reminded Americans of the fragile nature of republics and how easily they might be transformed into tyrannies because of moral decay. The character and spirit of the people, not the size of its armies or the wealth of its treasuries, determined whether a republic lived or died. The simple, sturdy qualities of the yeoman—courage, integrity, frugality, temperance, industry—comprised the true strength of a republican society. The love of luxury, elegance, and social distinctions gradually degenerated a people into dissipated, effeminate cowards totally unable, as well as unwilling, to serve and protect their commonwealth.

For Americans, the sacrifice of individual interests to a greater common good comprised both the essence of republicanism and the idealistic goal of the Revolution. Consequently the Revolution was to be more than a rejection of British corruption; it was to be a reformation within provincial societies as well, a reformation defined in republican terms. Emphasizing a morality of social unity, many Americans hoped to create an organic polity by joining individual citizens together into an indissoluble union of peace and goodwill: a true republic. Theirs was a lovely though delicate ideal because a republic, by definition, depended entirely on the character and spirit of its citizens. Republics required the total absence of selfishness and extravagance. They rested on virtue—the willingness of citizens to place the common good above their own private needs and desires. Thus, the presence or absence of virtue determined whether a society would remain republican.

In their articulation of these republican ideals, genteel American authors assumed that public virtue flourished most readily among citizens who privately displayed simplicity, frugality, temperance, and industry. Only a society characterized by equality, by natural rather than artifical differences, could foster a willingness among its citizens to accept authority and to subordinate themselves to the common good. Provincial gentlemen did not intend to create a leveled society; rather, they envisioned an organic hierarchy under the leadership of natural aristocrats who resembled the disinterested heroes of classical antiquity rather than the effete, money-hungry, tools of British ministries.

The republican concern with virtue pervaded the Revolutionary movement and exerted a shaping influence over American culture. Although seemingly opposed to natural human selfishness, it held out great promise. In an enlightened and optimistic age, the most hopeful among the American revolutionaries considered humans to be malleable and their own society to be in a particularly "plastic state" where "the benefactor of mankind may realize all his schemes for promoting human happiness." Americans in 1776 wanted to "form a new-era and give a new turn to human affairs." They intended to shine as the "eminent example of every divine and social virtue" by becoming that unique type of simple, upright, and egalitarian people whom enlightened authors since ancient Rome claimed to be the necessary prerequisite for a republican society.[17] For Americans, then, the moral character of their society would form the prime measure of the success or failure of their revolution. Republicanism in 1776 became a fresh attempt to confront and resist the temptations of luxury; it constituted a new, secular restraint on the selfish proclivities of men, a social restraint providing focus for the efforts of the entire community. For the great bulk of Americans, republicanism blended indistinguishably with revolution and regeneration.

With the outbreak of the Revolution, Americans embraced a distinctive set of political and social attitudes that permeated their society and united them against the British. Believing that history revealed a continual struggle between the spheres of liberty and power, American revolutionaries quickly formed a republican consensus aimed at protecting liberty from ceaseless aggressions of power. Republicanism meant maintaining public and private virtue, internal unity, social solidarity, and vigilance against the corruptions of power. United in this frame of mind, Americans set out to gain their independence and to establish a new republic.

Varied Expectations

Although the bulk of Americans espoused republican ideas in their struggle against the British, these ideas did not bear the same meaning for everyone. It soon became apparent that republicanism represented a general consensus solely because it rested on such vague premises. Only one thing was universally clear: republicanism meant an absence of an aristocracy and a monarchy. Beyond this, agreement vanished. What precise form a republican government should assume and, more important, what constituted a republican society remained vague. Differing perceptions of republicanism resulted from the fact that social and economic forces at work within eighteenth-century America had created a number of amorphous but nonetheless very real needs among various groups of people.[18]

Most Americans, living in isolated rural communities, drew meaning in their lives from a traditional corporate world rather than the entrepreneurial individualism of those advocating a market economy and a more open, competitive society.[19] The transformations affecting their lives throughout the eighteenth century latently mobilized large numbers of rural folk in support of a profoundly reactionary worldview based on essentially premodern, localist impulses. Living in an undercommercialized countryside, suspicious of higher authorities and commercial activity, these people desired above all else independence and homogeneity. Only such an environment would preserve them from outside interference, internal dissension, and the social disruptions created by the unequal distribution of wealth and power. Locally validated leaders served primarily to insulate local customs and traditions from larger outside interests and allegiances. Rural folk wanted to be left alone in their relative equality, with the means to prosper and the right to shape their own moral and political worlds.

The changes taking place during the eighteenth century threatened the integral worldview from which Americans drew meaning and identity in their lives. Disturbed by a growing certainty that the simple, organic world they cherished was slipping away in the face of malignant unintelligible forces, a great many rural Americans became particularly susceptible to calls for moral reformation. They became ripe for a unique form of political mobilization.

Revolutionary republicanism effected this mobilization by providing a crusading ideology that unified rural Americans behind political activity otherwise condemned by their own worldview. Theirs became a moralistic ethos that did not stop at the rational in its reaction to the bewildering changes of the time. Rural Americans drew particular meaning from the gentry's exhortations to political action cast in libertarian terms. They responded positively to country party rhetoric attacking aristocratic corruption and the hierarchical tyranny resulting from the invasion of power into the realm of liberty. The dark, conspiratorial suspicions of this rhetoric resonated with the localists' fears of change and distrust of hierarchy. They took seriously the gentry's exhortations to grasp control of their own lives, to escape from the oppression of corrupt outside forces, and to return their country to a virtuous course. Primed for a purgative, reactionary crusade and urged to participate in what they assumed to be just such an effort, rural traditionalists or localists shaped Revolutionary republicanism according to their deepest needs and expectations.

In areas that were experiencing widespread penetration by the market economy, several perspectives resulted. The sudden increase in the concentration of wealth in societies that were not overwhelmingly prosperous created widespread concern that a few were gaining wealth by abusing a system intended to serve all equally. These people, puzzled by and perhaps drawn to the values of the market economy, demanded equity within their societies, as well as the maintenance of social opportunity for themselves and their children. They joined their rural brethren in viewing republicanism as a means of returning their society to the corporate values of the past.

At the same time, however, a contrasting outlook emerged in urban areas as well as in increasingly open, diverse, mobile rural regions. There the aggressive, individualistic ethos driving Ethan Allen, new merchants competing with the Junto for economic gain in Boston, upstart planters challenging the Virginia squirearchy at the polls, and thousands of other Americans whose economic activities wrenched them out of the traditional corporate world of their forefathers created quite a different view of republicanism. Republicanism for them was a combination of the ideas of John Locke and English country party radicals like James Burgh and Richard Price. Their understanding of Locke, however, came through the writing of men like Burgh and Price, in whose hands the ideas of contract, of governors as trustees of the people subject to dismissal if they abused that trust, sprang from

Locke the advocate of personal autonomy and popular sovereignty rather than Locke the progenitor of social hierarchy. These men fused such a perception of Locke with a bitter middle-class resentment of the closed, aristocratic nature of the British constitution and the country party's deep distrust of the misuses of power.[20]

It was Burgh's *Political Disquisitions* (1774), a kind of bible for English radical reformers as well as American republicans, that fashioned a profound amalgam of middle-class radicalism, country ideas, and Lockean principles of contract, state of nature, and government as a trust of all the people. Burgh infused traditional opposition and republican ideas with individualist attitudes drawn from an insurgent middle class. When he attacked placemen, for example, his outrage stemmed not only from the threat to an independent House of Commons posed by these men but from the fact that they represented a nonmeritorious obstacle blocking the access of talented middle-class individuals to public office. He constantly attacked the British government for apportioning its lucrative and prestigious positions only to the nobles and gentry who dominated Parliament. Merit, not eminence, talent, not status, should dictate who gained public office.

Richard Price, in his *Observations on the Nature of Civil Liberty* (1776), skillfully combined Locke, Commonwealth principles, and middle-class radicalism. In his discussion of debt, paper money, and banks, he imbued the country party's suspicion of capitalism with a more modern middle-class ethos. Men who profited through artificial means such as banks and paper money, Price claimed, constituted an idle and unproductive element within English society, an immoral, nonindustrious class, who, like the nonworking poor, stood in stark contrast to the talented, hard-working middle class. Price and other reformers began, quite unself-consciously, to transform the traditional perception of a subsistence economy as natural and a market economy as artificial. Instead they considered a natural economy to be one characterized by diligence and industry, artificial economy by idleness and nonproductivity.

Consequently although the reformers employed the language of classical republicanism, corruption for them took on a new meaning; symbolizing idleness, profligacy, and an absence of talent and merit. A corrupt system rewarded unproductive and talentless drones by denying public careers to men of merit. The reformers called for a nation of virtuous, diligent, and frugal middle-class individuals as desirous of a meritocracy of ability as they were of a social order of civic virtue. They shaped Locke's ideas on natural equality to mean a natural right to equal opportunity.

Out of this perspective arose a new conception of virtue that integrated greater public good with industry and economic productivity; this entailed a transformation in how individuals viewed the essential nature of public behavior. Civic activity alone no longer defined virtue and morality; economic activity became important as well. Citizens still had a duty to work for the common good, but economic behavior directed toward private benefit became the best means of achieving this goal. The virtuous man thus became involved in self-centered economic behavior that resulted in a society based on talent, not artificial privilege.

The rising middle elements in America drew their republicanism from Price and Burgh just as did other Americans. Theirs, however, was a special perception: one of aggressive individualism, strident nationalism, interest group politics, and a focus on a market economy open to all. They looked forward to a society offering a wide array of opportunities to deserving citizens and to a government open to men of talent and ability. A deferential society was anathema to them; it meant an aristocracy of privilege instead of a republic of natural abilities.

The republicanism of the American gentry could not have been more different. They too drew upon the ideas of John Locke, but their perception of Locke was similar to that of their English counterparts. The English gentry had assumed that the publication of Locke's *Two Treatises on Government* merely dignified the established legal order of the English polity. His principles helped restore the right of political initiative to the English ruling class by demonstrating that just opposition to the crown could legitimately coexist with a hierarchy of social authority. Therefore a revolution such as the one in 1688 depended on the constant and firm psychological dependence of the majority of the population upon the ruling class—clergy, gentry, and aristocracy. While each individual might have the theoretical right to destroy the legal order of society in the face of an unjust tyranny, the necessities of the social structure were such that only a very few could exercise this right responsibly. And since the entire validity of the right of resistance rested logically on the responsibility with which it was employed, only gentlemen of the ruling class were, by definition, capable of assuming such an awesome moral burden. It was this doctrine that the great English lords readily embraced in 1690 and that served the ruling aristocracy so well throughout the succeeding decades of the eighteenth century. It provided the firmest support for their hierarchical order.

The American gentry absorbed these same principles; such ideas underlay their perception of republicanism. For them the affective force naturally linked to the duty to obey social norms—the internalized structure of social control so necessary to a hierarchy—had been irreversibly dissociated from the legal order of English society by the Revolution. This authority, this affective force itself, however, had not been dissolved; rather, for the American gentry, such an operative authority now resided within their own society. The gentry, long accustomed to viewing themselves as the embodiment of the "people" in the symbolic representation of king and people springing from the protection-allegiance covenant, thus assumed that the tremendous responsibility for leading the Revolution fell to them. In their minds, the Revolution was a revolt against corrupt officials, not a revolt against the principle of hierarchical authority. Consequently John Locke's ideas on social hierarchy admirably served embattled members of the gentry in their effort to solidify their position in American society by leading their countrymen in a revolt against their British oppressors.

Republicanism Triumphant

Americans who supported the Revolution did so for different reasons, but all professed a devotion to republicanism. Just what that meant, though, remained open to question. Some enthusiastically accepted the cash nexus of market relations; others remained profoundly anticapitalistic. Some wanted to retain a communal society based on social hierarchy; others desired an open, competitive society without regard for rank or status; and still others preferred a simple, homogeneous society of relative equality held together by deep corporate bonds. These disparate desires emerged as discrete fragments of two larger cultural impulses—republicanism and liberalism—coursing through the lives of late-eighteenth-century Americans. At times the two seemed to run parallel to one another, at other times they appeared in direct conflict, and at still other times they melded into a nearly indistinguishable whole. In many ways republicanism—a familiar ideology permeating all walks of life—shaped Americans' thoughts; it provided them with meaning and identity in their lives. Liberalism—an unarticulated behavioral pattern more than a sharply delineated mode of thought—unconsciously shaped their daily activity. Most Americans still clung to a harmonious, communal view of their society even while behaving in a materialistic, competitive manner. Republicanism ritualized a mode of thought that ran counter to the flow of history; it idealized the traditional values of a world rapidly fading rather than the market conditions and liberal capitalist mentality swiftly emerging in the late eighteenth century. Yet the confrontation with the British in the 1760s and the 1770s instilled new vigor into traditional republican values by stigmatizing the institutions and attitudes of a mother country poised on the verge of the Industrial Revolution. Consequently the Revolution sanctified virtue (defined as the subordination of self to the greater good of the community) corporate harmony, and unity at the very time that those values had become anachronistic.

Throughout the Revolutionary years, Americans continued to idealize an essentially premodern set of values while wrestling with changes that transformed their society. More and more isolated agrarian villages began to be tied into larger commercial networks; opportunities abounded that revealed the unlimited potential for human freedom; and the bonds holding together families, churches, and communities eroded. However, the conflict between traditional republican values and newly emerging liberal behavioral patterns never became so clear-cut as to set one specific set of ideas in opposition to another. Indeed this tension seethed as fiercely within individuals and groups as it did between competing elements within American society. The cosmopolitan gentry's competitive economic behavior tore at their own profoundly conservative social views, while the traditional localists' desire for individual equality increasingly conflicted with their professed communal values. Many Americans could, and did, believe simultaneously in corporate needs and individual rights. They never had a sense of choosing between two starkly contrasting traditions—republicanism and liberalism—between Locke the aggressive individualist and Locke the devotee of hierarchy, or between Burgh the embittered middle-class individualist and Burgh the libertarian fearful of corruptive tendencies emanating from the realm of power. Instead they domesticated classical republicanism to fit their contemporary needs; quite unself-consciously they amalgamated inherited assumptions with their liberal behavior.

The tension between republican ideology and liberal behavior carried throughout the Revolution. Yet the war itself, or rather its victory, prompted most Americans to view their efforts in republican terms and to enshrine republican values in the meaning of the war itself.[21] Most Americans had entered the Revolution with the millennial expectation of creating a new republican society comprised of virtuous citizens free of Old World corruption. The Revolution carried the promise of regeneration with a desperate insistence born of the uncertainties arising from societal transformations. During the course of the war, however, American behavior manifested disturbing signs of European vice. Factional and personal rivalries emerged; public officials and governmental contractors indulged in widespread corruption; farmers demanded usurious prices for their crops and merchants for their trade goods; many engaged in a lucrative trade with the enemy; and others employed a great variety of desperate means to avoid military service. The techniques employed to win the war also raised grave questions about the republican character of Americans. The continental government found itself forced to conscript citizens, confiscate property, and engage the mysterious and very likely corrupt financial and administrative talents of shrewd and ambitious individuals. Worst of all, the militia—the backbone of a republican society—proved ineffective; only the creation of a professional army with rigorously disciplined soldiers and self-promoting officers saved the cause.

Despite these disheartening experiences, Americans chose to believe that their victory was a splendid confirmation of their moral strengths, a magnificent testament to their republican ideals. At the war's end in 1783, Americans celebrated public virtue, not its failure. To preserve their millennial vision of the future, they could not recognize the reality of the many questionable expedients employed to win the war. The Revolutionary generation redefined its experiences and made them as virtuous and as heroic as they ought to have been. Thus, victory—gained by the fallible, partial, and selfish efforts of many Americans—allowed an entire generation to ignore these unpleasant realities and to claim that it had remained true to the republican standards of 1776. They offered those standards and the image of a unified, virtuous, republican citizenry to future generations.

Idealizing the Revolution and enshrining republican ideals did not solve the tensions that had pervaded America before as well as after the war. Although the Revolution had mobilized a vast number of Americans of different needs and expectations through its exhortations and political actions, its libertarian rhetoric and its optimism regarding national regeneration, what American leaders meant by this incitement may well have been quite different from the spirit in which many Americans—rural and urban, rising or declining—took them. Americans shaped the rhetoric of the Revolution to their innermost needs. What might happen when those needs were not met by the successful completion of the Revolution was obscured by the war itself, but the question would arise with renewed intensity once the war ended, for then Americans had to consider the form of government and the type of society that would develop within their new nation.

In the nearly two decades between the end of the Revolution and the turn of the century, cultural stress within the young republic increased greatly. The struggle between republicanism and liberalism intensified within individuals as well as between groups. These cultural strains profoundly affected the lives of Americans during the years 1783–1800 as they attempted to establish the arts, create new forms of government, and forge a republican culture within their new nation.

three

The Arts in the New Republic

Americans emerged from the Revolution filled with a buoyant optimism. For them, the Revolution was far more than a colonial war for political independence; it promised a fundamental restructuring of their political, social, and cultural world. A fresh new republican world of art, politics, literature, and social affairs would blossom once individual Americans, as well as American society as a whole, broke free of the shackles of the past. America would become not only the political ideal of the world but its cultural capital as well; republicanism would foster artists, writers, and playwrights to rival Rembrandt, Milton, and Shakespeare.

Such expectations of artistic greatness emerged from two sources: one an ancient belief and the other themes found within the opposition literature of the Revolution. When Benjamin Franklin observed that "the Arts delight to travel Westward," he was articulating the idea of *translatio studii* or the *translatio imperii*.[1] This belief—that civilization and culture inevitably traveled from east to west—originated in classical Greece and Rome, emerged during the Renaissance, and reappeared in Enlightenment thought. Franklin assumed, given the course of history, that America was destined to inherit the mantle of cultural greatness. John Adams recalled that "the observation that arts, sciences, and empire travelled westward" pervaded pre-Revolutionary Massachusetts, "and in conversation it was always added since I was a child, that the next step would be over the Atlantic into America."[2]

Country party writers were more specific; they linked artistic achievement to freedom. John Trenchard and Thomas Gordon, for example, expostulated in *Cato's Letters* that *"Polite Arts and Learning* [are] *naturally produced in Free*

States, and marred by such as are not free."[3] Opposition writers, however, never perceived cultural endeavors to encompass a transcendent realm of aesthetics and refined sensibilities separated from the common, everyday occurrences of the world. While they spoke and wrote of "the muses," "arts and sciences," "fine arts," or *"belles lettres"* (the word *culture* itself did not refer to a separate sphere of aesthetic tastes and sensibilities until well into the nineteenth century), these authors never divorced such phenomena from the political, social, or economic life of their communities. Social, aesthetic, political, and economic developments existed for them as indivisible strands in a single social fabric. Consequently, if civil liberty were the essential prerequisite for social happiness, political stability, and commercial prosperity, it must necessarily be the seedbed of artistic greatness as well. It naturally followed that as America appeared destined to become the bastion of political liberty, so too should it become the new Athens of the Western world.

Once fused with freedom and the regeneration expected to accompany the emergence of republicanism in America, however, the enthusiastic expectations for artistic achievement suffered the ambiguities and contradictory impulses affecting the larger society. What constituted "republican art" was no clearer than what comprised a republican society or a republican government. Art and artists in America became caught up in the same dialectical process affecting the social, political, and economic lives of Americans: a dialectic between freedom and order, license and restraint, virtue and selfishness, individual liberty and communal responsibility. No clear pattern emerged to guide individual artists or the community at large in their expectations for the arts in the young republic. Americans expected artistic greatness for their culture but remained uncertain over the place of artists within their society.

Art in America

By the 1780s a number of American artists living in London had begun to receive enthusiastic recognition from European admirers. Such artistic victories, scored by John Singleton Copley, Benjamin West, and Gilbert Stuart, became the source of tremendous pride for Americans. A Baltimore newspaper bragged that "the paintings of Copley and West find even in Europe, little competition." Such circumstances "ought to teach us very respectful ideas of American genius." Americans could not help but feel pride when the London press referred to Stuart as the Van Dyck of his time or when a London patron claimed Stuart to be "the first Portrait Painter now living."[4] Such accolades pleased Americans greatly, for they longed for cultural recognition from European nations. The tremendous prestige their artists living in London enjoyed seemed to indicate to Americans that their culture would quickly blossom and overcome the amateuristic and imitative character of the provincial years. At the same time, though, the place of art and artists within American society itself created tremendous anxieties for many Americans as tensions developed within their culture over the value of artistic expression in a republic.

These tensions resulted from the fact that American republicanism gave rise to an ironic paradox: it simultaneously spawned an excitement for artistic accomplishments generated by the idea of *translatio studii* and a hostility toward their development that crippled them at the very moment of their birth. On the one hand, it incorporated an enthusiasm for regeneration and progress, yet on the other, it feared corruption and the loss of virtue. At all times, though, republicanism linked the nature of a society with the character of its people. Here lay the true roots of the ambivalence and hostility elicited by artistic endeavors.

Classical literature taught that republics rested upon the virtuous character of their citizens. Consequently anything associated with passion and licentiousness—love of material possessions, overweening personal pride, sensual pleasures—threatened the health of society. Such beliefs forced many Americans to survey artistic creativity from a critical perspective. Some contended that paintings and sculpture "flourished chiefly in wealthy and luxurious countries." Mature societies always supported such artistic endeavors, but to a young republic they were "highly pernicious and destructive."[5] Art and artists thrived in an effete, dependent society devoted to sensual pleasures rather than in a robust, independent environment where each person must be able to spring to the defense of the nation's liberties. In a society where the arts flourished, "You would look, therefore, for shoeless beggars and brilliant equipage. And you will find them." Art, in the minds of many Americans, became firmly associated with luxury. "Wealth alone can requite the labour of the artist," observed the *Port Folio*.[6]

Many Americans believed that the fine arts sapped the cause of virtue and piety. They represented decadent, decaying cultures, not vibrant young republics. John Adams bemoaned the fact that the chisel, the brush, and the pencil had "been enlisted on the side of Despotism and Superstition" throughout the ages. By arousing the passions and enervating the spirit and the character of individuals, the arts served political and religious tyranny. Following a European visit, an American traveler confirmed this suspicion: "I have no doubt that the pencil of Peter Paul Rubens has contributed to strengthen the doctrines of papal supremacy, and to lead the minds of hundreds and thousands, more deeply into the shade of bigotry and superstition."[7]

Artists themselves often wrestled with similar feelings. In many ways, the lives of two such artists, John Trumbull and Charles Willson Peale, delineate the tensions affecting so many Americans in the post-Revolutionary decades.

Both men, one a gentleman and the other from an ordinary background, experienced the tension between personal ambition and public welfare, private gain and communal responsibility, and the demands of the marketplace and personal standards of taste. In addition, they struggled with the contradiction so many other Americans perceived between artistic creativity and public virtue.

John Trumbull came from a solid gentry family in Lebanon, Connecticut.[8] His father, Jonathan, owned the finest home in the area, headed a thriving commercial business, represented the town in the Connecticut Assembly, sat on the county court, served as a colonel in the Connecticut militia, and became governor of the colony in 1769. From his early youth John loved to draw. His pastime delighted his parents until he announced his desire to study under John Singleton Copley, the most prominent portrait artist in Boston. Jonathan announced definitively that gentlemen might draw as a diversion but never as a profession; John must therefore attend Harvard, where he could either take up the ministry or study law and return to the family enterprise. John did enroll at Harvard, but while there he frequently visited Copley's home and continued to draw. Upon his graduation in 1773, he gained employment drawing maps for his father, the governor. With the outbreak of the Revolution, John became an adjutant in a Connecticut regiment, served as second aide-de-camp to General Washington, and gained promotion to the rank of colonel when he was only twenty years old. In a fit of pique, he resigned his commission in 1777 and returned to Lebanon, where he painted portraits of relatives and friends. Life in Lebanon may have made Trumbull restless and anxious, however; community opinion considered art a frivolous endeavor, hardly worth the time and talents of a man of Trumbull's station and great intellectual ability. As a result, he left Lebanon in 1778 to serve in a military campaign in Rhode Island, where he experienced heavy fighting. By the summer of 1778 Trumbull had settled in Boston.

Boston brought no less uncertainty for him. Trumbull simultaneously kept up his own artistic work and attempted a number of business projects with his brothers. In addition he joined a social group of other young members of gentry families, who reinforced his status as a gentleman. They had little use for the local committees of safety, which they considered foolish and ignorant, nor did they trust the middling and lower classes because of their gullibility and lack of restraint. Committed to the Revolution, they envisioned its goal to be an ordered society resting on proper deference and respect for men of eminence. They expected the Revolution to foster a spirit of virtue that recognized that men of education, refinement, and wealth must be the natural leaders of society.

While Trumbull subscribed wholeheartedly to a genteel image of society, he remained uneasy with such a culture's view of the gentleman as artist. In an effort to please his family and friends, he embarked on a business trip to London in 1780, although he still longed to study painting, perhaps even as a profession. While in London, he visited Benjamin West, who placed him under the tutelage of Gilbert Stuart. In January 1782 he returned to Boston still torn between commerce and art. Nonetheless, Trumbull returned to London and Benjamin West late in 1783. There, however, he encountered another tension: the conflict between the luxurious life of London and the austere republicanism of his native land.

Raised in an environment of moderation and restraint, Trumbull had heard many Congregational ministers deprecate luxury and extravagance; his own reading in the classics taught him that the decline of Rome and Greece resulted from the self-imposed decay of excessive affluence. Americans must therefore not emulate Europeans, whose luxury supported magnificent art, literature, drama, and gracious living but also decadence and corruption. Trumbull worried over the direction American society might be taking: "Have we not too eager a spirit for Commerce, have we not too much ambition of Opulence, and are we not precipitating ourselves into the imitation of every species of Luxury and refinement:—and does not all this tend to the inevitable destruction of republican Virtue and national Character! I fear so."[9]

Trumbull decided to become an artist, to turn his back upon the commercial world, and yet this decision did not relieve him of uncertainty. His mood fluctuated wildly between excitement and optimism over his own personal goals and depression and anxiety over the condition of the world and the future of his country. He observed to his brother that "it appears to me a very ridiculous world & perhaps we are not the least ridiculous objects in it, you talking wisely of Oeconomoy, republican Virtue, & national Honor, & yet feeding Folly, Luxury, & Extravagance with Gauze, Ribbons & Tea— While I rail at Vanity & yet live for flattering it."[10]

The conflict between virtue and commerce did not, however, constitute the sole, or even the primary, anxiety for Trumbull. Rather, his insatiable urge to paint troubled him above all else. Not only did it fly in the face of the traditional values of his family, but it sprang from a selfish personal desire for individual achievement that contradicted his own republican principles. In the end, he transmuted this tension between personal ambition and the need to serve a larger communal good called for by republican teachings by resolving to achieve eminence as a painter of history. Painting scenes from the Revolution promised Trumbull a perfect resolution to his inner conflict. He could appease his personal ambition to achieve national prominence as an artist and at the same time contribute to the republican virtue and character of the nation by means of the moral examples his work would provide.

Trumbull gained inspiration from the work of Benjamin West and John Singleton Copley, who in turn drew upon the neoclassical style of the eighteenth century. This genre, influenced by Enlightenment thought, emphasized science and history rather than religion and the Scriptures as subjects for artistic creativity. This secularized art that emerged from a secularized society became part of a moralizing fervor that pervaded Western culture in the eighteenth century. Classical history accorded nicely with this didactic and historicizing mood by providing appropriate subjects for artists intent upon fostering moral values.

When West and Copley began their professional careers, they practiced this neoclassical mode. West, however, reasoned that modern battles were just as appropriate as ancient ones to depict virtue and that modern men should thereby be presented in contemporary clothing. The result was his masterful and innovative *Death of General Wolfe* (1771) in which he celebrated the death of a modern hero in neoclassical terms employing traditional Christian iconographical imagery. Wolfe lay in the same posture as Christ in the Pietá. He was, however, in modern dress, and the cross had been replaced by a national flag. Whereas neoclassical artists portrayed death scenes on couches or in beds, West, followed by Copley, placed these events on the actual grounds where they took place as close to the actual moment as possible and thus greatly heightened the effect of immediacy in his work.

This was the style Trumbull adopted when he initiated his pictorial record of the American Revolution. He completed the first scene, *The Death of General Warren at the Battle of Bunker Hill, 17, June, 1775*, early in 1786, to great acclaim. West considered it the finest portrayal of a modern battle ever painted. Yet important and quite illuminating distinctions existed between Trumbull's *Bunker Hill* and the battle scenes of West himself, differences that resulted from the backgrounds of the two men. West, born into a modest Quaker family, arrived in London a poor and barely literate man. Although he became thoroughly acquainted with the concept of decorum—proper facial and figure types, appropriateness in pose and gesture, correctness of fashion—he never acquired the mind-set of a gentleman. Common sense told him that individuals involved in life-or-death combat, regardless of whether they were officers or enlisted men, patrician or plebian, should be portrayed in passionate engagement. This was not the case with Trumbull's work. All officers, British and American, displayed calm courage and gracious dignity. As gentlemen, they were, in Trumbull's mind, naturally endowed with higher sensibilities. His officers appeared oblivious to the horror and violence enveloping them. Trumbull reserved passionate countenances for the common soldiers, whose faces he drew from standard art handbooks of expression.

A fellow student of West, William Dunlap, who considered Trumbull "awfully above me," offered a critique of *Bunker Hill* that graphically revealed Trumbull's purpose as an artist.[11] Critical of the selection of Bunker Hill as a subject, Dunlap declared: "The death of Doctor Warren . . . is an incident of minor consequences compared with the repeated defeats of the veterans of Great Britain by Prescott, Putnam, and the brave undisciplined Yankee yeomen. . . . Such a moment of triumph might have been chosen by an American painter."[12] Such was not, however, Trumbull's purpose. For him the Revolution carried a special meaning: morality, virtue, reason, and restraint resulted only when the masses followed the lead of gentlemen. He took seriously classical aesthetics. The intent of literature, poetry, and painting was to idealize virtue by capturing noble acts of history. Trumbull as artist intended to teach the value of deference and order. While his own life embodied the contradictions and ambiguities of a changing society, he remained intent on portraying the transcendent virtues of an aristocratic class and a traditional, organic culture.

Whereas John Trumbull became an artist by choice over a potentially prosperous commercial career, Charles Willson Peale became an artist after serving an apprenticeship to a saddler.[13] For a time Peale followed the saddler's trade, repaired watches, and painted portraits simultaneously in a desperate attempt to gain financial solvency in his native Maryland. He finally gained the trust and support of the wealthy Charles Carroll, who financed a trip to London for him so that he could study with Benjamin West. In 1767 Peale, a debt-ridden itinerant artist, left Annapolis for England. When he returned two years later, he quickly developed a reputation among the gentry of the middle colonies as an excellent portrait painter. Still, he had to travel about in order not to exhaust his market in any one area. In 1774 when he settled in Philadelphia, Peale remained in debt even though he had established himself as one of the premier portrait artists in the colonies. He still had to cast about for customers and often found it necessary to solicit payment. Peale desperately needed fresh subjects and a changed cultural environment in order to develop his artistic sense and aesthetic appreciation. The Revolution held out a bright promise in Peale's mind for the creation of an American Athens in which he and other artists could thrive within an appreciative climate of public opinion.

Unlike Copley, Stuart, West, and Trumbull, who resided in London for the duration of the war, Peale remained in America totally dedicated to the Revolutionary cause. Convinced that the future of the arts in America depended greatly on the manner in which artists behaved during the war, he joined the radical element within Philadelphia and spoke out in support of American liberty. In 1776 he enlisted in the Philadelphia militia. While fighting for liberty he intended to record this great epic in world history for future generations. He planned to create a collection of portraits of heroes of the Revolution to stand as examples to future generations.

Peale's wartime experience combined the roles of politician, artist, and soldier. His outspoken defense of American liberties in the prewar years gained him election to numerous committees responsible for regulating Philadelphia's economy and government between 1774 and 1780. During his service in the militia, Peale painted miniatures of his fellow soldiers that enabled him to record for posterity countless faces and scenes of the Revolution. In 1776 the Continental Congress awarded him the first commission for a portrait of George Washington.

Peale saw war firsthand, not as a romanticized ideal. His service in the militia exposed him to treachery, confusion, mud, ice, sickness, death, and dislocation. Yet when he resumed his collection of portraits in 1780, none of this reality appeared in his work. Instead the neoclassical style and mode of thought he absorbed while studying under West in London pervaded his creations.

The artistic style that Peale learned from West rested on certain conventions: the artist had a moral responsibility to educate and elevate the minds of those who viewed his creation; the best way to do this was to capture in his work eternal virtues that transcended time and place. Consequently Peale, committed patriot that he was, did not see America as unique; rather it simply became the New World vehicle for the transmission of classical virtues that had been snuffed out in Europe. His paintings screened out the social disorder, the personal pain and suffering, as well as the chaos and atrocities with which he was so familiar. Peale never believed he was imposing a false order upon the confusion about him; instead he firmly believed that his work revealed a preexisting natural order. His purpose was not to be original or creative but rather to capture the unity and order of the universe for the benefit of his countrymen.

If Peale's gallery did not accord with his wartime experiences, it did coincide with his view of republicanism, which called for subordination of individual desires to the greater communal good. With the gallery Peale could integrate his role as artist with that of public servant. Unfortunately for Peale, the republican perceptions of most of his countrymen did not lead them to consider him a beneficial public servant. Instead a great many of the individuals whom Peale desired to paint felt that the most beneficial thing any artist could do would be to emigrate. Peale found himself caught up in an irrational, but effective, bind with many of the most prominent men in America. On the one hand, responding to republican beliefs that associated art and artists with decadence and corruption, some viewed Peale as an agent of tyranny. Others, the more conservative among the gentry patrons Peale sought, felt he took the rhetoric about the rights of man altogether too seriously and thereby stood as a representative of democratic chaos. Peale's attempt to link the arts in America to republican principles constantly faced opposition inspired by those very principles.

Undaunted, Peale continued to pursue his goal of a gallery of prominent personages of the Revolution, only in order to do this, he had to become an artist-entrepreneur. He found himself forced to ferret out customers willing to pay for their portraits and then to dun these individuals for the agreed-upon fee. While Peale never gave up his gallery idea, he did find it necessary to search for a way to avoid becoming entirely dependent on the uncertain support of wealthy customers. "Public art" constituted one such attempt. He suggested that the national government subsidize work, to be hung in public places, that celebrated the virtues of the young republic. Peale thus meant to rescue art from the capriciousness of the marketplace by making artists subsidized public servants rather than private entrepreneurs. Although Peale never convinced legislators that American culture merited or needed such support, he remained a champion of public art throughout most of his life.

When Peale failed to gain government subsidies for his work from the representatives of the people, he took his case for public art directly to the people themselves. He created a series of transparencies from natural or historical scenes that could be manipulated so as to give the illusion of realistic movement. After a profitable initial response, the novelty of "moving pictures" wore off, and ticket sales disappeared. The people at large proved every bit as indifferent, hostile, and fickle toward the arts as the genteel. Peale then turned to the creation of Peale's Museum of natural history. Like his portrait gallery of prominent Revolutionaries, the museum reflected Peale's attempt to elucidate and to retain the beneficial values of harmony, order, and stability that he so urgently desired to find in the confusion of post-Revolutionary America. Virtue, if found no place else, reigned preeminent in his museum. Always supportive of the idea of civic responsibility, Peale could only hope that the order found in the museum might "influence public opinion [so] that republicanism will be highly promoted."[14]

Although the museum reflected Peale's attachment to republican ideals, its fate mirrored his relationship with the democratic and commercial forces encouraged by the Revolution. Throughout the years that he operated the museum, Peale was repeatedly forced to compromise his scientific methods. His constant augmentation of the collections overwhelmed any rational scheme of classification, and yet he had to keep increasing, shifting, and changing his exhibits in order to attract sufficient customers to keep the museum open.

In many ways Peale's experience as a museum curator replicated his career as an artist. He constantly experimented with various kinds of art and different sorts of exhibits, not in response to any personal aesthetic design or desire for artistic creativity but out of necessity. He found himself forced to adapt his work to the desires of his audience, to judge his art by the standards of the marketplace, to survive more by the sharpness of his wits than by the creativity of his brush. As long as he remained in America he had no choice; to survive as an artist necessitated the development of commercial instincts and ploys that inhibited the development of greater artistic creativity. And yet Peale would have it no other way. His deep commitment to republicanism would not allow him to abandon his effort to establish a link between a republican society and the arts. This caught him up in an ironic paradox: the republican ideology in which he so fervently believed fostered a deep hostility and suspicion of the arts themselves and stimulated a democratic marketplace that stifled artistic creativity. Peale the artist found himself forced to endure the effects generated by values and ideas championed by Peale the Revolutionary republican.

The work of Trumbull and Peale, though, taken with that of West, Copley, and Stuart, did stand as positive evidence of the progress being made by American artists. Their canvasses equaled the best European work of the day and surpassed most. These Americans had fully absorbed the neoclassical style of the age; indeed, any of their paintings could have been taken for the work of a European master. Their creations indicated that Franklin's hope for the westward transit of the arts did appear to be taking place.

Another artist, the obscure and enigmatic Ralph Earl of Connecticut, also attempted to paint in the current neoclassical style. A heavy-drinking spendthrift who spent time in debtors' prison, Earl tried to maintain himself as a portrait painter. His work simply could not compare in quality with that of the superior artists; he lacked their technical skills, their accomplished sense of color and shading. However, Earl's paintings offered something that the others lacked. Over time, the backgrounds Earl painted for his portraits began to differ greatly from those of his more successful colleagues. Rather than blurring his backgrounds in order to sharpen the focus on the subject or seating his clients in one interior setting or another, Earl set his portraits in the Connecticut countryside. He made the native background an integral part of the picture rather than simply a backdrop. His work suggested a special character about the American environment—a romantic spaciousness, an openness, a freedom. By taking the humble landscape seriously and on its own terms, Earl's paintings revealed a natural quality, a lack of restraint, about American life that set it apart from the timeless transcendent values of neoclassical art. His landscapes expressed a naturalism that went beyond the formal conventions of the day. They hinted at the unique qualities of spontaneity and naturalness that had begun to emerge with the Revolution and intimated that America might become more than simply the most recent exemplar of transcendent classical values; a fresh, new society might emerge in the West.

Music

Like the paintings of Ralph Earl, the musical compositions of William Billings suggested a similar freedom.[15] In *The New-England Psalm-Singer* (Boston, 1770), the first tunebook by an American composer, as well as the first collection consisting entirely of American music, Billings had displayed a complete mastery of the English church music of the day. Like Earl, he went beyond the established European conventions by integrating musical impulses drawn from his native environment and created a distinctive musical form and style.

Prior to the publication of the *Psalm-Singer*, the only hint of the Westerly progress of music came from the colonial response to changes in English church music. Anglicans had begun to incorporate more instrumental music into their services and to sing a more intricate kind of vocal music. At the same time non-Anglican sects, particularly the Congregationalists and Presbyterians, gradually allowed organs into their churches, and they too began to respond to vocal music. Psalm singing, where all members of the congregation sang Psalms lined out by an elder or a deacon, had been the sole concession to music within the early churches. Then hymns drawn from nonbiblical texts or from portions of the Bible other than Psalms gradually entered Congregational and Presbyterian churches. Finally, anthems, elaborate tunes characterized by an exuberant style punctuated with trills, graces, lively tempos, and ornate textual changes, predominated.

These ambitious pieces often strayed from the strictly devotional purposes of psalms and hymns. They gave free range to an aesthetic impulse by demanding increased sophistication from those attempting to sing them. Consequently a developmental spiral set in among Congregational and Presbyterian singers. As individuals became more skilled, they desired more demanding music; as the music became more difficult, it called for more sophisticated training; such training produced even more accomplished singers. This new environment created a demand for better-trained teachers, singing schools, and native composers who could provide local singers with more appropriate instruction, as well as music distinctive to their needs.

Billings's *Psalm-Singer* filled this need. Billings, the son of a shopkeeper and a tanner by trade, was a self-taught musician. Blind in one eye, with one leg shorter than the other and a slightly withered arm, Billings, negligent in his dress and totally without grace of manner or speech, had as prodigious an appetite for snuff as Ralph Earl did for alcohol. His *Psalm-Singer*, consisting of tunes and instructions designed specifically for singing schools, was a work of native genius, a masterful integration of English church music with provincial wit and melodies.

Billings's instructions included discussions of musical literacy, vocal exercises, lessons in trills and graces, and thoughts on the relationship between music and human feelings. He concluded the instructional portion of the book with the observation that little could be learned from formal rules and examples. Just as a knowledge of grammar did not produce poets, "all the hard dry studied Rules that ever was prescribed, will not enable any Person to form an Air." It followed, then, that others should not copy him, since the best rule to follow was "for every *Composer* to be his own *Carver*." "*Nature is the best Dictator.*"[16] Here and in his original tunes, which made up the vast bulk of the book, Billings drew upon his own inspiration rather than the conventional forms of Protestant church music coming into vogue.

The tunes, which quickly became immensely popular, included anthems similar in nature to the new English church music, but Billings also incorporated three fuging tunes, the first by an American. These songs included passages in which two or more separate voices simultaneously sang different words to the same or different tunes. Billings's songs exhibited a distinctive, peculiarly dissonant sound and employed literary rather than scriptural texts. For many of his tunes, Billings employed marked, dancelike rhythms characteristic of popular American folksongs, rarely if ever written down. Irish jigs and traditional Anglo-Celtic folksongs such as "Greensleeves" and "Lord Randal" echoed throughout his work. Billings wrote several of the texts himself and attempted to employ language conducive to musical word-painting. This resulted in sacred-secular compositions that exuded dancelike exuberance as well as pious spontaneity.

In his naive integration of folk and art music, secular and sacred texts, and traditional provincial rhythms with the forms of the emerging English church music, Billings gave voice to a democratic spirit that emerged with the Revolution. His early tunes, together with those published in *The Singing Master's Assistant* (1778), became increasingly popular among the common folk; soldiers carried copies with them from camp to camp. The new tunes in the *Singing Master's Assistant* incorporated events from the Revolution familiar to every individual and blended local place names and phrases with those from the Scriptures. In addition, Billings went far beyond his earlier work by emphasizing musical rather than religious aspects of the performance and in stressing a boisterous style particularly appealing to ordinary individuals. While commending soft, melodious sounds for training the ear and observing that singing schools rested on order and a master's rational judgment, Billings declared: "It is vastly more agreeable (at least to me) to hear a few wild uncultivated sounds from a natural Singer, than a Concert of Music performed by the most refined artificial singers on earth, provided the latter have little or no assistance from nature."[17] He much preferred the power and enthusiasm of fuging tunes to the slower, more orderly psalms and hymns. Spontaneity, ardor, and even blatantly secular raucousness appealed far more to Billings than the decorous hymns of traditional Congregational churches.

The end of the Revolution brought increased popularity for the music of Billings, but he no longer stood alone as a native composer. Hundreds of pieces by American composers appeared alongside European works printed in large collections or in American magazines devoted entirely to music. Music itself was attaining the standing of an independent profession and an art in America. Concerts gained in popularity and sophistication as more cities began to support them. Performing ensembles composed of two hundred to three hundred individuals sang songs by Handel, followed by those of Billings. In response to these changes more and more Americans became involved in composing and performing, and at the same time great numbers of European artists, music merchants, compositions, and instruments entered America. The *translatio studii* indeed seemed to be coming true in music as well as in art.

Such transformations did not come without social tension. The coarse and vulgar-appearing Billings and his joyfully dissonant music created dissension among many New England Congregationalists. His music encouraged the emergence of choirs composed of sophisticated singers separated from the congregation. These choirs, generally consisting of young people chosen on the basis of musical talent rather than social eminence, often displaced established members from their accustomed gallery seats. Worse, elder members accustomed to the order and decorum of a deferential social structure found themselves subjected to the increasingly secular, open, and democratic music of Billings.

A reactionary backlash against Billings gathered around Andrew Law, a musical compiler from a socially prominent family in Milford, Connecticut. Law had issued his first important collection, *Select Harmony*, in 1778. Like Billings's collections, it contained psalms, hymns, and fuging tunes, but there all similarity ended. Billings incorporated patriotic songs in his collections, while Law included none. Billings disdained "refined artificial singers"; Law emphasized "good or genteel pronunciation."[18] Billings constantly attempted to attain more elaborate sophistication, whereas Law worked to return to simpler, more straightforward compositions. Above all, Billings emphasized that singing should reflect the open, natural qualities of the American environment, while Law stressed staid, stable, religious precepts. Billings's work hinted at a release from ordered restraints; it stressed spontaneity, freedom, boisterous opportunity. Law's work epitomized decorum, order, gentility, stability. In many ways the differences between the two types of music reflected the social tension emerging within American society between individuals and groups anxious to retain a traditional, structured social order and those exemplifying the freer, more natural, and open environment of opportunity that emerged with the Revolution.

Literature

This same subtle tension gradually appeared within the literary efforts of Americans as they began to develop their talents for writing poetry and prose. By the 1770s, although no literary piece to match the gifted accomplishment of *The Death of General Wolfe* or *The New-England Psalm-Singer* had appeared, the prospects for an active literary scene showed marked signs of improvement. Provincial colleges began to encourage literary study, a few magazines appeared that had brief runs, but more important, vigorous signs of potential literary achievement began to appear in the work of four gifted young poets.

Phillis Wheatley, a slave, published her first poem in the *Newport Mercury* in 1767 at about age thirteen. She kept writing poetry, and by the time she accompanied the Wheatleys' son to London in 1772, she had achieved no little acclaim. While in London she published *Poems on Various Subjects, Religious and Moral* (1773), which helped to provide the celebrity so lacking in the provincial literary scene throughout the 1760s. Many Englishmen considered her living proof of the hypocrisy of the American Whigs regarding slavery and the mental capabilities of blacks; by and large, however, the English viewed her accomplishments as evidence of the spread of English civilization and the beneficial effects of empire.

Three other young authors emerged simultaneously with Wheatley. These men—John Trumbull (cousin of the artist), Timothy Dwight, and Philip Freneau—formed a fresh generation of poets determined to emphasize the new aspects of American culture, as well as to shape America's cultural destiny. They took seriously the idea of the westward transit of the arts and its theory of progress for America and intended not only to foster such an idea but to explain it as well. Considering the arts to be an integral part of human nature and human society, like commerce and agriculture, the three poets linked the rise of the arts to the rise of the larger culture of which they were a part. As a result, each man wrote a resonant Augustan poem exalting America's imminent cultural greatness.

Trumbull declared in 1771 that "America hath a fair prospect in a few centuries of ruling both in art and arms" in a long poetic addendum to his commencement address on the fine arts delivered at Yale in 1770.[19] He extolled the arts in America in terms of the inevitable facts of human nature that had cultivated or inhibited their development throughout history. In a discussion of the sequential rise and decline of the fine arts in Greece, Augustan Rome, and eighteenth-century England, Trumbull contended that each instance proved conclusively that virility and an aggressive drive to sustain national glory nourished the arts, while a self-indulgent effeminacy precipitated their decline. Given his belief that the fine arts responded with the certainty of natural laws to the increase of masculine virtue within a society, Trumbull had no hesitation in predicting future greatness for America. America would become "the first in letters, as the first in Arms."[20] Trumbull's ebullient prediction, however, did not represent a cry for cultural nationalism on his part. Instead, like most other eighteenth-century writers, he believed in a republic of letters that went beyond national boundaries, transcending both time and place to draw into one universal present authors from Athens, Augustan Rome, London, and, most certainly very soon, New Haven and

Philadelphia. The identical moral-historical forces that created great artistic achievements in Greece, Rome, and England would do the same in America. America would, however, stand beside these nations—not distinct from them—as the epitome of transcendent moral and cultural values.

Like Trumbull, Timothy Dwight predicted an Augustan age in his *America; or, a Poem on the Settlement of the British Colonies; Addressed to the Friends of Freedom and their Country* (1771). In this work, after charting the progress of civilization throughout the ages, he predicted that the glory of Rome would arise in America and with this would come a glorious flowering of the arts. Dwight created a "Spirit of Freedom" in his poem that predicted commercial and political greatness for America, for he too could envision only future glory as American society matured.

Freneau collaborated with his Princeton classmate Hugh Henry Brackenridge to write *A Poem, or the Rising Glory of America* (1771), the longest and most complex of the poems celebrating America's future. In this work, Freneau and Brackenridge adopted a spiraling perception of the *translatio studii;* civilization and the arts not only traveled westward but gained with each movement in the transit. Consequently America was destined not only to achieve the greatness of the past but to surpass it. American literature would rise as naturally and as inevitably as the sun.

By the end of the Revolutionary War, that sun seemed to be shining with an ever-increasing brightness. Literature, if not yet an accepted profession, was at least becoming professionalized. Native writers could look forward to a growing popular demand for their work. Not only did the printed word increase but, like tunebooks and singing schools, it spread rapidly throughout the new nation. The number of magazines devoted entirely to literature mushroomed. The two most prominent of these—*The Columbian Magazine* and *The American Museum*—appeared in Philadelphia, published by Mathew Carey, a recent Irish immigrant intent upon providing evidence of the progress of the arts in America by publishing American works both past and present. Americans not only appeared ready to accept the literary efforts of their countrymen but were enthusiastic about the eminent cultural achievements of their nation.

The Rising Glory seemed to have arrived: American authors exuded the same confidence and enthusiasm, the same high expectations, for republican America as the majority of their countrymen. However, with the victory in 1783 came a strange sense of ambiguity, an uncertainty: what kind of society would emerge as a result of the Revolution? Would the triumph of American arms usher in a new Augustan age in America? Or would chaos and anarchy ensue? American writers could not escape these dilemmas; indeed they personified them in their own lives and work. While some authors espoused an organic, hierarchical republicanism, others responded to the more egalitarian tendencies of the Revolution. Still others attempted to balance elements of both of these inherently contradictory impulses within their literary efforts.

America's first important literary coterie, the Connecticut Wits, reflected the strains and tension affecting their native New England and much of the rest of the new nation as well. All the Wits, whose most prominent members were John Trumbull, David Humphreys, Timothy Dwight, and Joel Barlow, attended Yale, and the majority came from solid gentry families in Connecticut. Many became prominent doctors, lawyers, and political leaders. They hoped to encourage American letters in a genteel manner in order to demonstrate that republican societies could produce an elevated style of literature. At the same time they wished to nurture an ordered and conservative republican society. John Trumbull captured the essence of these twin desires when he observed: "A just taste in the fine arts, by sweetening and harmonizing the temper, is a strong antidote to the turbulence and violence of pursuit."[21] The Wits espoused the balance and order of early eighteenth-century Enlightenment thought; they retained a gentlemanly distaste for extremes of thought and action.

The Wits came to maturity in a challenging time. The decade following the end of the Revolution initiated a period of restless equilibrium, a mix of innovation and conservative adaptation, a blending of fear and excitement. By and large, in the face of such turmoil, most New Englanders clung to Enlightenment, Protestant, and republican traditions. For many, these became interchangeable concepts within a single belief system. They took for granted a tradition of austere republicanism that subtly mixed a belief in equality with respect for one's superiors, accepted orthodox religious views, and supported a stable, organic social order. In the face of postwar economic, social, and political turmoil, the Connecticut Wits attempted to foster this New England brand of republicanism. Like most of their countrymen, they emerged from the Revolution filled with jubilation over the prospects of American republicanism, which they frequently equated with the beginning of the Christian millennium. However, with the passage of time, most of them became disillusioned with the direction in which their society seemed to be moving. They articulated this growing disappointment in increasingly hostile denunciations of, for example, paper money issued by the government, luxurious extravagance, the pretentious egalitarianism of the average clodhopper, and deism.

John Trumbull's *M'Fingal* (1782), the first of a number of epic poems that appeared in the 1780s, evolved from the disillusionment experienced by the Wits and articulated their contempt for the social changes taking place. When the poem appeared early in 1776, Trumbull intended it as propaganda: he cast it in terms of a dialogue between the Whig, Honorious, and the Tory, M'Fingal, in order to expose the false reasoning of the latter through pointed satire and heavy irony. As the Revolution drew to a close, Trumbull, in response to the urgings of his friends, determined to develop the poem as a piece of literature. The changes worked into the poem graphically revealed how he viewed the outcome of the war. He still ridiculed prominent Tories, as well as the ineptitude of British leaders, but his sharp scalpel of satire now appeared double-edged. While M'Fingal's position on the war remained clearly wrong, the squire no longer seemed absurd when appearing before a town meeting. Instead he delivered trenchant critiques of the noisy ignorance, low character, and lawlessness of the mob. He criticized radical patriots who had inflated the value of Continental currency, to the ruin of responsible business practices. In many ways Trumbull transformed the bumbling Tory into a spokesman for conservative American values. Indeed at one point M'Fingal exclaimed: "Each leather-apron'd dunce, grown wise, Presents his forward face t'advise / And tatter'd legislators meet. From every workshop through the street." Then, "For in this ferment of the stream / The dregs have work'd up to the brim / And by the rule of topsy-turvy / The scum stands foaming on the surface."[22] Much like his cousin the artist, John Trumbull had serious reservations about the direction the Revolution seemed to be carrying American society. His initial faith that ordinary people would dutifully follow the lead of the responsible gentry gave way to disillusionment over what he perceived to be democratic excesses spawned by the Revolution.

By the late 1780s most of the other Wits, like Trumbull, had abandoned their fervent ambitions for America and restricted their efforts to sporadic patriotic odes and heavy-handed preaching, as well as scolding denunciations and satires directed at the irresponsibility of debtors, the vulgarity of democrats, and the dangerous tendencies of deists. Twelve installments of *The Anarchiad*, a series of poems written by Barlow, Trumbull, Humphreys, and other lesser poets, published in the *New Haven Gazette* between October 1786 and September 1787, articulated the frustration the Wits felt over recent developments within the new nation. The specific target of those poems was Shays' Rebellion in Massachusetts. Offended by the lawlessness of the armed mobs of farmers that closed down courthouses in western Massachusetts to avoid prosecution for debt, the Wits expressed their anxiety that "Anarchia" might spread throughout the nation. They savagely attacked these farmers as subhuman herds of lawless, irrational creatures whose very existence tarnished the republic. A number of poems criticized the farmers' demand for state-issued paper money in order to pay their debts. The Wits perceived the demand for paper money as the effort of shrewd, but lazy, farmers to impoverish the genteel commercial class. "The drafty knave his creditor besets. / And advertising paper pays his debt: / Bankrupt their creditors with rage pursue. / No stop, no mercy from the debtor crew."[23]

Such barbs resulted from the Wits' belief that the farmers' plight resulted not from being unfairly taxed by a government controlled by commercial elements, but from the fact that they ate far too well, drank excessively, dressed inappropriately to their station, and insisted that their children attend college rather than remain on the farm. According to the Wits, farmers had not been impoverished by taxes but had fallen prey to luxury. Thus, Shays' Rebellion became for the Wits a grotesque blight on the bright promise of American life so jubilantly portrayed at the advent of the Revolution. In a somber parody of the Rising Glory poem, the Wits vented their sense of betrayal by following the emergence of the demon Anarchia rather than the ascent of the fine arts: "Here shall my best and brightest empire rise. / Wild riot reign, and discord greet the skies. / Awake, my chosen sons, in folly brave. / Stab independence! dance o'er Freedom's grave."[24]

That not all the Wits grew so bitterly reactionary became apparent in the growing divergence between its two most prominent poets, Timothy Dwight and Joel Barlow. Dwight expressed unbounded hope for American progress in such work as "Greenfield Hill" (1788)—an extended paean to the positive virtues of Connecticut life, American farmers, and sober habits—but became increasingly disillusioned with the egalitarian impulses beginning to appear throughout society. By the mid-1790s his fear of anarchy became obsessive and overwhelmed his hopes for an orderly, republican America. One of his first acts upon assuming the presidency of Yale in 1795 was to banish a portrait of his former compatriot, Joel Barlow, from the campus because Barlow had become an outspoken champion of international revolution.

Barlow had begun his literary career as an intimate friend of Dwight and a prominent member of the Wits. His heritage, however, differed greatly from most of his fellow Wits. The son of a poor farmer, Barlow eventually graduated from Yale in 1778. His earliest work—patriotic Revolutionary poems—like that of Dwight, dealt with visions of a Christian millennium in America. His epic poem, *Vision of Columbus*, which appeared in 1787, contained nothing that would disturb his Connecticut colleagues. In it Barlow saw the destiny of America culminating in a world united by Enlightenment virtue and harmony. The final vision of the epic poem pictured all of humanity united in thought, language, beliefs, and manners; every individual became a peaceable citizen of one great empire. Although Barlow appeared to support the orthodox view of the Christian millennium in his work, he may well not have accepted such an eventuality as the end and design of things. By the time he published *Vision*, Barlow was already beginning to undergo a transformation in his religious, philosophic, and political thought. This did not become clear, however, until he traveled to Europe and became embroiled in the French Revolution. While in Paris he revised *Vision* and in the fifth edition, published in Paris in 1793, made significant alterations in it.

These alterations indicated a change in social attitudes quite the reverse of those exemplified in Trumbull's *M'Fingal*. Barlow deleted passages, changed others, and added much new material. The end result made God and Christianity secondary to the rule of man in determining his own destiny. Further, by this time Barlow had become an ardent advocate of the French Revolution and espoused the rights of individuals over the ordered prerogatives of kings and aristocrats. In the fifth edition, Barlow articulated the promise of the egalitarian aspects of American republicanism rather than the hierarchical social order espoused by his former colleagues among the Wits.

Shortly before the new edition of the *Vision* appeared, Barlow also published (1792) *Advice to the Privileged Orders in the Several States of Europe*, a book meant to be a reply to Edmund Burke's *Reflections on the Revolution in France*. Written while Barlow's faith in the French Revolution was at its height, *Advice* breathed a faith that authoritarianism must give way to open opportunity for all. The book emphasized two premises that had become basic to Barlow's thought: *"all men are equal in rights,* and . . . *the government is their own."*[25] By this time Barlow's vision of the American Revolution had carried him a long way from the opinions of the other Connecticut Wits. In Barlow's mind, the promise of America had become one of freedom and opportunity for the individual to pursue political, social, and economic advancement untrammeled by the traditional restraints of an ordered past. For Barlow the tension between hope and fear that so troubled the Wits disappeared. Freedom and hope displaced pessimism and fear.

Philip Freneau, like Barlow, also emerged as a democratic radical. Yet Freneau's radicalism never assumed the smooth optimism of Barlow's. He could not foresee an age when all men, let alone all Americans, would be joined in the harmonious brotherhood portrayed in the *Vision of Columbus*. His poetry often dealt with disadvantaged people: the poor beggared soldier "bespatter'd around / With the grog he had vomited up"; selfless patriots like Joseph Reed, unheralded by "this ungrateful age"; men incarcerated for the lack of a few shillings in debtors' prisons "Appointed by the wisdom of your States / To shut in *little* rogues, and keep out *great*." He had only scorn for Peale's gallery of national heroes and the epic poems of the Wits because none of these represented the solitary "naked soldier, perishing with cold."[26]

Freneau could not support the idea of America's rising glory that he himself had helped to establish. His disillusionment, quite unlike that of Dwight or Trumbull, resulted from his belief that the Revolution had not fulfilled its democratic promise. To Freneau the very elements of tyranny against which the free men of America had fought the Revolution were gaining fresh footholds in the young republic. Avarice and ambition seemed to dominate governmental councils; national leaders advocated if not monarchy, then an elitist, aristocratic form of government. Revolutionary soldiers, small farmers, hard-pressed country merchants, and courageous settlers on the frontier were victimized by a vicious system of taxation and the manipulation of public securities by a privileged few. Only a thorough democratic commitment could possibly thwart such a system and preserve American republicanism. Still, while Freneau's fear always outweighed his hope, he never gave up his democratic efforts throughout the 1790s, when he turned to journalism to support his hopes for a better society.

For Hugh Henry Brackenridge, the road from the *Rising Glory* throughout the post-Revolutionary decades contained greater ambivalence than for either Barlow or Freneau.[27] Like Freneau, Brackenridge viewed the Revolution as more than simply a colonial struggle for independence; it represented a truly revolutionary attempt to establish an entirely fresh array of social institutions. At the outset of the Revolution, Brackenridge believed that freedom from the imperial shackles of Great Britain would mean the release of a flood of talent and ability. The duty of a republican author was to guide the common citizen—the American republican—to achieve such promise. In his mind every common mechanic, farmer, or artisan could become a governor, a senator, or a representative in Congress. Simple folk needed only sympathetic guidance and the opportunity to reach their full potential. Consequently, throughout the 1770s, Brackenridge concentrated upon his public responsibility as a republican author. He remained determined to subordinate his own aesthetic needs or desires to the common good. As a result, his writing between 1775 and 1779 constituted propaganda more than literature. An identical ideological fervor permeated his writing for the *United States Magazine* after he founded this monthly in 1779.

Perhaps owing to the public's lack of support for his magazine and its subsequent failure, Brackenridge became disillusioned with the American people as republican citizens. In a final editorial, written in 1779, he cynically announced his conclusion that the public at large "inhabit the region of stupidity, and cannot bear to have the tranquility of their repose disturbed." Brackenridge vowed to leave his readers in peace to *"sleep on and take your rest."*[28] The confident optimism in the common man's capacity for enlightenment—to become a republican citizen—that pervaded his *Rising Glory* had turned to a brooding realization of the paradoxical qualities of popular sovereignty. Americans had indeed become republican citizens, but that citizenship brought with it a stubborn capacity to behave in singularly independent, self-seeking, and at times unpredictable ways. Instead of becoming independent-minded individuals intent upon improving themselves and their society by supporting republican authors, the people responded blindly to impassioned, emotional rhetoric and to popular appeals to ignorance.

In 1781, disillusioned with this turn of events, Brackenridge moved to the frontier town of Pittsburgh, where he established himself as a lawyer and vowed never to write again. Within five years he had established the best legal practice in western Pennsylvania and helped found the *Pittsburgh Gazette*. In addition, he served in the Pennsylvania legislature, where he confounded many of his constituents by voting as he thought best rather than in response to their strident demands. When he ran for a seat in Congress, Brackenridge was defeated by an illiterate miller.

Brackenridge turned again to writing. Now, however, his youthful enthusiasm of the 1770s had given way to ambiguities, to the paradoxical view of an outsider: a man who was neither plebeian nor patrician, democrat nor aristocrat, easterner nor westerner. Brackenridge seemed a strange mix, a farrago of conflicting impulses, which set him off from other authors of the post-Revolutionary period. Unlike his contemporaries, Brackenridge investigated the anomalies, contradictions, and ironic paradoxes of his culture while attempting neither reconciliation nor advocacy.

As early as 1788 he had begun to write *Modern Chivalry*. Part One, a succession of loosely–related stories, appeared between 1792 and 1797 in four separate installments. Part Two, an even more scattered assortment of tales, was published between 1804 and 1815. All of the stories centered around Captain John Farrago and Teague O'Regan, Brackenridge's two main characters who neither changed nor developed throughout the work. Farrago, a well-educated, genteel, middle-aged American, remained wedded to ideas and principles "drawn from what may be called the old school: the Greek and Roman notion of things."[29] Teague, Farrago's Irish servant, was a blindly ambitious, totally unprincipled, ignorant "bogtrotter" who could not avoid getting into trouble. There was no plot development in *Modern Chivalry*; Farrago and Teague moved aimlessly from one encounter to another.

Although no story line emerged in Brackenridge's work, he did articulate several themes that reflected his political philosophy. Perhaps the clearest statement of Brackenridge's perception of American political life came when he observed that "genius and Virtue are independent of rank and fortune; and it is neither the opulent, nor the indigent, but the man of ability and integrity that ought to be called forth to serve his country." Continuing, Brackenridge observed that "on the one hand, the aristocratic part of the government, arrogates a right to represent; on the other hand, the democratic contends the point; and from this conjunction and opposition of forces, there is produced a compound resolution, which carried the object in an intermediate direction."[30] Brackenridge firmly believed that a class struggle existed between the aristocracy and the people, and he never abandoned his preference for the people's side in the contest. This did not mean that he overlooked the excesses of democracy or that he ever failed to support the paramount importance of the judicial exercise of the suffrage. He clearly saw the lack of intelligent discrimination on the part of the voters as well as the ambition of unqualified persons to rise to high places, and, above all, he abhorred demagoguery.

Many of those supporting an organic, hierarchical social structure in America praised *Modern Chivalry*, apparently considering the work a clever satire directed at the ignorance and excesses of popular democracy. This was not, however, the central thrust of the book. While Teague behaved like a fool and became the victim in many comic episodes, he could not be passed off as an ignorant buffoon. Teague, not Farrago, gained election to public office, and even the Captain realized the implications for the future of American democracy. Men like Teague would fill public offices "when the present John Adams, and Lees, and Jeffersons, and Jays, and Henrys, and other great men . . . have gone to sleep."[31]

Such a future did not please Brackenridge, who realized that the cultural and social transformations set in motion by the Revolution were irrevocable. He knew, too, that public opinion would have a shaping influence on not only politics but literature and the arts. In spite of all this, Brackenridge may never have entirely forsaken his ideals of the early 1770s. The public might still be influenced by literature and thus guided toward a slow but steady improvement. *Modern Chivalry* not only revealed Brackenridge's sensitivity to the ironic nature of the democratization of American society but also represented his attempt to instruct through laughter and the popular medium rather than the epic poem or formal, educated treatise. *Modern Chivalry* fell between the neoclassical Founders and the romantic Jacksonians. Brackenridge was far closer, however, to Mark Twain than to Alexander Pope.

In *Modern Chivalry* Brackenridge recognized the ambiguities of a democratic society and yet remained hopeful that Americans would recognize and live by republican principles of virtue and rationality. A writer who appeared in the late eighteenth century, however, questioned whether a good society would emerge even if all Americans adopted virtuous republican principles. Indeed, Charles Brockden Brown introduced quite a different sort of ambiguity into American literature.

Born in Philadelphia to Quaker parents in 1771, Brown suffered from poor health throughout his life and continually fell into spells of melancholy. His work expressed uncertainty about virtue, truth, and morality itself. In his novels events often degenerated into a moral mass in which good and evil came to the same unfortunate end. For Brown there was no "right" and "wrong"; great wrong could come from pure motives. The transcendent values of the neoclassical authors and artists had no power to shape society even if all people adhered to them. In fact, disastrous results could come from the best intentions of upright, virtuous individuals. Whatever tension existed between good and evil, virtue and vice, liberty and tyranny became part of an intricate combination of external circumstances, unrecognized motivations, and the involvement of many people. All these factors worked to stifle conscious purpose, to short-circuit virtue and vice alike. In Brown's work events seemed beyond human understanding and control.

Brown contributed little, if anything, to the art of fiction. His works contained improbable plots, an awkward style, and ponderous prose and showed all the signs of being hastily written. In a two-year period (1798–99), Brown wrote six full-length novels, including *Arthur Mervyn* and *Edgar Huntley*, and a number of shorter works, and he edited the *Monthly Magazine and American Review*. Often working on three or four novels simultaneously, Brown captured his thoughts on paper as rapidly as they flowed but took little time to develop them fully. The strength and value of his work lay in the manner in which he represented ideas in fiction. He never merely illustrated moral ideas; rather he explored them, tested them, exposed them to the perils of human behavior and human nature. Instead of simply reiterating principles such as austerity, frugality, moderation, sincerity or candor, Brown turned his imagination to the creation of fictional characters who attempted to live by these ideas. He then exposed both the characters and the principles to a world in constant flux, filled with false appearances and unexpected circumstances. His protagonists, regardless of their intentions and character, entered ever more deeply into a world defined by irreconcilable moral conflicts. Through a series of discrete episodes loosely analogous to the original theme with which the story sets out, Brown created a narrative within a narrative within still another narrative. He worked out his plots as he moved along, and consequently each separate event restated or deepened the original central idea, and yet out of these emerged a theme quite different from the original one. This theme arose out of the totality of the separate events and often defied simple, straightforward statement because it reflected the complex, often contradictory, conflicts within human nature and human behavior. Brown's work represented something very different from the formal, systematic, speculative thought of the eighteenth century.

Brown was groping toward a fresh vision of society. His thought encouraged the development of a democratic consciousness and a utilitarian outlook, but perhaps because he lacked the talent or the available vocabulary needed to articulate them, his ideas remained vague. Although he sensed changes within society, he remained unable to create a systematic mode of thought to articulate them. Clearly, though, the image of society that he was able to convey, however formless, did not resemble the organic hierarchy called for by neoclassical artists and political figures espousing classical republican rhetoric. Brown had little use for heroic aristocratic individuals who stood as examples to society; rather he emphasized the popular masses and the system of society that emerged from a natural order—the aggregate result of complex events emanating from the varied and conflicting motives of innumerable insignificant individuals. Whatever threats existed to the equanimity of the protagonists in his novels resulted not from political events but from psychological ones. Unconscious impulses rather than the rational thought upon which the Enlightenment rested controlled human lives. While the conscious efforts of men and women created ideas and institutions within their society, these creations soon took on a life of their own capable of controlling the lives of individuals within that society in ways those individuals simply could not comprehend. Within such an environment, the conscious motives of men and women—their character—counted for very little. Indeed they were just as capable of bringing about great harm as were the actions of selfish, mean-spirited individuals or groups.

Theater

In spite of its ambiguities, Brown's work, as well as that of his literary colleagues, enjoyed an excellent reception in post-Revolutionary America. Posing little threat to the moral fabric of society, poetry and literature stood only as mounting evidence of the success of the *translatio* and the future greatness of American society. This could not be said about the theater. Of all artistic activities in America, the professional theater was the least well developed and by far the most controversial. Throughout the Revolutionary era, it had remained problematical whether the theater would rise in glory along with the various other arts.

At the close of the French and Indian War, no American play had been published or produced and no American actor had ever performed professionally on the stage. Theater in America consisted of a single troupe, the London Company of Comedians (later renamed the American Company of Comedians) managed by David Douglas and the Hallam family. This mediocre group existed as itinerants traveling with their makeshift buildings and flimsy properties from city to city, while making stops at smaller towns along the way. Douglas and Lewis Hallam, Jr., nonetheless struggled to improve the troupe. They expanded repertoires, employed the talented singer-actor John Henry, and constructed permanent theater buildings in New York and Philadelphia, complete with attractive scenery designed and constructed in London. In spite of these efforts, the company still played to meager and sometimes hostile audiences. And in 1774 the Continental Congress included theater in the activities banned by the Continental Association calling for nonimportation, nonconsumption, and nonexportation as well as forbidding frivolous behavior. Early in 1775 the company scattered; some left for Jamaica and others for London.

Late in 1785 the American Company returned to New York, where John Henry announced on opening night that he and his colleagues had never wanted to leave America; he then declared their devotion to the principles of the Revolution. Despite this effort as well as their determined attempts to provide the latest London hits supported by the best European stagecraft, the company met with petitions against drama, rioting, insults, physical threats, and intense ideological opposition; the last resulting in a new wave of antitheater legislation that diminished audiences to pre-1763 numbers.

The American Company found itself caught up in a controversy concerning virtue and luxury. Americans, quarreling as much about the nature of their society as they were about the theater, couched their arguments in terms of morality and the survival of republicanism. Should the new nation purge itself of Old World corruption, or should it allow human nature unlimited freedom of expression? Antitheater spokesmen associated drama with the decadence and decay that had destroyed ancient republicans. Charles Rollins, a prominent historian, claimed that an attraction to the theater had been "one of the principal causes of the decline, degeneracy, and corruption of the Athenian State."[32] In his mind the success of the stage always accompanied the emergence of a rigidly structured class society that debased innocence, frugality, hard work, and virtue. In answer, supporters of drama countered such arguments point by point. The strength of their position, however, lay with the contention that if America was to achieve cultural greatness, it must have native theaters, plays, and actors, just as it must produce its own epic poems and historical paintings. American republicanism must be brought to life on the stage so that young people might receive inspiration from the graphic portrayals of virtuous individuals such as George Washington.

With this in mind, the American Company presented *The Contrast* at the John Street Theatre in New York on 16 April, 1787. This five-act sentimental comedy had been written by America's first successful playwright, Royall Tyler. Set in postwar New York, the play focused on the imminent marriage of the dandy, Billy Dimple, and Maria, a sweet, dainty, sentimental creature. The marriage had been arranged by Maria's father—the bluff, honest businessman, Van Rough. Colonel Manly's arrival in town, however, interrupted the plans for the upcoming nuptials. Manly, involved in suppressing Shays' Rebellion, came to the city in a noble attempt to petition Congress to vote pensions for the soldiers who had served under him in the Revolution. The plot of *The Contrast* emerged from a tension between Dimple and Manly, as well as a comic confrontation between Manly's Yankee servant, Jonathan, and Dimple's effeminate French-mannered manservant Jessamy.

Tyler had seen many plays at the John Street Theatre and borrowed extensively from these in his own work. By placing the structural and stylistic borrowings into a contemporary, post-Revolutionary social context, he created a distinctively American play. The conventional tension between hypocrisy and sincerity—a stock feature of social comedies of the day—became instead a richly-textured satire on the conflict in America between luxury and virtue. Tyler's characters represented stark contrasts between conflicting forces in the post-Revolutionary decades: republicanism versus aristocracy, family stability versus social chaos, sincerity and simplicity versus European affectations and devotion to fashion, and the rugged soldier versus the effeminate fop. More important, Tyler had his characters act out these conflicts in clearly recognizable contemporary social settings.

In his drama Tyler utilized American manners more thoroughly than any other author of the era and thus provided his countrymen with a wonderful reflection of their own lives. Rather than merely representing the conventional hypocritical rake, Billy Dimple became the Europeanized American representing the attempt to subvert American society by fostering luxury. Colonel Manly grew beyond the stock sentimental soldier to personify the virile, austere American republican. As the epitome of self-sacrificing virtue, Manly repeatedly spoke out against the evils of luxury and dissipation. Jonathan was Tyler's most creative character. As the archetypal Yankee, he expressed disdain for servitude and social distinction. When referred to as a servant, he exclaimed: "Servant! Sir, do you take me for a neger.—I am Colonel Manley's waiter . . . but no man shall master me. My father has as good a farm as the colonel." In conversation with Jessamy, Jonathan claimed that "we don't make any great matter of distinction in our state between quality and other folks."[33]

For the first time the American Company enjoyed an enthusiastic reception. In addition, *The Contrast* drew great praise as a work "honorable to American genius and literature."[34] Considering it an achievement ranking with *The Vision of Columbus*, the historical paintings of Trumbull, and the Handel-Billings concerts, reviewers praised *The Contrast* as representative of the robust health of culture in America and as solid evidence of the distance traveled by the theater since the end of the French and Indian War.

Most reviewers praised the manner in which Tyler portrayed virtue in its clash with luxury, but they failed to recognize a more significant and long-lasting cultural conflict running through the drama. The contrast between Manly and Jonathan comprised a much more subtle theme within the larger contrast. For Tyler, living within a rapidly changing cultural environment searching for identity, no clear model of the American predominated. Neither Manly, the austere republican patterned after George Washington, nor Jonathan, the brash unsophisticated Yankee, could legitimately function as a cultural ideal. Manly's classical republican rhetoric sounded strangely hollow and archaic, while Jonathan's independent manner still appeared slightly foolish and inappropriate. Manly, the self-sacrificing, communally oriented republican, and Jonathan, the aggressive, individualistic democrat, epitomized a tension within American culture. Tyler sensed it, but critics were not yet willing or able to recognize it. Instead they clung to the familiar in their praise for the victory of virtue over luxury.

Tyler himself could never be quite so sanguine. Born into one of the wealthiest families in New England, educated at Boston's Latin School and Harvard, and having served as a major on the staff of General Benjamin Lincoln during Shays' Rebellion, Tyler left New York four years after the appearance of *The Contrast*. He opened a law practice in the aggressive, competitive, open atmosphere of Vermont, where he became a leading Federalist, filled a number of judicial positions, and eventually served as chief justice of the state supreme court. Within his own life Tyler manifested the tension resulting from a drive to succeed in an individualistic, materialistic world, combined with a deep yearning or need for republican order and harmony. Like many of his countrymen, he found himself in a cultural environment filled with ambivalence and uncertainty.

Upon Tyler's departure for Vermont, the mantle of the foremost playwright, as well as the principal leader of the theater in America, fell to William Dunlap, a man firmly committed to the rising glory of America.[35] For him the freedom gained as a result of the Revolution promised cultural greatness for America. "If, as we believe, the world is to be in future a democratic world . . . It is expedient that every source of knowledge should be *opened* to the governors, *the people*, every obstacle to their improvement removed."[36] Convinced that the stage could become a "great engine" for social improvement, Dunlap devoted himself to creating "proper exhibitions to set before a free and well-ordered people."[37] His effort reflected his faith in republicanism, his unswerving belief that a free people would in fact be well ordered and eager to follow the leadership of "the wise and the good."

In many ways Dunlap resembled Brackenridge's Captain Farrago; he exhibited the same naive optimism, the same simple faith in the power of republican ideals to foster the progress of all facets of American culture. And like Farrago, Dunlap found himself awkwardly struggling to make sense of a cultural environment in flux. He lived in a transitional era separating, and yet blending, elements of republicanism and democracy, classical and romantic impulses, virtuous self-control and the unprecedented freedom of individual opportunity.

Dunlap's career in the theater began auspiciously when the American Company performed his *The Father, or American Shandyism* at the John Street Theatre on 7 September, 1789. The play enjoyed an enthusiastic reception that encouraged Dunlap's faith in the great potential for the arts in America. While aware of the handicaps that American artists and playwrights endured in comparison with their European colleagues, Dunlap believed this would be only a temporary condition. Over time America would blossom as the cultural capital of the world because all its citizens, not just a few nobles and aristocrats, enjoyed full freedom to consume and to create culture. Dunlap saw his role in helping America to achieve its tremendous cultural potential as one of enlightening the people to the worth of the arts so that they would enthusiastically embrace them and champion their advancement. Following the success of *The Father*, Dunlap sought to write plays that would guide the people to a more sympathetic understanding of the arts as well as to inculcate proper republican values in their minds. Acting upon this conviction, Dunlap wrote seven plays between 1792 and 1798. His best, *Andre* (1798), also articulated his resolution of his own personal uncertainties regarding freedom and order, liberty and restraint.

Dunlap based the plot of *Andre* on an actual event of the recent war: the execution in 1780 of the British Major John Andre, who, disguised as a civilian, had attempted to bribe General Benedict Arnold. His play did not dwell exclusively upon the patriotic celebration of its prominent events; rather, it explored the human conflicts and ideological uncertainties created by the war. In reality *Andre* presented Dunlap's own deliberations on virtue in the guise of its leading characters. He portrayed John Andre as the embodiment of virtue—brave, high minded, generous. The young English gentlemen made a single tragic mistake, which he refused to rationalize. He went to his death calmly, with neither animosity nor resentment. A young American cavalry officer, Captain Bland, argued throughout the play that the execution of so virtuous a man would be cruel and unjust. Dunlap skillfully presented the figure of Andre in such an appealing manner and couched Bland's soliloquies in such heartrending language that, like the conventional sentimental melodramas of the day, only a thorough blackguard would have carried out the execution. And yet the man who demanded Andre's death was George Washington. The general declared to Bland: "I know the virtues of this man and love them. / But the destiny of millions, millions / Yet unborn, depends upon the rigour / of this moment."[38]

Dunlap deliberately structured his play to present two separate perceptions of virtue, two contrasting views of what the nation should idealize: the traditional corporate world versus the emerging individualist ethos of the era. Washington stated the case for the corporate ideal clearly and forcefully. Recognizing both Andre's virtuous qualities and Bland's emotional attraction to the convicted spy, Washington realized that such feelings had to be subordinated to greater, less personal considerations. The general knew that the capacity to displace individual or personal desires with thoughtful considerations for the welfare of the larger community constituted the essence of virtue. In the end Washington—the man of feeling and reason—emerged as the ultimate embodiment of virtue. A man of compassion, he remained able to place communal interests, order, and harmony above the individual.

In many ways *Andre* represented Dunlap's statement regarding the tensions within American society between freedom and order. He had come to the realization that his own deepest loyalties lay with the traditional values of order and restraint. The new freedom must not be stifled but needed to be constrained by rational, enlightened individuals in order not to become dangerous to society. In its focus upon the past and in the figure of George Washington, the play emphasized classical conceptions of virtue, stressed self-restraint over individual autonomy, and exalted communalism over individualism.

This was not, however, to be the world of William Dunlap. Instead an increasingly aggressive and egalitarian public shaped his life in the theater. *Andre* had only three performances. The play would not be popular until Dunlap brought it out as a low comedy playing to simple folk's prejudices under the title *The Glory of Columbia—Her Yeomanry*. In order to alleviate the American Company's constant financial embarrassment, Dunlap found himself forced to offer what the public would support. Dunlap constantly had to compromise his aesthetic values and to vulgarize his idealistic standards and expectations for the American theater. By 1805 he had been forced into bankruptcy by his creditors, lost all of his property, and his theatrical career came to an ignominious end.

Throughout his life in the theater, Dunlap, like Peale, Brackenridge, and others, found himself on the horns of a dilemma. He wanted both to serve the people and to promote the arts in America. Early in his career Dunlap presumed a wonderful compatibility between these two impulses: an orderly people would appreciate and enthusiastically welcome instruction at the hands of the wise and the good. However, over time, it became ever more apparent that the people, growing increasingly "disorderly," exerted a tremendous influence over the arts. The public determined what kind of plays could be performed and, indeed, dictated whether the theater itself would remain open. Dunlap and his fellow American artists and writers directly confronted the essential paradox of a republican society: how can such a society hope to be well ordered, virtuous, and responsive to an enlightened few when the ultimate power within the culture resided with the people themselves?

The translatio *Accomplished*

This dilemma cut to the heart of the condition of the arts in late eighteenth-century American society. For all intents and purposes, the *translatio* had been fulfilled. Creative individuals in America had mastered the conventional neoclassical European forms of artistic expression; yet there was little new, fresh, or American about these creations. In order for the *translatio* to be effected, no need existed for a singular American style to emerge or to be validated. None did. A few hints appeared in the work of Charles Brockden Brown, William Billings, and Philip Freneau, but even these individuals remained unable to clarify their feelings or to work out a uniquely American mode of art or literature. American artists remained trapped within the limits of traditional republican thought. Determined to shape the character and opinions of the people through their art, intent upon fostering transcendent values drawn from an ancient republican heritage, they remained blind to whatever creative forces might emerge from the new American environment.

They became increasingly frustrated with a people who showed every sign of desiring to speak, act, and write their own thoughts.

Those Americans who had anticipated a revolution in the arts similar to the political revolution from Great Britain experienced severe disappointment. "The revolution that never was" best described the state of the American arts in the late eighteenth century.[39] Yet there were distinctive American ways of life and thought emerging in the era; there was innovation and newness within American culture. In their social, religious, and political attitudes, many Americans were, in fact, subtly shaping a unique culture. The clearest manifestation of this distinctiveness came with the new governments being formed within the young republic. Here, too, though, change was slow, and efforts to create these forms of government reflected the cultural tensions pervading the nation.

four

The Creation of Republican Governments

Just as the Revolution spawned euphoric hopes and expectations of the Rising Glory among those associated with the fine arts, so too did it engender an intense excitement over the prospects for new republican governments that would drastically reorder the world Americans had known. Freedom from the corruption and restraints of Great Britain created a chance for a new kind of politics, a new kind of government, that would change the lives not only of Americans but of all people. Given such an opportunity, Americans labored from 1776 to 1788 to perfect constitutions that would embody the republican principles for which they fought the Revolution.

Responsibility for initiating this process fell to the Second Continental Congress. When that body convened in May 1775, it was essentially a wartime gathering. Hostilities had broken out the previous month, and Congress had to deal with three important questions related to the relationship between the colonies and Great Britain. Should a call go out to the separate colonies to form new governments? Should a formal declaration of independence be issued? Should some form of confederation of the colonies be formed? Congressmen wrestled with these thorny problems for more than a year. Finally, on 10 May, 1776 they recommended that the colonies "adopt such Government as shall, in the Opinion of the Representatives of the People, best conduce to the Happiness and Safety of their Constituents in particular and America in general."[1] On 7 June, Richard Henry Lee moved that "these United Colonies are, and of right ought to be, free and independent States." He suggested that "a plan of confederation be prepared and transmitted to the respective Colonies for their consideration and approbation."[2]

Thus, previous to the Declaration of Independence of 4 July, 1776, several states were already at work preparing new constitutions, and a congressional committee was discussing a form of confederation. Within a year all the states had written new constitutions or revolutionized their old charters, and Congress had drafted a plan of union.

The Articles of Confederation

When Americans began the simultaneous drafting of state and federal constitutions, they embarked on the most creative period of constitutional development in their history. However, while the excitement occasioned by the opportunity to start afresh characterized discussions of the new state constitutions, the discussions over the creation of a central government remained perfunctory and produced little of intellectual significance.

The desultory nature of the debates leading to the Articles of Confederation resulted from the fact that few Americans in 1776 could conceive of the thirteen separate states becoming a unified republic with a single pervasive national interest. A man's "country" was his state. John Adams "supposed no Man would think of consolidating this vast Continent under one national Government." Instead he assumed that the separate states would, "after the example of the Greeks, the Dutch and the Swiss, form a Confederacy of States," with each member retaining full sovereignty. In 1779 when he composed a draft constitution for Massachusetts, he declared that "the people of this Commonwealth have the sole and exclusive right of governing themselves, as a free, sovereign, and independent state."[3] Several years later Ezra Stiles observed that the Confederation government was never intended to be "a body in which resides authoritative sovereignty; for there is no real cession of dominion, no surrender or transfer of sovereignty to the national council, as each state in the confederacy is an independent sovereignty."[4]

The observations of Adams and Stiles rested in large part upon their understanding of the works of the European philosophers Montesquieu and Vattel. The former, whose *Spirit of the Laws* exerted a shaping influence upon late eighteenth-century American thought, counseled that republican governments could be sustained only by small, homogeneous societies. A vast continental republic made up of a multiplicity of conflicting interests and diverse cultural habits could lead only to anarchy or tyranny. According to Vattel's *Law of Nations*, however, a union of sorts was possible, since "several sovereign and independent states may unite themselves together by a perpetual confederacy without each in particular ceasing to be a perfect state."[5] It was just such a confederation of sovereign republics—a "league of friendship"—that men such as Adams and Stiles had in mind.

When the public at large considered the possibility of a national government, more basic issues came into play. The same libertarian fear of the concentration of power that caused so many colonists to suspect the British government throughout the 1760s and 1770s affected their view of the Articles. With the Articles under discussion in Congress, the town of West Springfield, Massachusetts, cautioned its delegates to bear in mind the "weakness of human nature and the growing thirst for power." The localists' suspicion of distant authority made the town members express the fear that "the sovereignty and independence of particular states [is] nearly annihilated. . . . We entertain no jealousy of the present congress but who knows but in some future corrupt times there may be a Congress which will form a design upon the liberties of the People & will it be difficult to execute such a design when they have absolute command of the navy, the army & the purse?"[6]

Such anxieties had a distinct effect upon the deliberation in Congress. The Articles of Confederation presented to the states in November 1777 for ratification created a confederacy, the United States of America, that for all intents and purposes simply extended the existence of the Second Continental Congress and carefully observed the prerogatives of the separate states. A unicameral legislature composed of annually elected state delegations, each with a single vote, comprised the central government. Congressional committees with a continually changing membership assumed whatever executive duties might arise. The majorities required in Congress depended upon the relative importance of the matter under consideration. Routine business called for a simple majority; more significant issues such as making war, ratifying treaties, and coining or borrowing money demanded the consent of nine states; ratification of the Articles themselves, as well as their alteration in the future, required the unanimous consent of all thirteen states. Clearly Congress intended to protect the interests of the separate states.

Despite such deference to state sovereignty, an exceptional degree of union emerged under the Confederation government. The Articles specifically forbade the states to engage in foreign relations, negotiate treaties, or declare war. In addition, the new constitution guaranteed the privileges and immunities of citizens of each state in every other state, eliminated travel and discriminatory trade restrictions among the states, and provided for the reciprocity of extradition and judicial matters among the states. A substantial grant of powers to Congress—declaring war, making treaties and alliances, determining boundary controversies and other disputes between the states, minting coins, regulating Indian affairs, fixing the standards of weights and measures, borrowing money, appropriating levies on the states—appeared in Article 9. Collectively these resulted in the creation of as strong a republican confederation as any other in history and constituted an impressive effort in the direction of a truly national government.

Regardless of the privileges granted to Congress, however, the ultimate

These portraits by Copley and Peale exhibit the wealth and grandeur of the American gentry.

Nicholas Boylston (1767) by John Singleton Copley. Courtesy of the Harvard University Portrait Collection, Cambridge, Mass.; Bequest of Ward Nicholas Boylston.

The Edward Lloyd Family (1771) by Charles Willson Peale. Courtesy of the Henry Francis du Pont Winterthur Museum, Winterthur, Del.

Mob actions in North Carolina (1770) and Massachusetts (1786) in defiance of gentry domination contrast sharply with the calm demeanor expressed in the paintings of Boylston and the Lloyds.

Governor Tyron and the Regulators. Courtesy of the
Library of Congress, Washington, D.C.

Shay's Mob in Possession of a Court House (1884). Courtesy of the New York Historical Society, New York City.

In many ways the work of Trumbull and Earl represents the state of American art by the end of the eighteenth century. Trumbull's, by far the more skillful, is representative of the neoclassical influence in the United States; Earl's hints at a more natural quality emerging from the New World environment itself.

The Death of General Warren at the Battle of Bunker Hill 17, June 1775 (1786). by John Trumbull. Copyright Yale University Art Gallery, New Haven, Conn.

Daniel Boardman (1789) by Ralph Earl. Courtesy of the National Gallery of Art, Washington, D.C.; Gift of Mrs. Murray Crane.

These pictures—of Charles Willson Peale standing in his museum and of an evangelical revival—illustrate tensions within the republican culture of the late eighteenth century. Peale emphasized rationality and order in his museum, whereas evangelists stressed emotionalism in their efforts to throw off the influence of established authorities.

The Artist in His Museum (1822) by Charles Willson Peale. Courtesy of the Pennsylvania Academy of the Fine Arts, Philadelphia; Gift of Mrs. Sarah Harrison (the Joseph Harrison, Jr., Collection).

Camp Meeting (ca. 1835), lithograph from a painting by A. Rider. Courtesy of the New-York Historical Society, New York City.

Portrayals of womanhood in the late eighteenth century invariably glorified women even as the republican culture of the time restricted their individual development.

Liberty and Washington (ca. 1800–10). Courtesy of the New York State Historical Association, Cooperstown.

Keep within Compass (ca. 1785–1805). Courtesy of the Henry Francis du Pont Winterthur Museum, Winterthur, Del.

Federalist cartoons often depicted the disdainful reaction of genteel elements within American society in response to the emergence of the Jeffersonian-Republican party.

The Providential Detection. Courtesy of the American Antiquarian Society, Worcester, Mass.

A Peep into the Antifederal Club (1793). Courtesy of the Print and Picture Department, Free Library of Philadelphia.

Prints illustrating the Whiskey Rebellion (1794) and the emotional response to Jay's Treaty (1795) clearly reveal the tension between the Federalists and the Republicans in the last decade of the eighteenth century.

Tarring and Feathering an Excise Officer. Courtesy of the General Research Division, New York Public Library; Astor, Lenox, and Tilden Foundations.

Hanging of John Jay in Effigy. Courtesy of the New York State Historical Association, Cooperstown.

powers—the regulation of commerce and taxation—remained firmly in the hands of the states. Congressional "recommendations" to the states remained just that, and each state retained the freedom to accept or reject appropriations levied upon it by Congress. Article 2 made abundantly clear the form the Confederation was to assume: "Each state retains its sovereignty, freedom and independence, and every power, jurisdiction, and right, which is not by this confederation expressly delegated to the United States, in Congress assembled." The states, intent upon holding fast to their sovereignty, had, as stated in Article 3, joined to form a "firm league of friendship"—a loose alliance among sovereign states—and remained intensely suspicious of encroachments upon their rights and prerogatives.

State jealousies, rather than significant theoretical differences, protracted the discussion of the Articles for over a year and prevented their unanimous ratification until March 1781. State interests—representation in Congress, the apportionment of levies to support the central government, and the fate of western lands—fueled the most heated debates. Large states demanded proportional representation, small ones insisted upon equality; southern states wanted state apportionment to be based on the value of landed property, while northern delegates demanded that population, including slaves, be the basis for such apportionment; states without western land claims as well as those dominated by land speculators demanded that states with such claims cede them to the nation so that they might "become the common property of the whole" and thus serve the "national welfare."[7]

Regardless of the various interests involved in western lands, Virginia did demand in return for its cession a promise on the part of the Confederation government that such lands would be "settled and formed into distinct republican states."[8] This commitment resulted in the land ordinances of 1784, 1785, and 1787 that established the method of survey, sale, and political organization of the Northwest, as well as future acquisitions. These ordinances, the greatest achievement of the Confederation government, resulted from a widespread devotion to state sovereignty and the pervasive fear of the aggrandizement of centralized power that might result at some time in the future if the public domain remained under the control of Congress.

By the time of the passage of the land ordinances, it had become abundantly clear that the Confederation did indeed constitute a coalition of sovereign states. Most of the states not only guarded their prerogatives jealously, but even, in violation of the Articles themselves, assumed the power of making war, placing armies in the field, and undertaking diplomatic negotiations abroad. Indeed many Americans considered the Confederation a wartime expedient; with the coming of peace, they felt that the powers granted to Congress should lapse. As early as December 1783 Thomas Jefferson suggested that Congress had outlived its usefulness and that its delegates should "separate and return to [their] respective states, leaving only a Committee of the States." This would "destroy the strange idea of their being a permanent body, which has unaccountably taken possession of the heads of their constituents, and occasioned jealousies injurious to the public good."[9] With the coming of peace, Congress's ability to function suffered a precipitous decline. Quorums became increasingly difficult to form, and by the mid-1780s the body had all but abdicated its responsbility to govern.

State Constitutions

This was far from the case with the various states. Throughout the war years and after, the state governments worked vigorously to deal with the problems facing their citizens. Such intensity resulted from a sense shared by most Americans that the very success of the Revolution itself rested on their efforts to create new governments based on wise and lasting principles. For most Americans struggling to break free from oppressive centralized authority, the creation of republican governments in the states became the whole object of the Revolution itself. The richest and most provocative discussions of constitutional principles and political theory—sovereignty, representation, equality, the separation of powers, liberty, property, and the common good—took place in the states. There Americans began their quest to enshrine republican morality and virtue and to shield liberty from the encroachments of power.[10]

After the Declaration of Independence dissolved the covenant between king and people, it was a foregone conclusion that state constitutions would exclude any mention of a king. Only one source of power remained, the people. That much was clear: the new governments would be republican governments. The proper structure of republican government, however, was by no means self-evident. A great variety of Americans attempted to translate the Revolutionary experience as they perceived it into constitutional language. This resulted in a decade (1776–86) of intense political discussions focused on the restructuring of power—the creation of governments entirely divested of monarchical influence that now drew all their authority from the people.

Once Americans began this process, they did so not only in the light of their past experiences but also in terms of libertarian Whig ideology. They were constantly on guard against the encroachments of power upon the realm of liberty. The first essential step to protect the people was to remove all prerogative powers from their governors. Pennsylvania went so far as to eliminate the position altogether, and every other state stripped the governor's position of all aspects of an independent magistracy. Most instituted annual elections for their executive and limited the number of years one man could serve. No governors were allowed to share in the lawmaking authority, and none had the exclusive power of appointing judicial and executive positions. American governors came to be viewed solely as repositories of the executive functions of government.

To guard further against oppression at the hands of governors, state constitutions embodied the concept of separation of powers. While invoking Montesquieu's idea of separating the executive, judicial, and legislative functions, in practice Americans employed the concept only to protect the legislative and judicial branches from incursions by the executive. More precisely, they lodged almost all power—executive, legislative, and judicial—in the legislature, the true embodiment of the people in the government. The people now had the power not only to make the law but to enforce it as well.

Care needed to be taken to ensure that the legislatures remained free of corruption. Short and regular terms of meetings helped answer this threat, and increasing representation and broadening the suffrage helped bring the legislatures closer to the people. Even the most radical English libertarian, however, had remained suspicious of men in poor circumstances who might be influenced or intimidated by their betters and thus favored limiting the suffrage to those with a stake in society. Although by 1776 a number of Americans had come to question this, all the state constitutions called for some proof of attachment to the commonwealth, if only the payment of taxes and fulfillment of a residence requirement. The best safeguard of the integrity of the legislatures, though, remained equal representation. Assemblies, based on a full and free suffrage of the freeholders, should become exact replicas of the whole people.

A commitment to the idea of free, full, and equal representation was not void of ambiguities. Many Americans adhered simultaneously to the concepts of virtual and actual representation. Their belief in the unity and homogeneity of the people impelled them to support the idea that each representative served a single organic society (virtual representation); yet their desire for the legislature to be an exact replica of society called for an explicit consent from the people divided into equal electoral districts with intimate ties to their own representatives (actual representation). Many Americans began to press for the power to instruct their representatives on how to vote, to call for residential requirements for both voters and their assemblymen, and to view their legislatures as made up of clashing interests. However, to surrender the idea of virtual representation would be to threaten the intellectual foundations of their republicanism; consequently, most Americans held to a conception of republicanism based on a transcendent common good.

Most Americans remained wedded to the idea that only a correctly balanced government could check oppression. The educated gentry responsible for writing most state constitutions assumed the existence of a natural elite that should take its rightful place in the upper houses of their legislatures.

The senates would therefore become the repositories of the wisest and best men in society—men of superior ability and education who placed the public good above all else. How to distinguish and isolate the "senatorial part" of society raised perplexing questions. To set off an aristocracy, even a natural one, flew in the face of republican principles. To focus on property as a criterion for membership in the senate set up a separate interest that violated republican principles, and yet property seemed to be the only means of distinguishing the "wise and good" from the populace at large.

The attraction of balanced government combined with the fear of aristocracy caused Americans to change their perception of the nature and function of the senate. Gradually more and more Americans came to see the senate as merely another device to check the otherwise unrestrained power of the legislature—a check representing the people, not the embodiment of a special social or intellectual order in society. This resulted in a belief in a two-house legislature representing identical interests created to prevent hasty or ill-considered legislation.

Although few at the time had more than a vague awareness of the implication of the idea of double representation, it formed an integral element in a fundamental transformation taking place in American political thought. The basic elements of this transformation involved the character of constitutional restraints on political power, the relationship between the people and their legislatures, and, above all else, the meaning of the sovereignty of the people. Taken together, the deliberations over these issues—sporadic and without overall design or intent—carried Americans toward an entirely new conception of politics without their being fully aware of it. The changes were so subtle and disparate through the 1770s and early 1780s that few realized their full impact.

The most basic change taking place involved American attitudes toward a constitution. Their struggle against the British in the 1760s had convinced many Americans that in order to ward off the oppressions of Parliament, they must protect their most fundamental rights by removing them from the arbitrary power of any particular government. This could best be accomplished by creating a written constitution that existed distinct from and superior to government, superior even to the representatives of the people in the legislatures.

By 1776 such a separation of fundamental law from everyday legislation led Americans to see constitutions as written documents that guaranteed the rights and privileges of the people. Unfortunately, the legislatures themselves became the principal interpreters of the fundamental law under which they covened. The same blurring of fundamental and statutory law that helped bring on the Revolution remained to plague the new republic. In a single brilliant passage in a pamphlet entitled *Conciliatory Hints, Attempting by a Fair State of Matters, to Remove Party Prejudice* (1784), Thomas Tudor Tucker captured how American actions over the previous two decades had subtly re-shaped their perception of a constitution: "The constitution should be the avowed act of the people at large. It should be the first and fundamental law of the State, and should prescribe the limits of all delegated power. It should be declared to be paramount to all acts of the Legislature, and irrepealable and unalterable by any authority but the express consent of a majority of the citizens collected by such regular mode as may be therein provided."[11] This statement succinctly captured the new understanding that was emerging in a piecemeal manner throughout the states. Such a conception completely altered the old contract between the people and their rulers. Now authority in every part of the government was derived entirely from the people. Constitutions were no longer covenants between two parties; they now brought government itself into being and proscribed and limited its powers.

Once constitutions came to be viewed as being superior to government, the manner in which they were drafted became crucial. It became apparent that if constitutions were to be made genuinely impervious to legislative tampering, they must be created by a power greater than the legislatures themselves. Gradually, but surely, the institution of the constitutional convention developed. Years of Americans meeting "out-of-doors" in commit-tees, mob disturbances, crowd activities, and extralegal congresses, long considered legally deficient bodies, provided an essential foundation for such a development. Indeed the perception of a convention of the people came quite rapidly and without conscious forethought to be viewed by Americans as an extraordinary constitution-making institution quite different from and superior to their customarily elected legislatures. Such bodies provided a legal and peaceable means for the people to reassume the power to govern in their own hands, to make the necessary changes that would ensure their liberties and protect their interests from the legislatures set above them. Thus, the old contract between the people and their rulers had been com-pletely transformed in a revolutionary manner. The people now established their government, which ruled under their watchful eye.

Such a view of the relationship of the people and the government naturally raised questions about the meaning of sovereignty. Indeed the theory of sov-ereignty, basic to the colonial resistance to Parliament in the 1760s, became central to the emerging understanding of government and society in post-Revolutionary America. Discussions of sovereignty began and ended with the belief that absolute and indivisible sovereignty must reside somewhere in any society. By the time of the Revolution, Americans believed sovereignty resided in their legislatures. It was this belief that made the idea of a Con-federation government of real power difficult to envision. The possibility of divided sovereignty—two legislatures having power within a single state—was almost beyond conception. Thus, efforts by nationalists to expand the power of the central government ran counter to the intellectual perception of sovereignty, as well as the ideological thrust of the Revolution. However, efforts by people within the states to control their individual legislatures lay squarely within, and benefited from this ideological momentum.

A tension emerged between those who considered legislators mere tools or agents of the people subject to their binding instructions and those who considered representatives, once elected, to be independent of the people and free to deliberate for themselves upon the public good. The latter emphasized the concept of indivisible sovereignty residing in the legislature, while the former came increasingly to believe that an indivisible sovereignty did in fact exist in society but that it rested with the people themselves, not with their elected representatives. Some worried lest power slip away from the legislatures to the people at large, while others feared the loss of control over their local interests to a hierarchy of elected officials.

The logic of events and circumstances inexorably favored the position of individuals viewing their representatives as simply proponents of the local interests of those who elected them. As the people came to view representatives, senators, and governors alike as their agents, the several branches of government became increasingly indistinguishable. No longer did the people actually share in any part of the government; instead they directed their representatives in every part of it. The people enveloped the entire government; no separate branch could personify the whole authority of the people. In fact, not even all of the collective branches could incorporate the total powers of the people. Thus, Americans, caught up in the ideological thrust of their Revolution, moved increasingly toward an acceptance of the complete and actual sovereignty of the people.

The Gentry Lose Control

Gentry leaders throughout the various states enthusiastically espoused the sovereignty of the people. Their belief that republican virtue and morality called for a natural hierarchy led those in control of state legislatures during the Revolution to write constitutions based upon much broader suffrage and far more equitable representation than characterized the provincial governments. John Adams, for one, blamed the "tyranny" of the British, their mistrust of the people, for the problems within the colonies previous to 1776: "All power, residing originally in the people, and being derived from them, the several magistrates and officers of government, vested with authority, whether legislative, executive, or judicial, are their subordinates and agents, and are at all times accountable to them."[12] Given this perception as well as his conviction that virtue predominated in American society, he willingly allowed wide popular participation in the new state governments. Adams and other Whig leaders apparently had little fear that removing the influence of the crown would expose them as the only proponents of social hierarchy in America and endanger their position within society. Even if some of them had harbored private doubts, most assumed that their taking the lead in resisting the British would validate their legitimacy and make clear to all Americans the advantages of a native aristocracy.

Members of the gentry had welcomed their poorer countrymen's support in opposition to the British aristocracy but expressed shock and dismay upon hearing, shortly after the outbreak of the Revolution, their cries that "we have not cast off a British aristocracy to be saddled with an American one." In many colonies groups of individuals demanded "no governair but the guvernor of the univarse" and pressed for state constitutions eliminating governors and upper houses, as well as supporting annually elected lower houses based upon universal male suffrage.[13] Worse, in the minds of the gentry, the people insisted on electing representatives who were not gentlemen, men who would represent the local interests of their constituents. The whole fabric of social hierarchy seemed to be coming under concerted attack.

This resulted from the fact that, quite beyond the control of the gentry, the Revolution released commercial and acquisitive forces only vaguely experienced in the prewar years and then limited almost exclusively to the gentry themselves. It accelerated the development of capitalism in America as no other event of the eighteenth century.[14] In order to supply the armies of over 100,000, a multitude of new manufacturing and entrepreneurial interests sprang up, and subsistence farmers with little previous awareness of trade connections beyond their local neighborhood became market-oriented producers with greatly expanded horizons of opportunity. In order to pay for the goods required by the army, the Confederation government, as well as the individual state governments, printed vast sums of paper money. Men with no previous experience beyond a simple barter economy became caught up in buying, selling, trading, and dealing throughout the vast interior regions of the country.

As great numbers of new producers and consumers entered the market economy, previously latent acquisitive instincts sprang up throughout all orders of society, and inland trade expanded enormously. Caught up in the optimistic expectations of an unparalleled prosperity and happiness to be brought about by the success of their revolution, farmers, traders, and shopowners borrowed money to expand their operations in order to guarantee their inclusion in that roseate future. For the first time ordinary individuals found themselves capable of purchasing luxury items that had always seemed out of their reach. Suddenly the urge to acquire luxury consumer goods stimulated the productivity of farmers. Industry and frugality, long the characteristic trait of simple folk, began to give way to industry and consumption.

Many people had difficulty adjusting to the end of the war and the resultant cessation of government spending. The demand for debtor relief legislation and the continued printing of paper money following the war's end resulted from the desires of individuals who relished their newly acquired ability to buy, sell, trade, and acquire luxury items formerly denied them. To continue to do so required, above all else, the issuance of paper money by the government. Without such a circulating medium, prosperity and entrepreneurial activity would be limited to the established creditor-merchants who dominated the Atlantic trade. With their private bills of exchange, these men could continue to prosper. Only a publicly created paper money supply could expand economic opportunity to include the hundreds of thousands of small traders, ordinary shopkeepers, aspiring artisans, and newly emerging market farmers who had gone into debt.

Ordinary farmers and petty entrepreneurs throughout the various states began to elect representatives to their legislatures who would respond to their needs by using the government in the interests of a wider section of the public. Political divisions now involved more than family interests or factional disputes; they became conflicts between groups of men with fundamentally differing opinions and interests. The new legislatures reflected these changes. Now common farmers made up about a third of the membership, and manufacturers and artisans, combined with lesser shopkeepers and professionals, composed a fourth. Men from all walks of life, college educated and those totally lacking in formal education, men of broad interests and experience and extremely parochial ones, became representatives of the people.

In a word the post-Revolutionary state legislatures were more democratic than their provincial predecessors.[15] Those who had traditionally enjoyed the exercise of political power—merchants, planters, lawyers, members of orthodox and established churches, cosmopolitan inhabitants of commercial urban centers—now had to compete with artisans, petty traders, shopkeepers, debtors, subsistence farmers, dissenters—ordinary people of little education or experience from small towns or farms deep in the interior—for control of the legislatures. Out of this confrontation new political configurations began to emerge.

Cosmopolitans versus Localists

The various states faced a similar set of issues resulting from the war and the need to establish new governmental procedures.[16] The matter of loyalists had to be confronted. Should property confiscation, test oaths, and special taxes be imposed upon Tories? What should become of the property and persons of loyalists who wished to return? Financing the war presented even more complicated issues; after the war, liquidation of the debt embroiled the states in a decade of controversy. To pay the debt and to put the state governments in a solvent position required taxes, but the basis of taxation and the medium in which taxes should be paid became troublesome.

Beyond these issues loomed others equally formidable. Should state governments be responsible for providing a circulating medium of currency for their citizens? Should credit be extended by the state or restricted to private initiative? Should debtors be aided by the state governments or left to fend for themselves? Other matters involving state expenditures also arose: should public officials be handsomely rewarded for their services or minimally compensated? Should the state build roads, support education, promote manufacturing and trade? Should state religion be disestablished? Governmental institutions too—the creation of new counties, the structure of the court system, the location of the state capital, and the powers and limitations of the state government—occasioned bitter discussions. Finally, the proper relation with Congress—involving money, men, and power—created intense arguments. How much and to what extent should the state support Congress?

These problems fostered remarkably similar responses throughout the states. In each state legislature two relatively well-defined opposing political blocs emerged to contest the issues. These groups did not form systematic organizations, nor did they extend into the electorate through institutional forms or organized electioneering. Rather they provided political expression within the legislatures to socioeconomic and cultural tensions that had been building for several decades. While no party labels or appellations appeared during the period, the terms *localist* and *cosmopolitan* best capture the essential nature of these opposing legislative blocs.[17]

The opposing perspectives of cosmopolitans and localists resulted from their contrasting experiences. Cosmopolitans resided along the Atlantic coast or major navigable streams in long-established counties and townships, as well as the urban and more heavily populated districts. Cosmopolitanism thrived in those areas that had been most thoroughly Anglicized. The cosmopolitan delegate pursued an occupation—merchant, trader, laywer, commercial farmer—that compelled him to deal with a broader world and permitted him to share in the cultural and social activities of his community. He enjoyed wealth, or at least comfortable circumstances. He very likely owned slaves or employed servants, had assets well beyond his debts, had served as a Continental officer during the war or in an important civil capacity, and had the benefit of formal education. His view of the world, particularly when compared to his localist colleagues, was extensive.

Localists represented isolated, independent, and relatively egalitarian communities scattered through the inland regions of the nation located far from or inaccessible to established trade routes. The localist delegate was very likely a farmer and might also, like most of his constituents, be in debt. If he had seen military service, it was as a militia officer, and so the experience was brief and likely did not take him far from home. Few localist delegates had held previous civil office, and if they had, it entailed only local responsibilities. They had little if any formal education and, given their restricted experiences, had difficulty perceiving a world much larger than their own neighborhoods or counties. Their goal was to represent the needs of their own people—their fellow debtors, small property holders, and newly emergent market farmers.

These divergent cultural backgrounds were reflected in the voting patterns that emerged in the state legislatures. Localists worked constantly to reduce governmental expenses. They did not fill newly created governmental offices or hold redeemable state certificates or notes. By and large localists took care of their own needs. They built roads, paid their ministers' salaries, supported what schools they had, and took care of their poor. In essence they wanted to be left alone. Consequently they resented having to pay taxes on land and other necessaries when that tax revenue seemed to benefit others. Localist delegates pressed for many forms of debtor relief. They consistently supported inflationary policies that eased the conditions of debtors, provided relief for taxpayers, and supplied publicly supported money or credit at low interest to promote economic expansion and prevent foreclosures. Above all, they demanded a plentiful supply of money that would be considered legal tender in the payment of debts and taxes.

Localist representatives took negative stands on a number of other issues. They opposed the creation of banks and legislation to aid businessmen in urban areas. They resisted the unimpeded return of loyalists, who, once they had regained their property, would support the cosmopolitan cause. They were cynical about state-supported colleges and systems of public education, hesitant to support congressional demands for enlarged powers, and violently opposed to the idea of strengthening the central government. These people, trusting no one but their own kind, supported a simple egalitarian form of democracy that left them in control of their own affairs and free from hostile and corrupt outside forces.

In contrast, cosmopolitans believed most governmental activity fostered the greater good of society. This was particularly true if they themselves exercised political power. They supported payment of the debt in full, not merely because they held most of the state certificates and would thus benefit directly but also because they believed that government must, in order to maintain a good reputation, create solvent economic substructures with an outstanding basis of credit among the world at large. As the personal beneficiaries of good government, they supported higher salaries for public officials.

Cosmopolitans also supported a solid judicial system, improved transportation, subsidies to promote economic expansion, a stable monetary system, and the maintenance of good order. Never hesitating to pay their portion to receive such benefits, they demanded that all residents of the state share in these expenses by paying their taxes promptly, and preferably in specie. All private debts as well should also be paid promptly and in full. To these men, paper money and debtor relief schemes appeared ill conceived and dangerously irresponsible. Cosmopolitans supported the authority and majesty of government. They consistently voted in favor of granting requests from the Confederation government for greater powers and looked favorably upon the creation of a stronger national government. Being broad-minded, urbane individuals, they quickly forgave loyalists, favored state-supported colleges, and endorsed the cultural and economic development of towns. Therefore the sort of democracy the localists advocated seemed like no government at all. It meant the domination of rational, educated, and propertied men by those of little property and even less insight into what responsible government was all about. Localism, to the cosmopolitan, meant narrow, selfish interests being pressed by ambitious provincials with little regard for order, decorum, station, and morals. It stood, in short, for the destruction of the sort of government that gentlemen had known—and controlled—for ages.

Beneath the tension within the legislatures coursed a deep cultural antagonism that repeatedly surfaced in newspaper essays, pamphlets, and public orations. In the minds of cosmopolitans, American society faced a crisis resulting from a combination of licentiousness and excessive democracy. Legislatures should be composed of men of property, independence of mind, firmness, education, and a wide knowledge of history, politics, and the laws of their society. Unfortunately, according to a Boston newspaper, such "men of sense and property" were being rapidly displaced in the legislative halls of the states by "blustering ignorant men." A Massachusetts gentlemen claimed that government was increasingly falling into the hands of those who, though perhaps honest, "yet from the contractedness of their Education, and whose views never extended further than a small farm or a bond of 50 or 100£ cannot, from long habit, be persuaded to view Matters on a large or national scale." Such men, "being unacquainted with the nature of Commerce view the Merchants as real positive Evils hence as well from Obstinacy as Ignorance, Trade, by which only a Nation can grow rich, is neglected." Cosmopolitans worried over the future, "when almost every office is in the hands of those who are not distinguished by property, family, education, manners or talents."[18]

For their part localists remained suspicious of gentlemen who constantly assumed it to be their privilege to draw power into their hands at the expense of the common people. An incident in South Carolina in 1784, involving an alleged insult to John Rutledge by a tavern keeper, William Thompson, became a *cause célèbre* and led to a clear articulation of localist resentments—resentments that had festered for years.[19] When the state legislature threatened to banish Thompson for his indiscretion against one of its own, the tavern–keeper and ex-captain in the Revolutionary service struck back. His public address of April 1784, a classic articulation of the resentment building against social superiority, spoke out on behalf of the people, or "those more especially, who go at this day, under the opprobrious appellation of, the *Lower Orders of Men*." Thompson not only attacked those aristocratic "Nabobs" attempting to humiliate him but upended the predominant eighteenth-century belief that only a natural aristocracy was peculiarly qualified to rule. He argued that the "persons and conduct" of Rutledge and other "Nabobs" of South Carolina "in *private* life, may be unexceptionable, and even amiable, but their pride, influence, ambition, connections, wealth and political principles, ought in *public* life, ever to exclude them from *public confidence*." All that republican leadership required was "being *good, able, useful,* and *friends to social equality*," because in a republican government "consequence is from the *public opinion*, and not from *private fancy*." Then, in tones heavy with irony, Thompson related how he, a tavern keeper, "a *wretch* of no higher rank in the Commonwealth than that of Common-Citizen," was debased by "those *self-exalted* characters, who affect to compose the *grand hierarchy* of the State, . . . for having dared to dispute with a *John Rutledge*, or any of the NABOB *tribe*." No doubt, Thompson exclaimed, Rutledge had "conceived me his inferior." However, the tavern keeper, like so many others in similar circumstances, could no longer "comprehend the *inferiority*." The animosity between those considering men like Thompson as their inferiors and those like Thompson who would no longer accept such treatment underlay the social ferment that boiled just beneath the surface of the legislatures and throughout American society in the 1780s.

Democratic Excesses

Within this environment many cosmopolitan gentlemen became convinced that their society faced a social crisis. For men well versed in eighteenth-century political theory, it was not difficult to diagnose the illness plaguing their society. If British rule twenty years previously had degenerated into a perversion of power, the excesses of the people now had become a perversion of liberty. By this the gentry did not necessarily mean mob violence, although Shays' Rebellion in the winter of 1786–87 shocked them; rather they meant the quite legal democratic actions of the state legislatures. The delegates, elected in as fair a manner and based upon as equal a representational scheme as the world had ever seen, openly perpetrated the excesses that so disturbed the gentry. In those assemblies paper money schemes, the confiscation of property, and the whole panoply of debtor-relief legislation that undercut creditors and violated property rights achieved legitimacy.

James Madison's experience in the Virginia legislature from 1784 through 1787 epitomized the unease cosmopolitans throughout the nation endured.

Madison quickly discovered that not all of his fellow legislators were gentlemen. In his opinion most cared little for public honor or honesty and seemed intent upon serving only narrow, local interests. Calm reason and order gave way to clamorousness and chaos. Lawmakers during Madison's tenure appeared to him to scramble to secure the demands of their constituents with little regard for consistency or the systematic creation of a body of laws to promote the overall interests of the state. Government, in the hands of "Individuals of extended views, and of national pride," could enlighten, but that standard would never be served by "the multitude," who could rarely conceive of issues except in terms of their own pocketbooks and their own neighborhoods.[20]

Such a perception was by no means unique to Madison. Gentlemen everywhere grew increasingly disillusioned with the "characters too full of Local attachments and Views to permit sufficient attention to the general interest" who disgraced the state legislatures by ceaselessly advancing particular causes and pandering "to the vulgar and sordid notions of the populace."[21] For Madison and his gentlemanly colleagues, the legislative branch of state governments, long considered the expression of the people's will as well as the best protector of their liberties, now seemed to have become a democratic despot. A tremendously important shift occurred in their thoughts; the fear and suspicion of political power long associated with the executive now became fixed upon the individual state assemblies.

Again James Madison offered the most cogent insights into the matter: "Wherever the real power in a Government lies, there is the danger of oppression. In our Governments the real power lies in the majority of the Community, and the invasion of private rights is chiefly to be apprehended, not from acts of Government contrary to the sense of its constituents, but from acts in which the Government is the mere instrument of the major number of the constituents." The people were just as capable of becoming despotic as any king or prince. Consequently the classical perception, in which the people's liberties faced a constant threat from the power of their rulers, made little sense. In America, rather than the many fearing the few, "It is much more to be dreaded that the few will be unnecessarily sacrificed to the many."[22] This fear of the power of the majority, when combined with the gentry's growing apprehension regarding the character of the American people, created the most profound despair for men like Madison and his colleagues. In Madison's mind Americans must discover "a republican remedy for the diseases most incident to republican government."[23]

Others agreed with Madison and set about reforming the state constitutions that had been written in 1776–77, adopting the Massachusetts Constitution of 1780 as their model. With a legislature balanced between a House that embodied the people and a Senate apportioned according to property valuation, a strong executive, and a judiciary appointed by the governor, this constitution represented a check on the unrestrained power of the people. A bill of rights spelled out the principle of the separation of powers in great detail. Some genteel reformers wanted to go beyond the Massachusetts Constitution as a model. They hoped to change the very character of the lower houses, first by decreasing the number of delegates so as to make the assembly more stable and energetic, and second by reducing their powers.

These efforts did not go unnoticed. Localists, who had welcomed changes in their state governments wrought by the Revolution, became apprehensive. For them the Revolution, by granting greater powers to much-enlarged legislatures, had been a success. From their perspective, the Revolution was just beginning to achieve its goals: a more equitable republican society where each individual and locale could gain autonomy and control.

Still, the reforms being made in the state constitutions did not seem terribly threatening to most Americans. Since perceptions of government experienced constant flux during the decade after 1776, it had become extremely difficult to find a single fixed definition of good republican institutions. Those in favor of reforming the original state constitutions could employ republican ideology for their purpose: a strengthened upper house stood as a second representative of the power of the people and made it more difficult for designing men to control two governmental bodies than just one. Senates thereby became bulwarks of the people against the usurpation of power by the house. A powerful executive, too, might have evoked distrust and fear when controlled by the crown, but now that he stood as a representative of the people, he could help protect them from one branch of government gaining overweening power at the expense of the others.

Those arguments gained credence through a subtly refined and much expanded understanding of the doctrine of the separation of powers, making alterations in the power of the executive or the senate seem like logical extensions of republican ideology rather than repudiations of it. Once all branches of the government—executive, judicial, and legislative—were considered simply as separate and equal servants of the people, it made perfect sense that no single one should wield more power than any other. The idea of the separation of powers, which had originally been used to protect the legislatures from the executive, now came to mean that the executive, legislative, and judicial branches should be forever separate and distinct from one another.

This view of the separation of powers became the most important maxim for legislative reformers during the 1780s. They elevated it into a central, if not the key, principle in American politican thought. The traditional theory of balanced government that called for an equilibrium among social orders within society became blurred. The separation of powers now called for a proper balance instead among the executive, judicial, and legislative functions. From this perspective senators, representatives, judges, and governors became servants of the people, and it made little sense to give one branch of the government more power than any other. In fact to do so violated the most basic republican principles; it drew excessive power into the hands of one body that would enable its members to tyrannize over the others.

Even with all the changes wrought in state constitutions the anxieties spreading among cosmopolitans would not subside. Many came to feel that the reform effort must be extended to include the federal government as well if the crisis in the state governments was to be truly resolved. No matter how well structured they might be, state governments did not seem capable of creating responsible laws and virtuous citizens. By 1786–1787, the reformation of the central government became the primary concern of those worried about America's ability to sustain republican governments and a prosperous republican society. As a result, when the Constitutional Convention gathered in Philadelphia in 1787, it represented the culmination of reform efforts to curb the democratic excesses of the state legislatures and to provide an institutional framework that could safely accommodate the dynamic changes taking place within American society.

The Constitution

The convention that met in Philadelphia throughout the summer of 1787, attended almost entirely by men of a cosmopolitan frame of mind, effected a political revolution as great as the one that gained independence from Great Britain. The delegates scrapped the Articles of Confederation and created a truly national government, a single continental republic that penetrated the state governments to the people themselves. At its head stood a powerful executive with broad appointive powers within the executive and judicial branches, who also served as commander in chief of armed forces and exercised virtual control over the nation's diplomatic affairs. Chosen by electors elected by the people rather than by the legislature, the president gained further independence during his four-year term of office, and he was eligible for perpetual reelection. The Constitution also created a separate, potentially powerful national judiciary branch, whose justices would hold office during good behavior and so gained immunity from the vagaries of popular election. The legislative branch consisted of a House of Representatives elected by the people and apportioned according to population and a Senate selected by the individual states composed of two senators from each state, each with one vote. Both houses of Congress enjoyed extensive legislative prerogatives, and Congress gained wide powers under the Constitution that had been denied it by the Articles. Most important, it now had the power to tax and to regulate commerce. In addition the new document specifically denied certain prerogatives to the states; they could no longer print paper money, impair the obligation of contracts, be involved in foreign affairs, or lay imposts or duties on imports and exports. The Constitution, unlike the Articles, created a true national state with extensive coercive powers.

The new government reflected the central cosmopolitan tenets of its authors. According to Alexander Hamilton, it suited "the commercial character of America"; John Jay felt that it mirrored the true "manners and circumstances" of the nation, which were "not strictly democratical."[24] The new arrangement must control the democratic excesses of the states by insulating the federal government from the populist forces that had sprung up with the Revolution. In addition, it should restore political influence to selfless gentlemen of broad vision and education. Madison believed that the best way to ensure this was to create "such a process of elections as will most certainly extract from the mass of Society the purest and noblest characters which it contains; such as will at once feel most strongly the proper motives to pursue the end of their appointment, and be most capable to devise the proper means of attaining it."[25] This desire to attract the best men to the government and then to allow them to exercise independent judgment resulted in the complexity of separate constituencies, staggered terms of office, and elaborate mechanisms of election created by the new form of government. Only such a filtration of talent and modification of the undiluted expression of the people could safeguard the hierarchical world of America's gentlemen.

At the same time the creation of an active, energetic government promised to unleash the commercial potential of the nation that had been inhibited by state control over commerce. With a national framework within which to work, the entrepreneurial interests of the gentry could develop the tremendous economic potential of the young republic. The new government, empowered to deal aggressively with foreign powers and to control the nation's commercial activities, could now actively promote national prosperity. Geographical expansion, commercial development, and the consolidation and mobilization of mercantile capital seemed a real possibility at last.

James Madison and the Constitution

These two impulses—to control democratic excesses and to create a more beneficial commercial environment—lay at the heart of the cosmopolitan's view of the good society; yet they also constituted the source of his greatest tension and frustration. Backward looking in his political beliefs—desperate in his desire to hang on to the neoclassical political and social world of the eighteenth century—and yet modern in his economic outlook, the cosmopolitan became a victim of his own success. The capitalistic practices of his economic world fostered an individualistic ethos that eroded his neoclassical world of hierarchy and deference from which he derived his sense of identity and security.

James Madison's intellectual search for a way to preserve republican government and society from its own worst excesses led him to a careful reconsideration of what American society had become by the mid-1780s. Struggling to comprehend the changes that were transforming the new republic, he caught glimpses of the weaknesses in the conflicting sources of authority—hierarchy and localism—that struggled for dominance. Out of his effort to think through the work accomplished at Philadephia, he arrived at the conclusion that the Constitution provided a framework for government and society resting on entirely different principles of authority than any previous governmental system. He presented this new understanding of political science, as well as his still inchoate perceptions of America's changing culture, in his contributions to the *Federalist* essays, published with those of Hamilton and Jay to support the ratification of the Constitution.

In these essays Madison spoke to the tension emerging in American society between the individual and the community. He attempted to find a system to oblige self-interested, self-governing men to respect the rights of others and to promote the interests of the larger community. He thus explored a middle ground between the potential tyranny of unrestrained majorities and the potential oppression of a hierarchy of centralized power. "The practicable sphere of a republic," he reasoned, must be large enough to "break and control the violence of faction," but it should never be so large as to sever the democratic bond between governors and the governed.[26] While republican government should restrain the undiluted will of the people, that will must never be denied. In Madison's view governments existed solely to protect and enlarge the freedom of the people as well as their equality of opportunity. The best guarantee of such a purpose was to be certain that governmental power and authority rested on the consent of the governed. This constituted the most vital republican principle to which all just government must adhere. Therefore Madison's primary intent became to discover the proper mechanism that would provide such insurance while at the same time maintaining order and integrity in government.

Madison believed this mechanism existed in the federal structure created by the Constitution. That system would be able to refine and purify the will of the majority by causing it to pass through the successive filters of state and national governments while simultaneously guaranteeing that government at either level, however purified, always rested upon the will of the people. State authorities would attend to issues requiring a particular understanding of the parochial needs of local situations, while federal representatives would handle national issues requiring broader vision and scope. Because each level of government had been carefully balanced, no separate branch of either the state or federal government would be able to operate in opposition to the interest of the whole people. In addition, the state and national governments acted as checks upon one another. Given the creation of these safeguards, future generations of American's would be able to enjoy as much self-government as human nature would allow.

Within this system Madison could constantly seek the middle ground. If the heedless pursuit of local interests threatened to overwhelm national authority or erode republican principles, Madison could throw his support to the central government and emphasize majority rule. Such was the case in 1787. If, however, a group of power-hungry leaders were to capture the central government at some future time and thereby threaten to destroy republican government through an oppressive oligarchy, he could emphasize anticentralist, libertarian principles and organize the countervailing powers of the state governments. For Madison, such a shifting of forces to achieve a proper equilibrium was necessary in order to ensure a lasting American republic.

In *Federalist* No. 10, Madison offered his clearest statement of the diseases that most commonly threatened a republic and their proper remedies. Sensing the emergence of a diverse individualism within the new republic, Madison knew that to gain legitimacy within this society government must rest upon the sacredness of the individual and each citizen's right to the fullest and freest expression of that individuality. He knew also that "as long as the reason of man continues fallible, and he is at liberty to exercise it, different opinions will be formed." Such "diversity in the faculties of men" must always be given free reign. Indeed, for Madison, "the protection of these faculties is the first object of government."[27] In making such a commitment, however, Madison realized full well that a diverse society composed of self-interested individuals must inexorably result in the creation of fiercely competitive antagonistic factions. Such factions naturally resulted from the liberties cherished in a republican society. To remove their causes was to destroy the very essence of a republican society. Thus, since the causes of faction could not be eliminated, "relief is only to be sought in the means of controlling, its *effects*."[28] This meant creating a governmental structure that simultaneously protected the peoples' liberties from the emergence of a single oppressive power and vitiated the power of factions themselves.

In Madison's mind, the Constitution accomplished this by dispersing power between state and central authorities and by dividing and balancing it among the executive, legislative, and judicial branches of the national government. While nearly every element of government at both the state and federal levels was elected by the people, these elections took place at different times and within such a variety of diverse electoral districts as to make it extremely difficult for one self-interested faction to gain simultaneous control of all branches of government throughout the nation. If a faction did control several state legislatures and gained a majority in the federal House, the Senate, the president, and the judiciary still stood as checks upon its excesses.

The surest means to control the effects of faction, however, lay in extending the geographic extent of government. The larger the republican government is, contrary to Montesquieu's dictums, the more secure the republican society is. Thus, "The influence of factious leaders may kindle a flame within their particular states, but will be unable to spread a general conflagration through the other states: a religious sect may degenerate into a political faction in a part of the confederacy; but the variety of sects dispersed over the entire face of it, must secure the national councils against any danger from that source: a rage for paper money, for an abolition of debts, for an equal division of property, or for any other improper or wicked project, will be less apt to pervade the whole body of the union than a particular member of it."[29]

Madison's view of American society rested on the realization that a self-interested and diverse population had emerged within the young republic. No longer could an outmoded hierarchy or a localism based upon majoritarian sentiments offer entirely legitimate bases of authority. The one smacked entirely too much of aristocracy, and the other promised only chaos. For Madison, then, the Constitution fostered a diverse individualistic society, but at the same time it produced a checked and balanced government of real authority and power. The Constitution had indeed designed a government to protect a republican society from itself.

The Federalists

Like Madison, the great bulk of Federalists—the name assumed by the cosmopolitan supporters of the Constitution—believed that the new government could preserve American republicanism from the democratic excesses they saw all around them. Republicanism to these gentlemen meant mobility, equality of opportunity, and careers open to men of talent. Such a perception of equality, however, was not incompatible with their commitment to hierarchy. In their minds all societies consisted of gradations of social orders held together by the deference owed to individuals in higher stations by those in lower ones. In a republic any person of ability should be free to move upward, but Federalists naturally assumed that individuals who rose in a republican society would first acquire the requisites of social superiority—property, education, social connections, broad experiences—before they took on the responsibilities of political authority. For this reason respectable people stood aghast as they witnessed men "whose fathers they would have disdained to have sit with the dogs of their flocks, raised to immense wealth, or at least to carry the appearance of a haughty, supercilious and luxurious spendthrift." Worse, state legislatures, the traditional Whig bastions of liberty, filled up with "men without reading, experience, or principle." Authority rested in "the Hands of those whose ability or situation in Life does not entitle them to it."[30]

In spite of, or perhaps because of, the changes taking place in their society, Federalists clung desperately to classical traditions of disinterested public leadership. For them the Constitution promised a last hope to preserve the republican ideal of a government in the hands of the "worthy" rather than the "licentious."[31]

Many Federalists accepted Madison's argument in *Federalist* No. 10. The "better sort" might be overpowered by localists in the many small electoral districts required by state legislatures, but in enlarged congressional districts men of broad contacts and experience would surely gain election and thus control of the national government, which, with its enhanced powers, now had the opportunity to shape American society. Thus, the Constitution offered a filtration of talent that seemed to promise the reassertion of genteel authority.

To accept the logic of *Federalist* No. 10, however, enmeshed the Federalists in several paradoxes. First, by recognizing that American society had become fragmented into a multiplicity of conflicting interests—interests that could become overbearing local majorities in particular state legislatures—they accepted a conception of society that undermined the traditional social justification for a natural aristocracy and an elitist style of politics. The notion of the organic unity of society had always undergirded the existence of a disinterested natural aristocracy. Now Federalists seemed to believe that such a society no longer existed.

Also, by depending upon the new governmental structure to solve the social and political problems arising from the Revolution, Federalists acquiesced to the very democratic politics that they blamed for the ills of their society. Indeed democratic elections became the basis for the perpetuation of the natural elite's continued domination of politics. So long as constituencies could be made large enough to stifle the opportunities for social upstarts to gain office, the popular vote would elect natural leaders. Democracy could be made to support an elitist style of politics, and, Federalists hoped, an ordered society as well.

Federalists had little difficulty in presenting the Constitution as continuing the libertarian tradition of republicanism and the embodiment of the people's interests. This was possible because since 1776, political ideals had taken on new meanings, and republican principles had undergone subtle transformations. In their effort to defend the Constitution, Federalists drew together the disparate strands of thought that had emerged throughout the previous decade. Gradually, still not always aware of the consequences, the Federalists created an entirely new conception of politics out of these previously disconnected republican ideas.

At the heart of their emerging persuasion lay the idea of federalism. Here Federalists had to wrestle with the paradoxical idea of simultaneous jurisdiction by two legislative bodies—a clear contradiction of the fixed idea of supreme and indivisible sovereignty. James Wilson, a prominent Pennsylvania jurist, solved this problem at his state's ratification convention. There he claimed that those who argued that competing independent taxing powers—Congress and the state legislatures—could not exist within the same community had entirely misunderstood the nature of sovereignty in America. For Wilson, sovereignty was indeed indivisible, but it did not rest in either the state or the national legislature. Supreme power in America emanated from the people; they were the source of government. The people never surrendered this sovereignty. They merely dispensed portions of it to the various branches and levels of government as they saw fit.

Once sovereignty had been located in the people, the new system of government made perfect intellectual sense, and the Federalists could not restrain their enthusiasm for introducing the power and control of the people into every aspect of the newly created governmental structure. To attack the Constitution now meant to attack the people themselves. "We the People" assumed a transcendent new meaning. Indeed, given the fundamentally different principle upon which the new Constitution rested, it became entirely logical for the Federalists to defend the absence of a bill of rights. Since all power resided in the people, what they did not specifically delegate to Congress they reserved to themselves. Therefore it was not within the national government's power to grant specific rights to the people. For the government to do so would have meant that it comprised the fountain of all power, just as it did in the decadent and despised societies of Europe.

Such contentions revealed the gradually emerging assumptions about government and society that made up the Federalist system. The traditional libertarian division of rulers and people into separate and opposing interests became irrelevant. Instead the old spheres of power and liberty had been fused. The people now held all power; their representatives in the various branches of the government became their servants. Consequently the government itself became the shield of the people's liberties, not a potentially dangerous threat requiring constant scrutiny. Governmental power became, in Federalist literature, indistinguishable from that of the people. Once this view had been established, the Confederation government no longer made any sense. With all power lodged in a single unchecked branch of the government, what was to keep a combination of men from oppressing the very people they were supposed to serve?

The clearest theme that ran through Federalist arguments in the ratification conventions was the need to distribute and separate traditionally mistrusted governmental power. The old conception of a mixed polity no longer made any sense. America, the Federalists argued, was a new, unique republican society of talent and ability with no distinct social orders, only the people. To create a government in which all branches represented the people made perfect sense. All that was necessary was to separate power into distinct executive, judicial, and legislative branches and to balance them against one another. In this way, the entire government, not just the legislature, became a democracy. Thus the Federalists presented the new government as a thoroughly democratic entity based on the needs and desires of the people. The Constitution, in their rhetoric, epitomized traditional republican maxims and represented the culmination of the popular thrust of the Revolution itself.

The Anti-Federalists

Opponents of the Constitution, the Anti-Federalists, did not see it that way. Indeed if any central theme coursed throughout their arguments, it was that the Federalists meant to erect an oppressive aristocracy that would stifle the democratic tendencies fostered by the Revolution. In the New York ratification convention Melancton Smith warned that the new government "will fall into the hands of the few and the great." A Marylander, Timothy Bloodworth, exclaimed that "the great will struggle for power, honor and wealth, the poor become a prey to avarice, insolence, and oppression." A newspaper essay claimed that the Philadelphia convention had created "a monstrous aristocracy" that would "swallow up the democratic rights of the union, and sacrifice the liberties of the people to the power and domination of a few."[32]

Such observations revealed that Anti-Federalists opposed the Constitution for the very reasons that Federalists supported it. They recognized that the new governmental structure would prevent ordinary individuals from gaining election to Congress and would thereby exclude local interests from actual representation in that body. Samuel Chase objected that "the government is not a government of the people" because only the rich and well born would gain election to Congress.[33] Members of the minority in the Pennsylvania ratifying convention recognized that because of the election process, "men of the most elevated rank in life will alone be chosen. The other orders in the society, such as farmers, traders, and mechanics, who all ought to have a competent number of their best informed men in the legislature, shall be totally unrepresented." Melancton Smith in New York remained convinced "that this government is so constituted that the representatives will generally be composed of the first class in the community, which I shall distinguish by the name of the *natural aristocracy* of the country."[34]

These feelings of resentment sprang from a widespread sense of suspicion, hostility, and fear of a hierarchy of outsiders that permeated Anti-Federalism. The Constitution instituted a government of strangers; worse, those strangers were gentlemen who not only had no fellow feeling with simple folk but felt superior to them. Old Amos Singletary during the Massachusetts ratification convention voiced the defiant hostility and deep insecurities of localists: "These lawyers, and men of learning and moneyed men, that talk so finely, and gloss over matters so smoothly, to make us poor illiterate people swallow down the pill, expect to get into Congress themselves; they expect to be managers of this Constitution, and get all the power and all the money into their own hands, and then they will swallow all us little folks like the great *Leviathan;* yes, just as the whale swallowed up Jonah."[35]

These attitudes—antagonism toward aristocracy, commitment to the most intimate participation in government by the widest possible variety of people, devotion to the egalitarian impulses of the Revolution—spawned majoritarian attitudes toward state legislatures but not toward the proposed new Congress.

Although the leadership of the Anti-Federalists included a number of prominent gentlemen—Rawlins Lowndes, George Mason, Richard Henry Lee, George Clinton—these men opposed the Constitution out of a philosphical and intellectual commitment to state government. Anti-Federalism itself emerged from much more visceral emotions. As much a social and a cultural phenomenon as a political movement, it sprang from a reactionary localism that pervaded American society. In the mid-1780s Anti-Federalism was handicapped because its ideas had yet to coalesce into a coherent political ideology. Consequently, in one state convention after another, Anti-Federalists found themselves bullied and embarrassed by their polished, articulate, unified Federalists opponents.

While the Anti-Federalist cause floundered, some individual adherents displayed a keen understanding of the social and political world emerging in America. This was particularly true of William Findley of Pennsylvania, a man who was far more representative of Anti-Federalist thought than gentlemen such as Mason or Clinton. Findley, an Irish immigrant who began life in America as an apprenticed weaver, had risen to become a spokesman for the debtor–paper money interests in the Pennsylvania legislature by the mid-1780s. A self-made man, Findley had never assumed the refinements of gentility—education, affluence, sophistication in speech and dress. Instead he remained an outspoken advocate of middling aspirations, achievements, and resentments. Indeed, he felt a special antagonism toward members of the gentry who looked down upon him and his kind.

Findley never denied serving the interests of his constituents. Indeed, he prided himself upon it and declared that whenever an individual had "a cause of his own to advocate, interest will dictate the propriety of canvassing for a seat" in the legislature. Findley saw nothing wrong with this. To him self-interest was the driving force within American society: "The human soul is affected by wealth, in almost all its faculties. It is effected by its present interests, by its expectations, and by its fears."[36] Findley freely admitted to being self-interested, but he belligerently refused to believe gentlemen were any different. He had no patience with the argument of the genteel that they served in political positions simply to promote the common good. Throughout his terms in the Pennsylvania legislature, Findley had intimate contact with the gentry; the mystique of disinterested aristocratic authority had no power over him. He knew that for all their claims of superiority emanating from knowledge, experience, education, and extensive connections, gentlemen differed from their neighbors only in having more money.

In Findley's mind American society was a heterogeneous mixture composed of "many different classes or orders of people, Merchant, Farmer, Planter Mechanic and Gentry or wealthy Men;" each group with equal claim to the rights and privileges of government. In such a disparate and egalitarian society, no group or class or men could possibly represent the interests of the entire community: "No man when he enters into society, does it from a view to promote the good of others, but he does it for his own good." Consequently the only fair system of representation must be one in which "every order of men in the community . . . can have a share in it."[37] Each local interest must be directly represented in order for the pluralistic society emerging in America to be embodied fully and completely within the government. This belief, combined with their conviction that the Constitution would keep ordinary individuals out of the national government, fed the antagonism Findley and his Anti-Federalist colleagues felt toward the Federalists.

Findley's attacks upon deference and the ability of gentlemen to govern in the interest of a common good was part of an entirely new perception of politics and society. Rather than a harmonious unity that solidified all orders into an organic whole, he saw society divided into disconnected and antagonistic interests. Whether he realized the implications of what he was saying or not, when he and other Anti-Federalists attacked the traditional idea of a natural aristocracy governing in the interest of all, they also indirectly undermined the belief in an organic social order that underlay their own localist brand of republicanism.

Not all of the Anti-Federalists sensed the changes taking place in their society as clearly as Findley, but all expressed an eighteenth-century libertarian distrust of hierarchy that came from a traditional local sense of community. They knew no other language. As they stumbled toward a new understanding of their world, they remained dependent on an anachronistic vocablulary. Bred upon the hostility believed to exist between the spheres of power and liberty, they felt certain that a republican government could exist only in a small geographic region of homogeneous interests and that they must distrust all executive and aristocratical power. Now, however, they watched in horror as the Federalists turned each weapon in their republican arsenal against them. When Anti-Federalists attacked a powerful executive or an independent Senate as potential sources of oppression by rulers set against the people, Federalists scoffed at them and replied that the president and senators were only agents of the people, not a separate and potentially oppressive interest at all. Whenever Anti-Federalists attacked the Constitution on the grounds that it divided sovereignty, they met the rebuff that sovereignty lay with the people and that to attack the Constitution was to attack the people. When Anti-Federalists demanded a bill of rights—the essence of libertarian republicanism—their opponents made them appear foolish by asking how a government could guarantee rights to the people when the sovereign people themselves limited and restricted the government. Everywhere Anti-Federalists found their own arguments turned back upon them. Republicanism, democracy, the sovereignty of the people—all seemed to have found a home in the Federalist camp.

As long as the powerful localism that permeated American society remained disparate, inchoate, and disconnected from its natural roots within the New World environment, it could not overcome the well-articulated ideology of the Federalists. Still, the Anti-Federalist cause enjoyed tremendous popularity. Even without many brilliant debaters, clever parliamentarians, newspaper editors, or men of great individual prestige within their ranks and little, if any, organization, the Anti-Federalists suffered only the narrowest of defeats.

A Changing Culture

The struggle over the Constitution produced a number of paradoxes and ironic consequences. The Federalists, elitists who wished to create a powerful centralized government controlled by the rich and the well born, constantly spoke in terms of the sovereignty of the people; they presented their case in the most democratic and radical language. Under this guise they managed to create a government that answered their needs—or so they imagined. In 1787 they had little reason to believe that the Constitution might also provide a national framework that could, under changed circumstances, just as easily accommodate the rise of a national democracy. The Anti-Federalists, on the other hand, who wished to create a decentralized government with direct participation by all classes of people, employed an archaic and anachronistic libertarian language of communalism. Yet, in actuality, their behavior belied such an ideal.

An embryonic individualsm was tearing at both the hierarchical and localist bases of authority represented by the Federalists and the Anti-Federalists. On the one hand, capitalistic economic practices of the Federalists eroded the social foundation underlying their traditional perception of a natural aristocracy. On the other, the egalitarianism characteristic of localism became increasingly manifested in an individualistic, self-interested behavior that fragmented the communal substructure of localism. As Federalists looked backward to an eighteenth-century ideal of politics and society, Anti-Federalists groped toward a new conception of society and politics more consonant with the transformations taking place within American society. Both groups exhibited thought and behavior characteristic of the newly emerging culture of the American republic.

five

A Republican Culture

In 1786 Benjamin Rush, a prominent Philadelphia physician and statesman, observed that it was a mistake to believe that the American Revolution was over: "This is so far from being the case that we have only finished the first act of the great drama." Americans had changed their form of government, "but it remains yet to effect a revolution in our principles, opinions, and manners so as to accommodate them to the forms of government we have adopted."[1] Americans must establish a republican culture to complement their republican political system.

For most Americans this did not seem a difficult task. Released from the artificial and decadent constraints of Great Britain, a new republican culture would emerge spontaneously from the benign New World environment. Convinced of the efficacy of such a culture to effect wide-ranging social transformations, Americans set out to apply republican principles to all aspects of their society. Their certitude that the institution of republicanism would be sufficient to bring about positive cultural change caused Americans to become infected with a boundless enthusiasm for the future of their infant nation.

Joel Barlow captured this optimism in a Fourth of July oration in 1787 when he exulted that "neither the pageantry of courts nor the glooms of superstition have dazzled or beclouded the mind" in America. Within such a beneficent atmosphere surely the millennium was "actually to commence in the territories of the United States."[2] Republican education, republican laws, and a republican environment of equality would create that unique kind of virtuous, egalitarian, and austere society of independent citizens devoted to the common good that men had yearned to achieve since ancient Greece.

In the two decades following the end of the Revolution, American society did indeed become republicanized but hardly in the manner envisioned by so many Americans in 1783. Tensions besetting those involved in the arts and tearing at the political and social beliefs of both Federalists and Anti-Federalists affected the larger culture as well. The materialistic, individualistic, and utilitarian actions of so many Americans during and after the Revolution continued to spread throughout society, with anomalous consequences for republican culture within the new nation.

Education in a Republic

In 1788 Noah Webster, an outspoken exponent of cultural independence, called upon his countrymen to "unshackle your minds, and act like independent beings. . . . You have an empire to raise and support by your exertions, and a national character to establish and extend by your wisdom and virtues." The only way to accomplish this grand mission was "to frame a liberal plan of policy, and build it on a broad system of education."[3] Such a system must break free from the decadence and corruption of Europe in order to blossom. In Europe, "grown old in folly, corruption and tyranny . . . laws are perverted, manners are licentious, literature is declining and human nature debased." Consequently, for Americans in their "infancy to adopt the present maxims of the Old World, would be to stamp the wrinkles of decrepit age upon the bloom of youth and to plant the seeds of decay in a vigorous constitution."[4]

Webster articulated feelings of excitement shared by a great many Americans in whom the Revolution had created a sense of opportunity, a chance to create a unique new society. Since the very existence of a republic rested upon the presence of solid republican citizens, Webster, Benjamin Rush, Thomas Jefferson, and a host of others attempted to delineate the educational environment critical to the realization of the goals of the new republic. They took as their objective the creation of a new type of individual—virtuous, patriotic, wise, just—molded by education into an independent-minded yet fiercely steadfast citizen. They believed that an appropriate education incorporated not only the dissemination of knowledge but the cultivation of virtue as well. In their minds public schools and colleges, rather than private tutors, academies, or parental training, offered the best means for achieving their desired ends. As a result they and a great many of their fellow countrymen drafted proposals for state-supported common schooling.

Jefferson, in the preamble to his Bill for the More General Diffusion of Knowledge (1779) presented to the Virginia legislature, had clearly stated the logic behind state-sponsored schools within a republic. In such a society the responsibility for guarding basic liberties, for maintaining a check upon ambition, corruption, and tyranny within the government, fell to the individual citizen. Since every citizen should be eligible to vote and since a republic required wise and honest legislators, Jefferson reasoned that the entire citizenry must be educated and virtuous in order to cast an intelligent vote. Further, since lawmakers in a republic must be chosen "without regard to wealth, birth, or other accidental condition," all citizens must be well educated since any one of them might be called to service.[5]

All people could not, however, afford a solid education. Consequently, in order to achieve the best possible representative government, every citizen should share the cost of education within the state. Jefferson proposed free elementary schools in every county in Virginia, twenty regional academies that offered free tuition for selected boys from the elementary schools, and state assistance at the College of William and Mary for the ten outstanding graduates of these academies. He also called for the faculty at William and Mary to oversee a statewide curriculum and to assume the responsibility for regional-level supervision.

Benjamin Rush offered a similar proposal in 1786 for a state university in Philadelphia, four regional colleges, and free schools in every town in Pennsylvania. It was Noah Webster, though, who provided the most thorough analysis of the role of public education in America. In an essay, "On the Education of Youth in America" (1788), Webster argued that "the *sine qua non* of the existence of the American republic" became the economic freedom of every citizen to acquire "what his industry merits" and "a system of education as gives every citizen an opportunity of acquiring knowledge and fitting himself for places of trust."[6]

Since republicanism, more than any other form of government, rested on the virtue, intelligence and integrity of its people, the condition of education in America greatly alarmed Webster: "No provision is made for instructing the poorer rank of people, even in reading and writing," and yet the separate states allowed "every citizen who is worth a few shillings annually" to vote. For Webster this situation constituted "a most glaring solecism in government. The constitutions are *republican*, and the laws of education are *monarchical*."[7] Worse, where community-supported schools for younger children did exist, they were "committed to the most worthless characters." The education of young people, "an employment of more consequence than making laws and preaching the gospel," had been allowed to sink "to a level with the most menial services."[8] Webster expressed astonishment and dismay at the fact that colleges and academies were staffed by men of good character and intelligence while the primary schools were left to incompetent and often immoral hacks.

Webster suggested a system of state-supported public schools: "Every small district should be furnished with a school . . . [that] should be kept by the most reputable and well informed man in the district." Such a system, which included girls as well as boys, should demand the greatest attention of American legislators, for "until the statesman and Divine shall unite their efforts in *forming* the human mind, rather than in loping its excrescences, after it has been neglected; until Legislators discover that the only way to make good citizens and subjects, is to nourish them from infancy; and until parents shall be convinced that the worst of men are not the proper teachers to make the *best;* mankind cannot know to what a degree of perfection society and government may be carried." Webster had high hopes for such republican system of education, since "America affords the fairest opportunities for making the experiment and opens the most encouraging prospects of success."[9]

Yet although few themes were as universally articulated through the last decades of the eighteenth century as the need for a self-governing people to be well educated, education throughout the states remained haphazard and elitist. The various proposals of men like Jefferson and Webster failed to gain legislative majorities. Jefferson, for example, offered his plan of 1779 to the Virginia legislature in the 1790s and again in 1817, only to meet repeated failure. A supporter of the bill informed him that neither the people nor their representatives would consent to the property taxes necessary to support a statewide system of common schools. In 1795 the legislature did grant approval to the portion of the bill providing for elementary schools but incorporated a local option clause that gave the county courts the power to decide whether to institute the program. This effectively emasculated the bill; the local gentry on these courts saw little need to tax themselves to educate their poorer neighbors. In the absence of a general system of education, Virginians depended upon private academies for those who could afford them and charity schools for those who could not. Rush's plan suffered the same fate in Pennsylvania, where controversy over free public schooling lasted into the 1830s. Although some states attempted different methods of funding common school programs, none managed to create a state-supported system to educate the masses.

The struggle over general systems of common schooling often reflected cultural tensions between cosmopolitans and localists within the states. An English visitor to Virginia in the 1780s observed that Jefferson's bill failed because "the comprehensive views and generous patriotism which produced the bill have not prevailed throughout the country."[10] A localist impulse opposed the bill, which created a great deal of skepticism toward new taxes assessed by the state, as well as the imposition of institutional regulations controlled by a distant centralized authority. Legislators from isolated areas refused to accept the idea that their republican society would collapse in the absence of a state system of common schooling. In their minds, local efforts as well as parental guidance remained adequate and certainly less threatening to local prerogatives.

Resentment of the gentry also created dissension. William Manning, a poor, unlettered farmer from Massachusetts, observed that "larning is of the greatest importance to the seport of a free government," and yet "to prevent this the few are always crying up the advantages of costly collages, national acadimyes & grammar schools, in ordir to make places for men to live without work, & so strengthen their party."[11] The same men were, however, "always opposed to cheap schools & woman schools, the ondly or prinsaple means of which larning is spred amongue the Many." Manning suggested that every state should support as many regional colleges as feasible and for every county to maintain grammar schools in areas convenient to the population. These schools would be open to both sexes free of tuition. Instead of such a system, however, Manning contended that "the few are always striving to oblige us to maintain grait men with grate salleryes & to maintain Grammer Schools in every town to teach our Children a b c all which is ondly to give imploy to gentlemens sons & make places for men to live without work." By the 1790s people like Manning had little patience for high-sounding rhetoric linking education to disinterested public service. He demanded the opportunity for individual advancement. Republican education for Manning represented a means to further an egalitarian urge for social mobility and economic self-aggrandizement.

Republican education meant something quite different to men like Rush and Webster, and herein lay another obstacle to the creation of general systems of public education in the young republic. Rush, in an essay on common school education written in 1786, revealed his perception of the role of education in a republic: "In the education of youth, let the authority of our masters be as absolute as possible. . . . By this mode of education we prepare our youth for the subordination of laws and thereby qualify them for becoming good citizens of the republic. I am satisfied that the most useful citizens have been formed from those youths who have never known or felt their own will till they were one and twenty years of age."[12]

Webster too believed that republican education should instill respect for authority and deference to superiors. For him "all government originates in families, and if neglected there, it will hardly exist in society; but the want of it must be supplied by the rod in school." Just as families should not be divided in authority between mother and father, so, too, in school "the master should be in absolute command. . . . A proper subordination in families would generally supersede the necessity of severity in schools; and a strict discipline in both is the best foundation of good order in political society."[13]

Rush and Webster supported public schools so long as they promised to fulfill their conception of the good republican society: ordered, deferential, and structured toward furthering the common good. However, the increasing presence of men sharing Manning's attitude within the state legislatures caused Rush, Webster, and others like them to become disillusioned with the direction republican America seemed to be taking and to lose interest in educational reform. Indeed, with the passage of time, they became critics of popular education. What appeared to him to be an increasing vulgarization of society led Rush to approve of practical knowledge being "as common and as cheap as air," but *"a learned* education" ought to "become a luxury in our country." If ever education became *"universal,* it would be as destructive to civilization as universal barbarism."[14]

By the late 1790s, when he retreated from active public life to begin his great dictionary, Webster too had grown increasingly conservative. Indeed, his dictionary, when it appeared, was not an impartial treatment of American words and their definitions at all. Rather it represented the final disillusionment of a republican intent upon shaping the language and values of his society in such a way as to counteract his country's growing commitment to egalitarian individualism. *People,* for example, he defined as "the body of persons who form a community. . . . The vulgar; the mass of illiterate persons. The communality, as distinct from men of rank." In old age he bemoaned the fact that "the true principles of republican government are now abandoned by all parties . . . and instead of expecting things to grow *better,* I am confident they will grow *worse*."[15] Webster's excitement with the possibilities of the Revolution had turned to fear when he encountered its liberal consequences: republicanism to him meant order, stability, and communal values, not social equality, individual autonomy, and personal freedom. When he presumed that his fellow citizens shared this perspective, he actively supported systems of public education, which would strengthen his republican world. When, however, he perceived that many Americans had quite a different view of what their nation should become, he withdrew his support.

Although little practical action was being taken to create public school systems, a belief in education as vital to the existence of the republic became, nonetheless, part of the culture. Americans adhered to the idea that the very health of their society depended on the proper education of its youth. And yet they remained steadfastly unwilling to tax themselves to institute a system of free public education. They simultaneously glorified and demeaned education.

Crime and Punishment

Faith in the efficacy of republicanism to effect beneficial change within American society penetrated throughout the culture. Americans believed that, for example, crime within their midst stemmed from colonial criminal codes imposed by the British. The natural benevolent instincts of Americans had been stifled by the imposition of cruel and arbitrary European measures totally inappropriate to the New World environment. As a result of such archaic and draconian laws, criminal behavior persisted unabated.

Such beliefs had gained strength from Americans' reading of Cesare Beccaria's *On Crime and Punishment*, translated shortly after its publication in 1764. A wonderful confluence existed between Beccaria's work and Americans' perceptions of their own colonial experience. Indeed, John Adams had quoted from this work extensively in his defense of British soldiers involved in the Boston Massacre. Beccaria's observation that when "we glance at the pages of history, we will find that laws, which surely are, or ought to be, compacts of free men, have been for the most part, a mere tool of the passions of some" merely confirmed the libertarian perspective of most Americans.[16] Such comments as this blended not only with the American colonial experience but with the optimistic belief that a benevolent republican environment could bring about beneficial transformations in American culture, too long constrained and perverted by Old World customs and institutions. Within a republican environment of freedom, order, and virtue, reasonable laws supported by the worthy instincts of all citizens would strike at the roots of criminal activity.

Such a conviction inspired William Bradford's widely circulated pamphlet, *An Enquiry into How Far the Punishment of Death Is Necessary in Philadelphia* (1793). Here Bradford exclaimed: "It is from ignorance, wretchedness or corrupted manners of a people that crime proceeds." In America, "where these do not prevail moderate punishments strictly enforced, will be a curb as effectual as the greatest severity." A New York reform society echoed Bradford's sentiments, describing America as "a land where the theatre of experiment is boundless. The relations of civil society were few and simple, and the complex abuses of long existing systems, in social order, were unknown."[17]

The belief that a republican society possessed an innately different character from the decadent cultures of Europe and that its laws should reflect that character caused the American states to amend their criminal codes. New laws stressed incarceration, restricting the use of the death penalty to the most serious crimes. These milder sentences were, however, to be strictly enforced. Such a commitment led to the establishment of state penitentiaries. By 1800 Philadelphia had converted its old Walnut Street jail into a state prison, New York had opened the Newgate State Prison in Greenwich Village, and New Jersey, Virginia, and Kentucky had constructed new facilities. Soon other states followed suit.

Americans, caught up in the flush of excitement over the boundless possibilities of their new republican culture, had high hopes for the reasonable system of corrections they were creating. Passage of the proper laws and construction of the necessary structures for incarceration were all that was necessary. Time proved them wrong. Crime did not disappear; instead the prisons became scenes of riot and excess, and American society itself seemed to grow more chaotic and restless. Clearly the roots of deviancy penetrated more deeply than the structure of the laws, deeper even than a benign environment, perhaps even so deep as to be impervious to republican culture itself. Signs of disillusionment with the criminal system began to appear sporadically even before the end of the eighteenth century, but, like the disparity between the republican commitment to education and the paucity of public schools, these failures did not lessen Americans' belief in the efficacy of republicanism to prompt salutary changes within their society. The power of republicanism to shape the minds of Americans had not been weakened by the realities of their everyday lives.

The Legal Structure

While the alteration of criminal codes involved a few reform-minded individuals, the larger structure of American law affected the lives of all citizens and drew the attention of a great many Americans. Here too they had tremendous expectations for qualitative change. Many "rejoice[d] in the amelioration of their form of government" and desired above all else "to establish a system of laws . . . dictated by the genuine principles of Republicanism." At the same time they responded to an ideological impulse contained within their commitment to republicanism—a belief in their destiny to achieve national greatness through commercial prosperity. Many Americans felt that with their victory over the British, they had "an empire to raise and support." With an "abundance of the means of subsistence," "a sturdy, independent, and intelligent people," and "a territory as exhaustless in moral and physical treasures, as it is wide in its expanse," the possibilities seemed limitless.[18] A legal structure must be created to release this potential for commercial greatness. Together these interrelated themes—republicanism and the demand for economic development to achieve national greatness—led to a transformation in the legal structure of America, but in unforeseen ways.

The new governments created as a result of the Revolution inherited a legal structure reflecting a society believed to be an organic whole. In such a society, the legal system encouraged a sense of ethical and moral unity. Reflecting this emphasis upon consensus, juries rather than judges often determined the applicability of laws; only in an environment characterized by agreement on traditional values throughout the broad base of the citizenry could this be possible. Provincial laws were therefore intended to further common ethical values and to promote economic and social stability.

To this end, colonial assemblies had enacted legislation meant to inhibit rapid or substantial alterations in the distribution of wealth and the social hierarchy. Laws, for example, impeded men from entering into speculative contracts by making the required formalities intricate, expensive, and inconvenient. By ensuring monopolistic privileges to those who first exploited the natural resources of the land, provincial assemblies similarly inhibited economic and social fluidity. Thus, while provincial contract and property laws served a variety of uses, their most important function was to promote economic stability in such a manner as to curtail competition and the resulting animosities between individuals within local communities. In the absence of competitive hostilities, men could more easily draw together in support of fundamental ethical values that promoted the process of consensus building upon which the entire legal structure rested and without which it could not function.

While the ethical unity and the socioeconomic stability so necessary to a legal system based on consensus faced severe strains throughout the late colonial period, those elements collapsed with the Revolution. The new state legislatures mirrored the transformations affecting American society and began to voice the majoritarian demands of conflicting interest groups. In such a milieu, the old laws became increasingly inappropriate, and a legal structure intended to serve as a stabilizing influence had quite the opposite effect. More and more individuals, intent upon taking advantage of the equality of opportunity promised by the republican rhetoric of the Revolution, demanded a legal system that would accommodate their socioeconomic desires, promote their newly won autonomy, and strengthen their ability to exploit economic opportunity.

In the face of such demands, laws dealing with such issues as contracts, property, and corporations began slowly to be transformed. While ethical standards of an earlier era such as the concept of fair exchange had formerly prompted individuals to employ their property in ways that promoted the moral and social stability of the community, men now demanded the freedom to dispose of their property as market conditions dictated. As a consequence contract cases in the post-Revolutionary years saw litigants argue that they should be allowed to engage in the free exchange of goods regardless of whether such transactions were judged fair by traditional standards. All that was important was the contracts be freely entered into by all parties. As such arguments gained credibility, individuals began to enhance their stature at the expense of their fellow citizens.

A similar development resulted from changes in the courts' perception of corporations. Throughout the colonial era most corporations had existed as inferior governmental agencies—parishes or townships—with the power to tax and to compel allegiance from individuals in order to further the needs of the entire community. Following the Revolution a new sort of corporation slowly emerged: the business corporation. Over time, courts, anxious to protect the private property rights of entrepreneurial individuals, distinguished between municipal corporations and private business ones. The latter escaped the restraints that required them to serve communal rather than private ends. These new economic institutions would mature into powerful mechanisms that allowed groups to amass great wealth and power that completely undermined the traditional economic and social order.

The greatest change in the legal structure resulted from transformations in the economies of the states. The Revolution had brought about massive economic dislocations as well as exciting new economic opportunities. Victory removed most economic constraints, and Americans found themselves free to create their own banks, to issue their own currency, and to control their own trade legislation. Independence gave a growing number of entrepreneurs the chance to structure the various state economies in order to exploit the opportunities revealed by the Revolution. Throughout the states commercial activity that in the past had been restricted to a small number of coastal towns spread to the interior as a market-oriented economy increasingly replaced one based on subsistence. As a result law assumed an innovative and transforming nature.

The most fundamental transformation to take place in the post-Revolutionary years embodied changes in the function of the common law. Throughout most of the eighteenth century the rules of the common law had served as a fixed body of doctrine based on precedent. Their primary function was to perpetuate communal order by ensuring equitable results between private parties involved in individual cases. Legislatures, not the courts, produced legal change. Consequently the rules of the common law stood as bulwarks of the established order, the very underpinnings of an organic community.

American judges inherited this understanding of the common law and throughout the Revolutionary years seldom, if ever, examined common law rules from a functional or purposive perspective. Over the last several decades of the eighteenth century, however, a gradual shift began to take place in the manner in which American judges viewed common law rules. A perception of common law adjudication as a process for creating, rather than simply discovering, legal rules slowly emerged. This led many judges concerned with shaping social and economic policies to formulate doctrines of general applicability in order to bring about beneficial results.

Lawyers and judges increasingly began to take into consideration the social or economic consequences of the legal rules brought under their consideration. The attorney general of South Carolina argued in 1796 that landowners should not be compensated for property taken by the state for road-building purposes because this would "thwart and counteract the public in the exercise of this all important authority for the interest of the community." Jurists throughout the nation began to articulate legal arguments in terms of "the importance of the present decision to the commercial character of our country" (Pennsylvania, 1785) and to weigh particular common law rules in terms of their ability to promote the "improvement in our commercial code" (New York, 1799).[19]

Observations such as these revealed the emergence of legal doctrine that took into consideration the increasing materialism of the age and accorded legitimacy to the competitive ethos of a market economy. By the late eighteenth century a great many common law rules appeared as impediments to economic growth and development. Over time, then, judges, increasingly sympathetic to an entrepreneurial urge for economic development, overturned common law rules granting property rights to initial users of various resources. These decisions legitimated a competitive ethic that fostered efficient use of natural resources to the betterment of the community. A classic example of a the emergence of such a legal mentality came in 1805 in the New York case of *Palmer* v. *Mulligan* in which the court denied the claims of a downstream mill owner for damages resulting from the obstruction in the flow of water occasioned by the construction of a similar mill upstream. One judge noted that under the common law, "He who could first build a dam or mill on any navigable river, would acquire an exclusive rights, at least for some distance." To uphold such a principle meant that "the public, whose advantage is always to be regarded, would be deprived of the benefit which always attends competition and rivalry."[20]

As American society became increasingly less unified and stable, as separate interest groups vied for ascendancy within the political and economic sphere, legal certainty became ever more important. As jurists began to conceive of the matter of certainty in more instrumental terms—to foster economic development—the control of juries assumed increased significance. In order to avoid unpredictable fluctuations in decisions resulting from the varied interests or passions of jurors, the legal system gradually deprived juries of the right to decide the law in civil cases. As one judge declared in 1792, to allow juries to determine the law "would vest the interpretation and declaring of laws in bodies so constituted, without permanence, or previous means of information, and thus render laws, which ought to be an uniform rule of conduct, uncertain, fluctuating with every change of passion and opinion of jurors, and impossible to be known til pronounced."[21]

With the passage of time, the legal system moved toward a more substantive conception of the law that drew sharp distinctions between law and facts. Nathaniel Chipman, conservative chief justice of the Vermont Supreme Court, argued as early as 1793 in his *Dissertation on the Act Adopting the Common and Statute Law of England* that principles of right that emerged from the nature of the case under consideration should be considered superior to precedents, previous decisions, or forms. Chipman insisted that once a court clearly identified the intent of the parties involved in a transaction, its purpose should be to find the best means to allow the concerned individuals to gain their primary desires. Such arguments marked the early beginning of the ascendancy of substance over form and contributed to a remaking of the legal landscape. Law would no longer stand for eternal verities protecting a traditional organic social order. Instead Americans moved toward a perception of the law as an innovative process, an instrument of policy, that enabled judges to create legal doctrine in order to bring about social changes within their society.

The social changes fostered by such a view of the law helped move American society away from an emphasis on communal unity as the primary social value toward one in which individuals became free to choose their own values. The law itself was not, however, value blind. The emerging legal structure in late eighteenth-century America consistently distributed resources and structured distributional rules—paper money, relations between debtors and creditors, property law, contracts—in favor of an entrepreneurial ethic. No longer could the legal system be viewed as a means to preserve local power, support a local consensus-building process, or as a mirror of stable, homogeneous moral and ethical values. It had become in large part a mechanism that encouraged individuals to make their own choice of ethical values and to enforce whatever decisions resulted. The primary function of the law, however, became the resolution of disputes arising over control of economic resources. In its resolution of such distributional contests, the law became a tool in the hands of the victors that enabled them to appropriate the bulk of the nation's wealth to themselves and to enforce that appropriation upon the losers.

As an integral part of this transformation in the legal structure of American society, the status of lawyers changed dramatically. Late in the eighteenth century the legal profession began an ascent toward a position of intellectual and political dominance. Within America's republican culture the courtroom became one of the most dynamic focal points of social order. There society's principal ideas melded with its principal institutions and gave rise to a newly emerging elite composed of skillful practitioners of the law.

The increasingly powerful position of the American bar resulted from an alliance created in the 1790s between legal and commercial interests. The most prominent and successful lawyers who emerged in the 1790s engaged in commercial law, not in the land conveyances or debt collection that their colleagues from an earlier era had worked on. As procedural changes took the power to decide points of law out of the hands of juries and gave it to judges, development of a uniform and predictable judge-made body of commercial rules was made possible. And once courts consistently began to overthrow the anticommercial doctrines of the eighteenth century, the bar assumed a vital part in the process. A shrewd understanding of subtle points of law became essential to the innovative use of the law to transform social and economic policy. Thus, a vital partnership emerged between the American bar and the American commercial community to affect the direction that law would carry their society.

A number of important consequences emerged from both the transformation in American law and the partnership between legal and commercial interests that accompanied it. One of the most paradoxical arose from the fact that many social conservatives, the men most desirous of maintaining the stability of an organic community, pressed for the creation of legal doctrine to further economic development. These doctrines enabled individuals to act on their environment uninhibited by the ethical and moral unity of a traditional legal order. The forces of change encouraged by these men completely destroyed the basis for the traditional organic hierarchy they so desired. In its place arose a competitive materialistic atmosphere intolerant of any order that inhibited the free development of individuals and their opportunities for social as well as economic advancement. Individuals no longer had to consider whether a fair exchange resulted from their bargains; they no longer assumed that honest productive labor constituted the sole legitimate means to accumulate wealth. Rather, the new perception of contracts allowed individuals to enrich themselves by executing a sharp bargain or by exploiting fluctuations in the market.

Traditional contract law had assumed a fixed nature of economic relationship that would inhibit men from changing their inherited status in the economic order. The new laws of contract, however, rested on quite a different set of assumptions. A fluctuating marketplace became the central feature of a dynamic environment that freed individuals to manipulate its operations in such a manner as to enhance the prospects that they rather than their neighbors or the community would benefit from it. Property, too, no longer stood as a stabilizing influence within the community. Instead a man's property simply became the starting point from which he might promote his own success. The entrepreneurial impulse had, in short, helped to transform American society from one in which men and women assumed a fixed place in a stable economic milieu organized around the moral unity and good of the community to a fluid one where individuals employed their property and wealth primarily as a means of gaining greater prosperity. Individual opportunity rapidly replaced communal good order as the primary social value in the economic atmosphere sought by those interested in the commercial development of the nation in the late eighteenth century.

The transformation of the legal structure in America had particularly ironic consequences for the development of republican culture. Jurists creating a more liberal economic environment, as well as the lawyers and commercial elements who supported them, articulated their goals in terms of republican equality. They therefore gave a peculiarly libertarian emphasis to the doctrine of equality—the very heart of republicanism. Their perception of equality emphasized equality of opportunity, not equality of social and economic condition. Indeed these men had a nearly irrational fear of the threat posed by individuals and groups demanding substantive equality. In their minds equality of opportunity faced constant dangers from the leveling impulse of those who would redistribute wealth through legislative majorities. They too feared the tyranny of the majorities formed in state legislatures that passed debtor legislation and threatened to undermine legitimate contracts and property settlements. Consequently, in association with the Federalists' creation of the Constitution, the legal community worked to establish a structure of legal and political ideas and institutions that would erect barriers (the sanctity of contracts) against the redistribution of wealth while simultaneously providing assurances to the clever, the artful, the ambitious, and the capable—those most skilled in the newly emerging world of market relations—that their accumulations of wealth would be protected.

In an age in which the opportunities for economic advancement burgeoned and the gap between rich and poor widened appreciably, the legal reforms promising to make people more equal only freed Americans to become increasingly unequal as they released individuals from the restraints of a corporate society. Ironically jurists intent on liberating Americans from an eighteenth-century mercantilist legal environment employed the language of republican equality while inadvertently helping to produce extremes of inequality far beyond those of the early eighteenth century. Yet since these arose within an environment wedded to republican principles, such inequalities became embedded within the emerging culture itself, where they did not seem to represent inequities or injustices at all but rather the honest fruits of able and industrious republican citizens who prospered in an open land of opportunity for all.

Republican Wives and Mothers

Social and economic changes of the sort that led to transformations in the legal structure of the nation caused a great many Americans—particularly free, white, adult, males—to become sensitive to the character of their society. Desperately committed to becoming republicans, these men clung to attitudes and ideals that reassured them of their success. At the same time, their intense desire to become a new sort of citizen—a republican citizen— affected the manner in which they viewed others within their society who were not citizens. Their self-conception, their commitment to republicanism, shaped their perception of women, Indians, blacks, and, in turn, the republican culture emerging in post-Revolutionary America.

The Revolution disrupted the lives and challenged the abilities and courage of both men and women.[22] Women found themselves responsible for the independent management of family affairs and often took over the operation of their husband's business in his absence. The republic that emerged after the war, however, offered little recognition of the autonomy characteristic of so many women during the war years. Divorce remained almost impossible for a woman to obtain. Married women found it increasingly difficult to gain or retain control of their own property. Trusteeships grew ever more complicated, while at the same time equity courts became less and less accessible to women. Woman's inclusion in the marketplace extended primarily to those areas in which it facilitated male transactions. It became quite common, for instance, to take a married woman's property in compensation for her spouse's indebtedness.

Regardless of the independence and responsibilities assumed by many women during the war, few legislators viewed women's lack of civil capacity as a contradiction of American republicanism. They apparently did not care to examine with any precision or rigor the socially radical content of that belief system. Consequently citizenship for women elicited little serious consideration. Instead quite a different status in society emerged for women: republican marriage and motherhood.

Americans expressed concern over the ability not only of their own generation but of future ones as well to continue to exhibit the moral character necessary to maintain a republican government and society. Government could not be counted on to develop civic virtue; indeed it drew its own character from that of the people. Instead the church, the community, and the family must assume this vital responsibility. Most Americans came to believe that "all government originates in families, and if neglected there, it will hardly exist in society."[23] Within the family the crucial role of guardian and molder of republican virtue came increasingly to devolve upon wives and mothers. Through their intelligent management of the household as well as their steadfast opposition to immorality and selfishness, women had it within their power to shape the moral character of the male members of society. Women's influence over the development of their children, particularly their sons, placed the ultimate responsibility for the future of the young republic in their hands.

The emergence of the conception of republican wives and mothers had important implications for the development of American culture in the late eighteenth century. More than anything else, by enlarging the significance of their activities within the home, it exalted the domestic function of women. Women's pre-Revolutionary domestic activities had required little, if any, ideological justification. These remained implicit in the biological and political economy of the female's world. The nursing mother naturally remained in the home, where she could tend the fire, make the meals, and keep the spinning wheel turning. The Revolution changed this in significant ways. By creating a public ideology of virtue based upon individual self-sacrifice at the very time when such a communal world seemed to be fragmenting about them, Americans argued with a shrill insistence that women, in their capacity as the guardians of traditional morality, would remain in the home. There, as models of piety, purity, morality, and self-sacrifice, they would guide the lives of their husbands and shape the character of their sons in such a manner as to preserve the organic community and virtue so essential to the success of the republican experiment.

At the same time that Americans began to glorify the domestic role of women, a consensus formed that wives and mothers could also serve an important political function. While their supposedly limited mental and physical abilities, as well as their vital function within the home, kept them from active political participation, they still had an essential role to fulfill. Republican mothers should encourage their sons to participate in civic affairs while educating them in the paths of virtue and communal stability. They should never, however, interfere with a husband's or a son's vote. While citizens, women were not truly political constituents. As a consequence late eighteenth-century women developed a deferential posture toward politics. As in all other facets of life during that time, a disjuncture existed between the politicization of men and women. When men considered themselves deferential citizens, women perceived themselves as loyal subjects. As men shed their deferential stance to assume a more aggressive egalitarian posture in the political world, women assumed a restrained, deferential political role. Consequently Republican motherhood legitimized a minimum political awareness of the most generalized nature. It encouraged women to remain content with such a slight role and not to desire a fuller, more meaningful, participation. As a result republican motherhood contained an inherent paradox: women were responsible for teaching men how to behave but were themselves incapable of an active participation in the outside world where that behavior was to have its greatest impact.

The appearance of cultural images of women as republican wives and mothers belied a society undergoing dynamic transformations. On one hand, society idealized the woman in the home, and women could at last take pride in their special role within the home and throughout the larger society. On the other hand, however, republican marriage led to a dead end for the wife. Women accepted a deferential political status so that men could advance within an increasingly egalitarian society.

In a culture ostensibly dedicated to the virtuous self-sacrifice of individuals to the common good, ever larger numbers of men became engaged in aggressive, materialistic, individualistic behavior to secure their own advancement in an increasingly fragmented and competitive society. That responsibility for maintaining public virtue and a self-sacrificing character had been channeled into the domestic life of women both obscured the emerging disjuncture between rhetoric and reality and eased the consciences of those men who might be troubled by it. By constraining women within the confines of an ever more rigid domestic ideology, by holding women strictly accountable to republican ideals that they themselves had been actively flouting for several decades, men became free to explore the outermost boundaries of a revolutionary rhetoric dedicated to equality, freedom, autonomy, and opportunity with little sense of contradiction or ambivalence.

The Indian and the Republic

The Revolution's promise of republican regeneration caused Americans to become acutely aware of distinctions between themselves and those of different races or cultures. Republicanism, however, provided the rationale for two quite distinct perceptions of the Indians with whom Americans came into contact—the noble savage and the brutal savage—as well as two separate modes of dealing with them—the philanthropist's desire to incorporate them into American society and the frontiersman's urge to destroy them.[24] Ironically, little practical difference resulted from the philanthropists' concern for Indians and the frontiersmen's hatred of them: both views resulted in the decimation of Indian tribes and the taking of their land. Both incorporated elements of republicanism that either obscured or idealized the deadly consequences of its actions for Indians and eased any anxieties that might trouble Americans.

Most American intellectuals attempted to understand the Indian in terms of the chain of being. Their belief in the dynamic capabilities of the New World environment, however, allowed them to conceptualize movement along the chain toward the ultimate form of the human species, the white man. The Indian—a simple child of nature—was only a short step away from the white man along the chain's hierarchy; his evolution should not take long. All that was necessary was to break the bands of savagery in order to allow the same forces of nature that shaped American republican culture to transform Indians into good republican citizens.

Defined as noble savage, the Indian in effect became a foil in the American's post-Revolutionary involvement in self-conceptualization. To perceive of Indians in terms of a noble simplicity that required only contact with republican culture to transform them into civilized yeomen lent credence to the American belief in the efficacy of republicanism to transform the character of their own culture.

With the objective of incorporating the Indian into white society, missionary agencies, with the support and guidance of the federal government, established schools on tribal lands to spread white values among the natives. These schools strove to inculcate improved farming techniques, home manufacturing, a sense of individual independence, and a fundamental work discipline within their students. At the same time the distribution of manufactured goods among the tribes destroyed the subsistence infrastructure so essential to the Indian way of life. Those who became ever more dependent upon civilized goods became increasingly less self-sufficient and thereby more malleable in the hands of the missionaries or government factors responsible for distributing the goods.

Throughout their efforts, however, philanthropists faced a great stumbling block to acculturation: the cult of the warrior stood in direct contrast to the republican cult of the yeoman farmer. To be a warrior meant to roam freely over the land hunting, fishing, and making war on rival tribes. The philanthropist concluded that tribal possession of vast acreages of land held in common fostered savagery. Civilization required individual ownership of just the amount of land that could be cultivated with the tools and disciplined work habits of white society. This could be achieved only if Indian tribes gave up the vast tracts of land held in common and adopted individual, fee-simple landownership. The choice, however, must always be a free one: the Indian must voluntarily choose to surrender tribal lands in order to take up individual plots.

Ideally the philanthropic plan for the civilization of Indians called for a gradual transformation. Indians would slowly surrender land in accordance with the level of civilization they had acquired; an orderly advance of white society would absorb the land not taken up by individual Indian farmers. Unfortunately the realities of a burgeoning white society intervened. Frontiersmen could not be controlled by the federal government. Their lust for land, as well as their hatred for Indians, drove them to intrude by the thousands on Indian land. The urge of state governments for territorial aggrandizement further complicated an orderly procedure for the cession of Indian lands.

Indians themselves proved increasingly intractable as well. Even where cultural change took place, many Indians proved adamant in their desire to retain their lands. Therefore, gradually, nearly imperceptibly, even the most idealistic philanthropists recognized the need to complete their civilizing plan by manipulation of those Indians who stood in its way. As president, Thomas Jefferson suggested to William Henry Harrison that the latter, in order "to promote their disposition to exchange lands," should foster the Indian's dependence upon government factories so that "the good and influential individuals among them run into debt, because we observe that when these debts get beyond what the individual can pay, they become willing to lop them off by a cession of lands."[25]

In the face of such manipulation at the hands of friends and violent intrusions at the hands of enemies, Indian culture rapidly deteriorated. Rather than becoming civilized, Indians often became demoralized, adrift in a culture that they did not understand. Yet republican emphasis on freedom of choice and equality of opportunity obscured these disastrous consequences even from the eyes of the most idealistic philanthropist.[26] The same language of the marketplace that permeated the jurist's commitment to foster economic development portrayed the Indian as the victim of an impersonal, fragmented social process for which no one was responsible except the Indian himself. Any cession of land had been a free choice; any contract signed had been voluntary and legal. White Americans' enthusiastic commitment to republican progress blinded them to the fact that the golden rule could not work in a cross-cultural context. To treat Indians as they themselves would be treated—as independent individuals competent to sign contracts, to buy and sell land in fee simple—and to extend republican civilization to them seemed best for all concerned. A blind egocentrism, a faith in republicanism's ability to regenerate all under its purview, impelled republican intellectuals and philanthropists unwittingly to destroy other cultures.

The proper relationship between civilization and the Indian meant something quite different to most frontiersmen than it did to American intellectuals. The frontier environment encouraged violent action rather than slow acculturation; it placed a high premium on the ability to master the red enemy rather than to welcome the noble Indian into white society. As a great many Americans migrated to wilderness areas following the Revolution, the destruction of Indians came steadily to be perceived as vital to the taming of the wilderness, to the progress of civilization. More and more Americans seemed to achieve self-realization through the willful destruction of the wilderness and its inhabitants. In the process, hunters and frontier farmers left devastation in their wake: trees were toppled and left to rot; animals were hunted down out of a pride of destruction as much as a desire for gain; and Indians were ruthlessly slain. All had been destroyed in the name of the advance of civilization. An ethic arose that called for men to take what they could in a profligate manner from a territory and then move on, depending upon a bountiful nature to replenish the wasted game and timber.

In a manner, the activities of the hunter-Indian fighters exemplified a manifestation of republican thought. Americans of the Revolutionary generation had made a profession of virtue and committed their republic to the escape from corruption. But Enlightenment thought taught them that natural laws of social and economic development gripped all societies in an evolutionary process that carried them inevitably from brutal savagery to the decadent civilization of commerce and corruption. In response, following James Harrington's reasoning that commerce could not corrupt so long as it did not overwhelm agrarian interests, Americans believed that in order to accommodate both virtue and commerce, a republic must be as energetic in its search for land as it was in its search for commerce. A vast supply of land, occupied by an armed and self-directing yeomanry, might establish an endless reservoir of virtue. This belief gave point to Jefferson's observation that "our governments will remain virtuous for many centuries; as long as they are chiefly agricultural; and they will be as long as there shall be vacant lands in any part of America."[27] Thus, if the increase in commercial activity following the Revolution threatened American virtue, it could revitalize itself on the frontier through the efforts of the armed husbandman.

A violently activist democratic ideology, based on nature's abundance and vitality, began to emerge by the late eighteenth century. Americans would not have to create their history in closed space, which could only foster decadence and decay. They could perpetually return to youthful vigor on the frontier. There they could begin again and regenerate themselves and their society through heroic combat with the wilderness and its creatures. The frontiersman gained self-realization through the prideful display of individual prowess and by a manly independence of social or other restraints. The myth of the frontiersman became one of self-renewal or self-creation through acts of violence. Believing in the possibility of regeneration, hunters, Indian fighters, and farmers gradually destroyed the natural environment that supported their economic and social freedom as well as their democracy of social mobility. Yet the mythology and the value system it spawned served long after the objective condition that had justified it disappeared. The armed individual, free to act on his environment as he saw fit, free to control his own destiny, became an important element of late eighteenth-century American republicanism.

Although philanthropists and intellectuals felt that the violence of the frontiersman represented the antithesis of civilization and sincerely abhorred it, the result of the two approaches to the Indian was nearly identical. The cultural life of the tribes gained little comfort or protection from the solicitude of the philanthropist. His plan for civilizing the Indian was as destructive of tribalism as the advance of the frontiersman was dangerous to the lives of individual Indians. Hating Indians and hating Indianness came to the same result.[28] If the frontiersman was more direct in his slaughter of Indians, the philanthropist's more circumspect ideas called for the cultural suicide of the various tribes. The ironies of the situation were particularly full. In the end the white man's love was as deadly as his hatred: frontiersmen desired the death of individual Indians; philanthropists plotted the elimination of an entire race and culture. Even when it became evident that the civilization process was not working with a tribe, philanthropists could not give up the optimism and hope bred of their commitment to republicanism. They simply proposed the same approach in each succeeding location. Ironically the elimination of Indian culture sprang from the regenerative powers attributed to American republicanism. The death or demoralization of Indians seemed to strengthen the commitment of white Americans to their ideal republican society.

Blacks in the New Nation

A commitment to republican principles of freedom and equality caused many Americans to intensify their consideration of those within their society who were neither free nor equal. Consequently the presence of blacks and slavery came under close scrutiny in the post-Revolutionary years.[29] Americans' emphasis on natural rights and the beneficence of the New World environment led many to assume that slavery would soon be eliminated. At the same time, however, forces at work within American society, including the commitment to the grand experiment of republicanism and to the economic development of the nation, created ambivalent feelings about blacks and mitigated the Revolution's antislavery impulse.

Throughout the southern states antislavery feelings and behavior varied widely. Georgia and South Carolina never experienced an antislavery movement at all, and in North Carolina such feelings became manifest only among Quakers. There were, however, widespread public attacks on slavery in Virginia, Maryland, and Delaware, as well as the embryonic organization of antislavery societies. Shortly after the outbreak of the Revolution, the legislatures of these states considered plans for the gradual abolition of slavery. While these came to nothing, the states in the Upper South did pass legislation facilitating private manumission, or freeing, of slaves. The new states of Kentucky and Tennessee followed the example of their sister states in 1798 and 1801. In North Carolina the legislature struggled with this issue for over twenty years. After taking a few halting steps toward easing manumission by private owners within the state, the legislature slipped back to a more rigid stance that made such actions difficult and expensive. Georgia and South Carolina, while never assuming a lenient policy toward private manumission, took steps by the turn of the century to make the procedure even more difficult. Owners in Georgia, for example, could free their slaves only through an appeal to the state legislature.

Ironically the movement toward more restrictive legislation in the southernmost states witnessed a parallel development in the Upper South, where the trend toward encouraging freedom underwent a marked reversal in the last decade of the eighteenth century. In 1795 the Virginia legislature strengthened the master's prerogatives in suits against him involving the freedom of a slave. By 1798 it forbade members of antislavery societies from serving on juries deciding such cases. Finally, in 1806, in response to a strenuous campaign to slow the tide of private manumissions throughout the state, the legislature passed a law requiring that any slaves freed after that time must, under penalty of law, leave the state within twelve months after being manumitted. Within a year the prospects for the abolition of slavery in Virginia and throughout the Upper South appeared dim indeed. The bright promise of the 1770s had proved illusory.

Upon passage of Virginia's law of 1806 requiring manumitted slaves to leave the commonwealth, the free states that bordered Virginia quickly enacted laws prohibiting the immigration of free blacks. Such laws revealed most northern antislavery advocates to be far more concerned with idealistic opposition to the institution of slavery than they were with the well-being of the freedman. This became abundantly clear in the gradualist approach characteristic of laws abolishing slavery in the North. Even these laws, conservative as they were, had been achieved only after prolonged struggles. In 1780 Pennsylvania enacted the first emancipation law in the United States. It freed no slaves; instead blacks born after its enactment gained their freedom upon reaching their twenty-eighth birthday. Judicial decisions wore away at the institution in Massachusetts and New Hampshire in lieu of legislative action, while in Connecticut, Rhode Island, New York, and New Jersey legislatures grudgingly granted emancipation but only upon the most conservative terms. New York's emancipation act of 1799, for example, imposed the same conditions as those of the earlier Pennsylvania law. As an additional compensation, owners could abandon slave children at any time and transfer the cost of their upbringing to the town in which they resided or to the state. When New Jersey finally passed an abolition law in 1804, it was so conservative and gradual in its effect that for all intents and purposes the state still had slaves, termed apprentices, at the outbreak of the Civil War.

Such gradualism resulted from a social conservativism that had as its beneficiaries the immediate welfare of masters far more than the ultimate good of the freedman. In the North calls for freedom and equality confronted the hard realities of concrete economic interests and ingrained social customs. With respect to the free black, northern society's commitment to equality seemed more symbol than substance. The two institutions one might expect to have raised the freedman to the status of a republican citizen—education and religion—failed him at every turn. Education, considered the key to the formation of a republican society, was by and large denied the black. In the absence of state-supported systems of education, the free black, like the poor white, had difficulty gaining anything more than rudimentary learning. White churches too shunned the black. Instead of being welcomed into the community through Christian egalitarianism and acceptance in the church, blacks found themselves forced to create separate churches in the major northern cities.

By the 1790s antislavery sentiment had weakened considerably. Ironically the Constitution's successful destruction of the foreign slave trade sapped the antislavery impulse of much of its reformist energy and caused it to sputter and stall out by 1 January 1808. Elimination of the slave trade convinced most Americans that something had been done to weaken slavery. While attacks upon the trade voiced an assumption of human equality, thus salving the nation's conscience, they said nothing about the evils of an institution within their own society. At the same time, however, many Americans came to see that their own revolutionary heritage carried with it dangerous potential for social disorder and chaos. As revolutions broke out in France and then among blacks in the West Indies, the ideology of the American Revolution became for many a threatening "cancer of revolution" that must be contained. The fear occasioned by Toussaint L'Ouverture's successful creation of a black republic in Haiti in the 1790s cooled American revolutionary fervor considerably.

While the weakening of American revolutionary ideology throughout the 1780s and 1790s contributed to the enervation of the antislavery impulse, that ideology itself incorporated ambiguities and contradictions that helped shape white Americans' perceptions of blacks and slavery. One of the many stumbling blocks to emancipation resulted from the manner in which Americans incorporated property rights within the basic natural rights for which they had fought the Revolution. They could not distinguish the right of private property from their other natural liberties and certainly did not view it as antagonistic to these cherished human rights. Indeed, most Americans associated freedom and independence with property. This had constituted the fundamental basis of their revolt. Property-owning yeomen declared themselves the enemies of every form of tyranny and rose up against the British. Their Revolution inclined toward defining liberty in terms of the just reward of the righteous struggle of independent freemen. Such a definition made it extremely difficult to conceive of freedom being granted to a passive, dependent order of men. Liberty rested upon an independent citizenry, whose independence, in turn, rested upon freehold property. A man arbitrarily deprived of his property became a slave. In this sense a revolution fought in the name of natural rights could become a positive impediment to the abolition of slavery.

In late eighteenth-century America the literature upon which so many Americans depended to help define their republicanism saw no inherent incompatibility between slavery and an ideal utilitarian state. Philosophers of the Enlightenment such as Thomas Hobbes and Samuel Pufendorf considered slavery an efficient means of social control that could prove useful in dealing with Europe's problem of the dangerous and idle poor. For Francis Hutcheson nothing encouraged industrious habits among the lower orders of society quite so well as perpetual bondage. Slavery, in his mind, should constitute the "ordinary punishment of such idle vagrants as, after proper admonition and trials of temporary servitude, cannot be engaged to support themselves and their families by any useful labours."[30] John Locke's classic exposition of the rights of revolution did not incorporate the poor. Instead he offered children of the poor working schools where they would become inured to labor and nothing else from the age of three. Such schools were nearly indistinguishable from slavery.

Commonwealthmen like John Trenchard and Thomas Gordon, whose *Catos' Letters* comprised the American textbook of equality, addressed themselves to independent men of substance. They harshly attacked charity schools and denigrated the dependent poor as threats to a republican society. While they never suggested enslaving troublesome poor people, some of their fellow Commonwealthmen did. James Burgh, for example, desired that idle and vicious individuals be enslaved, while Andrew Fletcher suggested that some 200,000 Scotsmen be forced into servitude. Such men, so influential in shaping American republicanism, taught that an enthusiasm for freedom, equality, and liberty could coexist with a contempt for the poor and was by no means incompatible with proposals to enslave them.

Commonwealthmen like Trenchard, Gordon, and Burgh exalted the role of the independent yeoman farmer in republican thought while denigrating that of the less-than-independent poor person. Republics rested upon the strength and virtue of self-sufficient individuals to ward off the encroachments of tyranny upon the sphere of liberty. At the same time, however, they warned that those whose will might be dominated or controlled by others represented a serious danger to republican liberty. Consequently the able-bodied poor, those who were nominally free but not independent, posed the greatest threat to a free society. These people became drones upon such a society. Not only did they fail to contribute to the communal well-being, but they sapped the strength of those who had to support them. Such people easily fell prey to unscrupulous demagogues who could use them to launch tyrannical attacks upon the liberty of the independent populace.

These attitudes about the dependent poor permeated American republicanism by the late eighteenth century.[31] In Thomas Jefferson, for example, they gave rise to two obsessive concerns: his deep-seated fear of debt and his suspicion of manufacturing. Each of these eroded individual independence, he believed, and thereby invited an end to liberty. By undermining independence, each "begets subservience and venality, suffocates the germ of virtue, and prepares fit tools for the designs of ambition."[32]

While they would never consider enslaving free people, no matter how dependent, Jefferson and others were extremely hesitant to extend the benefits of republican liberty to individuals whom they believed to be totally incapable of preserving it and who might thereby endanger the very existence of that liberty. Since the bulk of dependent poor people residing in Virginia were already slaves, republican leaders there hesitated to question that status. While some Virginia republicans expressed misgivings over the presence of slavery, they shrank from freeing 200,000 slaves and allowing them to participate in free society. They could only believe that if freed, blacks, whom they perceived as totally incapable of becoming independent republican citizens, would pollute society and undermine republicanism itself within the state. Consequently, regardless of one's feelings about slavery, it was far better to keep blacks in servitude. Republicanism itself depended upon it.

Virginia's commitment to slavery replicated that of the other southern states. At the same time the economic opportunities and political freedoms of the remainder of the states also rested in large part upon slavery. The carrying trade with the slave-based economies of the Caribbean had nurtured New England prosperity as well as its republican society. By the time of the Revolution Massachusetts alone had over sixty rum-producing distilleries, whose exports constituted a primary source of hard coin for the state. And although the state had only 5,000 black slaves within its boundaries, the West Indian trade provided employment to over 10,000 seamen, exclusive of all the workers who built and outfitted the ships. The singular social circumstances of Americans, North as well as South, resulted from a great many conscious choices. Consequently their language of freedom and equality rested on the existence as well as the perpetuation of black slavery. Any calls for conformity between principles and practice, regardless of how heart-felt they may have been, became irrelevant. Revolutionary ideas did not possess an autonomous power; rather such rhetoric conjugated differently in separate areas of the nation and, depending on the interests of different classes of men, could be employed in a variety of ways. Contempt for the poor and the black, however, pervaded American culture and constituted a serious flaw in the new nation's vision of itself as a nation of equals.

Cultural forces within American society obscured this flaw regarding the black. Whenever whites confronted blacks, they found themselves torn between separate impulses.[33] On the one hand, Christian benevolence and republican emphasis upon liberty and equality obligated whites to consider blacks as equal and accept them into the community as full citizens. On the other hand, the specter of slave revolts, the fear of race mixture, economic imperatives arising from a bountiful new world environment, and racism moved many Americans to treat blacks as a despised lesser being. White society projected despicable traits onto the black and translated the white man's worst into his best. Violent sexual behavior against blacks became the protection of racial purity, while the harsh domination of blacks in slavery reflected fidelity to the preservation of civilized restraints and a virtuous, independent social order. Such translations achieved peace of mind for the white—so vital to his continued faith in the regenerative powers of republicanism—at a terrible cost to the black. White Americans were not only absolved of any sense of guilt at holding blacks in bondage, such servitude suggested no contradictions or hypocrisy in their constant exaltation of the republican freedom and liberty that thrived in their nation—the last best hope of the Western world.

A Unique Republican Culture

By the end of the eighteenth century, the American commitment to republicanism had grown even stronger than it had been in 1776. Republicanism existed as a social fact, a cultural system whose tenets permeated throughout American society. However, America had hardly attained the kind of culture envisioned for it by its Revolutionary leaders. For these men the Revolution had offered Americans the opportunity to put Enlightenment ideas into practice by creating the kind of harmonious society envisioned for republics by philosophers since the ancient Greeks. Rather than generating an increased commitment to order, harmony, and virtue, however, Revolutionary republicanism appeared to be fostering an acquisitive individualism heedless of the common good or the benevolent leadership of a natural elite. Post-Revolutionary America, instead of becoming the New World embodiment of transcendent classical values, appeared increasingly materialistic, utilitarian, and licentious. Austerity gave way to prosperity; virtue appeared more and more to connote the individual pursuit of wealth rather than an unselfish devotion to the collective good.

The changes taking place in American society throughout the last decades of the eighteenth century helped create a far more open and unstructured society than had been anticipated by most Revolutionary leaders. The transformations taking place were so complex and undeliberate, so much a mixture of day-to-day responses to a rapidly changing socioeconomic environment, that most Americans were unaware of the direction in which such changes were taking them. Their commitment to republicanism, however, allowed them to continue to perceive of themselves as members of a virtuous, harmonious organic society long after the social foundations of such a society had passed.

Republican language's increasing disembodiment from the changing cultural context made self-awareness more difficult. Cries of republican equality became ever more insistent at the very time that Americans rigidly excluded blacks from their society, decimated Indian tribes in an attempt to transform them into republican citizens, restricted women to a separate, limited sphere, and created a markedly stratified society. The presence of an ideology as powerful as republicanism fostered an unconscious tendency among the dominant majority of Americans to make reality amenable to ideas, and ideas to reality, so as to create an integral worldview credible enough to foster a collective as well as an individual sense of identity and security.[34] Adherence to republican ideals helped to ease the strains present within late-eighteenth-century American society by allowing groups and individuals to dissociate themselves, their institutions, and their society from harmful and evil actions. The ideology of republicanism allowed—even impelled—men to view themselves as committed to the hármony, order, and communal well-being of a republican society while actively creating an aggressive, individualistic, liberal one.

six

The Emergence of a Democratic Society

By the last decade of the eighteenth century, American society was in a state of cultural ferment. The nation's population grew at an astonishing rate and began to spread rapidly out from the original states. Vast numbers of people accustomed to a subsistence life became drawn into the market economy. An environment of rising expectations stimulated the acquisitive instincts of many, as well as strained the customary paternalistic social relationships between parent and child, gentleman and servant, master and journeyman or apprentice, merchant and client, landowner and tenant. Set loose from the traditional bonds that had joined people over the years, thousands of simple folk were determined to take advantage of the expanding opportunities to get ahead with nothing but their own ingenuity and hard work.

Within such an atmosphere upward mobility no longer hinged upon proper breeding and social connections, restricted political privileges, or, least of all, a genteel education. Learning had not been rejected; it had been popularized. By means of chapbooks, almanacs, broadsides, handbills, and pamphlets, simple folk began to gain snatches of information about matters that had always been considered solely within the ken of the genteel. Literature of all kinds came at a rapidly increasing rate into the hands of individuals previously accustomed to only the family Bible.

Booksellers in the major cities multiplied in numbers, but the greatest stimulant to the popularization of knowledge was the increased publication and widespread distribution of newspapers. The number of newspapers published in America increased from 100 in 1790 to over 250 a decade later. Within another decade Americans would have the largest circulation of newspapers of any country in the world. In addition, the creation of an active central government led to the rapid development of mail service and post roads that helped carry newspapers far beyond coastal urban areas. In the single decade of the 1790s, American post offices increased in number from 75 to 903. The miles of post roads soared from 1,875 to 21,000 within the same decade.

With this increase in circulation came a change in the nature of newspapers. While some editors followed traditional habits, most adapted to the increasingly popular tastes of their ever-widening audience. "A Farmer," "A Republican," or "A Friend to Liberty and Equality" replaced classical pseudonyms, and editorials became noticeably simpler in style and content. Not only did editorial policies change to meet the needs of a popular constituency, but newspapers in the 1790s included a vast outpouring from ordinary citizens as they grasped the medium reserved in the past for gentlemen. Truth itself gradually underwent a process of democratization: ordinary individuals began to consider themselves as capable as the best educated of discovering and acting upon what was best for society.

Revolutionary republicanism prompted ordinary farmers, mechanics, and shopkeepers to challenge the idea that a gentlemanly few should provide direction for their society. Throughout the final decades of the eighteenth century, an egalitarian impetus brought together those inherently suspicious of power with others who had traditionally been powerless in an attempt to shatter the hegemony of gentlemanly elites. Quite spontaneously individuals and groups in a variety of areas—religion, commerce, politics—actively began to challenge the authority of mediating elites. They opposed any manifestation of social distinction as well as all but purely voluntary societal bonds. Any claim by an elite to speak for all the people appeared increasingly anachronistic and self-serving. Such a crisis in confidence in hierarchical society gave rise to fundamental demands for reform in religion, the law, commercial activities, and politics. Slowly, then, in an erratic and piecemeal fashion, ordinary workingmen, preachers, and political leaders began to articulate their feelings and to provide form, content, and legitimacy to their pent-up frustrations. Their efforts would culminate in the creation of a political movement to oppose hierarchy in America—a movement that finally formed the democratic and egalitarian impulses of localism into a powerful national ideology.

Antilawyer Sentiment

As more and more people took seriously the egalitarian rhetoric of the Revolution they became impatient with artificial constraints that impeded their chances to get ahead in life, impugned their worth, or bestowed special privileges upon a select few. Such attitudes led to criticism of the legal profession and the common law. Many Americans demanded "a system of law of our own, dictated by the genuine principles of Republicanism, and made easy to be understood to every individual in the community." Those people openly wondered: "Shall we be directed by reason, equity, and a few simple and plain laws, promptly executed, or shall we be ruled by volumes of statutes and cases decided by the ignorance and intolerance of former times?" The answer was obvious: in the United States faith should be placed in the ordinary citizen's ability to recognize and administer justice. "Any person of common abilities can easily distinguish between right and wrong," particularly "when the parties are admitted to give a plain story, without any puzzle from lawyers."[1]

A growing distrust of the legal profession became particularly acute in the post-Revolutionary period as a result of the rapid spread of the market economy and the egalitarian thrust of Revolutionary rhetoric. The emergence of a "lawyer class"—well-born, college-educated, socially well-connected men allied with powerful mercantile and commercial interests—appeared to fly in the face of popular expectations of equality. Rather than becoming part of an open, fluid society, lawyers formed a closed elite that was able, through familiarity with the law as well as legally vulnerable aspects of the economic structure, to reap tremendous advantages for themselves and their clients. These circumstances gave rise to the opinion that lawyers used legal chicanery to gain unfair advantage over diligent, honest folks or charged such people exorbitant fees to fulfill the simplest duties required by the law. Lawyers thus were perceived as men who inhibited free access to economic and social advancement.

Such feelings prompted a warning from the citizens of New Braintree, Massachusetts, to the state legislature in 1786: "With regard to the Practitioners of the Law in this Commonwealth, daily experience convinces us of the horrid extortion, tyranny and oppression, practiced among that order of men, who, of late years, have amazingly increased in number, opulence, and grandeur."[2]

John Dudley, a New Hampshire trader and farmer who sat on that state's supreme court from 1785 to 1797, shared this suspicion. In one instance Dudley observed: "You have heard, gentlemen of the jury, what has been said in this case by the lawyers, the rascals! . . . They would govern us by the common law of Europe. Trust me, gentlemen, common sense is a much safer guide for us; the common sense of . . . [the towns] which have sent us here to try this case between two of our neighbors." In conclusion, Judge Dudley exclaimed: "It is our business to do justice between the parties, not by any quirks of the law out of Coke or Blackstone, books that I never read, and never will, but by common sense and common honesty as between men and men."[3] In his *Letters from an American Farmer* (1782) J. Hector St. John de Crevecoeur voiced a similar view of lawyers: "They are plants that will grow in any soil that is cultivated by the hands of others; and when once they have taken root they will extinguish every other vegetable that grows around them. . . . The most ignorant, the most bungling member of that profession, will if placed in the most obscure parts of the country, promote its litigiousness and amass more wealth without labour, than the most opulent farmer, with all his toils."

An obscure Boston artisan with little formal education placed the emerging popular attitudes toward the legal profession squarely within the democratic and egalitarian context of Revolutionary republicanism. Benjamin Austin, a follower of Sam Adams during the Revolution, assumed the leadership of the "mob" in Boston throughout the 1780s and early 1790s. Writing as "Honestus," Austin published a pamphlet, *Observations on the Pernicious Practice of the Law* (1786), in which he offered a radically egalitarian critique of lawyers and the common law. Since lawyers rendered intricate even the most evident principles of the law and needlessly prolonged the judicial process for their own gain, Austin believed they should be abolished from the courtroom along with the numerous and complex codes of the common law. Austin proposed instead that petty cases be decided by referees who were neighbors of the litigants. In more serious cases judges should simply present the relevant evidence to the jury with an explanation of whatever points of law were necessary. Thus, all appeals to the law would be on the plainest principles possible; law would not be made to serve a privileged few by lawyers hired as much for their cunning as for their knowledge.

Austin articulated the frustrations of Americans beginning to challenge the position of elites in all walks of life. He declared that legal truths should be, like all others, accessible to ordinary men. Deference to special knowledge was every bit as unnecessary as deference to social connections and family names.

Artisan Republicanism

The resentment that characterized the animosity toward the legal profession emerged simultaneously among urban artisans and mechanics growing restive under political subordination to mercantile elites. Workers in the various urban centers of the nation began to break free of the dependent economic and political positions in which they found themselves at the end of the Revolution. They began to organize on their own behalf, to challenge elite control, and to develop a distinctly egalitarian political tradition. Through their efforts to achieve identity and self-respect, urban craftsmen contributed to the creation of a unique "artisan republicanism."[4]

Two parades staged in New York City symbolized the emergence of a new consciousness among American workingmen. The first, held on 23 July 1788, included nearly six thousand craftsmen, who turned out to march in celebration of a Federalist-artisan alliance in support of the Constitution. Such a coalition between conservative Federalists and democratically inclined artisans could not, however, last long, and by the early 1790s it was dead. Disheartened by the Washington administration's pro-English foreign policy, its backsliding on a variety of issues important to workingmen and Washington's own attack upon "self-created" societies much like the Mechanic's Committee so central to directing the interests of laborers within the city, many of the most politically conscious artisans joined with political opponents of Federalism within the city to form the Democratic Society of New York. The influence of this society spread downward into the artisan wards as Federalists replaced their formerly conciliatory rhetoric with outspoken attacks upon the Democratic Society, the French Revolution, and the lower orders themselves. Instead of being courted as they had been in the mid-1780s, artisans were called "the mindless multitude," "the ignorant masses," and "the rabble" by Federalist leaders who now displayed contempt for mechanics who might wish to participate in governing the city or the state. To most artisans it seemed like the 1770s all over again. An aristocratic elite looked down upon the "rabble" and intended to dominate it in their own interests.

The Democratic Society responded with an egalitarian interpretation of the America Revolution. In terms drawn from Tom Paine's *Rights of Man* the society's members maintained that the Revolution rested upon "sentiments of Democracy, founded upon the Equal Rights of Mankind."[5] Given such a premise, the society attempted to redeem the democratic impetus of the Revolution that had been lost amid the Federalists' claim that the Constitution represented the sovereignty of the people. For the members of the Democratic Society, democracy became an integral, if not the essential, element within American republicanism. At the same time they attacked deferential forms of all kinds, challenged traditional social and political customs, and led an ever more vitriolic attack upon Federalist financial programs as the basis for a newly emergent aristocratic elite within America. Most important for the development of an artisan consciousness, the society's leaders suggested that political virtue rested with the producing classes rather than with groups such as bankers, speculators, stockjobbers, and merchants who were amassing great wealth without pursuing a productive trade.

By 1794 when a massive procession of craftsmen paraded through the streets of New York in opposition to Federalist policies, a distinctive artisan republicanism had emerged to provide workingmen with a sense of political cohesion. This variant of republicanism incorporated strands of egalitarian political thought with an exaltation of the crafts celebrated in classical republican terms of independence, virtue, simplicity, and commonwealth. Viewing the small shop as embodying the quintessential values of republicanism, artisans stressed individual ability and equality while simultaneously emphasizing virtuous cooperation and a mutuality of interests. Their celebration of "the Trade" rested on a careful balancing of individual rights with communal responsibilities. Industry, independence, and hard work should be undertaken for the public good, not for personal gain alone. For this reason artisans became increasingly distrustful of mercantile and financial elites that seemed to practice modern entrepreneurial skills for self-aggrandizement rather than for the benefit of the commonwealth. When artisans attacked elites as unnatural impediments to the advancement of the ordinary individual, they did so to foster a collective or affective individualism that recognized human obligations to the larger society, not to foster a competitive individualism.

Evangelical Religion

The desire to integrate individual autonomy with communal unity, so central to artisan republicanism, spread beyond the world of craftsmen in the post-Revolutionary decades. Thousands of individuals, caught up in a simultaneous quest for personal independence and new ways to relate to one another, sought comfort from their sense of detachment by participating in the establishment of a wide variety of voluntary associations and organizations that sprang up following the Revolution. These included egalitarian and affective organizations such as Democratic-Republican societies, humanitarian groups like the New York Society for the Relief of Distressed Debtors, moral reform organizations such as the Columbia Moral Society of New York, educational associations like the American Academy of Arts and Sciences, and private fraternal groups such as the Freemasons.

The great majority of ordinary Americans, however, joined in an unprecedented proliferation of new religious groups.[6] By the end of the eighteenth century, America was no longer a land of Presbyterians, Episcopalians, Congregationalists, and Calvinist Baptists. It had become a seething mixture of, among others, Christians, Methodists, and Universalists, as well as Freewill, Free-Communion, and Primitive Baptists. These sects arose within a new religious culture that accompanied the crisis of authority brought about by the Revolution. As a result of the egalitarian language of Revolutionary republicanism, the evangelical pietism of ordinary people took on a different character than it had assumed in the late colonial period. In many ways the Revolution released and provided clarity and form for powerful currents of popular evangelical emotions coursing just beneath the surface of public life. These needed only the democratic impulses released by the Revolution to bring them to the surface, where they would rapidly transform the lives of great masses of previously apathetic and apolitical individuals. Gaining strength from the democratic secular thrust spawned by the Revolution, the evangelical piety of ordinary people overflowed into public life where it flooded customary structures in a wave of popular religiosity.

Everywhere established ministers looked, religion seemed to be in shambles. The Revolution had wreaked havoc: churches had been destroyed, ministerial training had been suspended by some and discontinued entirely by others, and the minds of many parishioners had been so politicized as to make them restive with orthodox doctrines and practices. Traditional established churches, even when they were neither dismantled nor faced with serious challenges, seemed ill equipped to deal with the huge increase in size, mobility, and personal autonomy of America's post-Revolutionary population. In addition, college graduates increasingly turned to law rather than the ministry, and membership in the traditional churches fell off precipitously. The influence of enlightened liberalism seemed to be spreading; it suffused the First Amendment to the Constitution and pervaded the thought of the genteel throughout the nation. It undermined the basic foundation not only of Calvinism but of all orthodox Christian beliefs by convincing people of their innate goodness. Rather than teaching people that they were sinners, it taught them that they possessed a benevolent moral sense or instinct and that evil emanated from corrupt secular and religious institutions rather than from the people themselves. Such beliefs led some individuals to mock Christianity and others to struggle mightily to harmonize liberal rationalism with their more orthodox religious beliefs. Still others adhered to a rational deism or to the more popular antireligious writings of Thomas Paine, Elihu Palmer, or Ethan Allen.

For great numbers of ordinary citizens, however, the Bible remained the primary source of meaning and guidance, and Christianity retained its centrality in their lives. Bewildered by the social disintegration of the postwar generation yet finding themselves freer than ever before to express their religious emotions, these people sought new ways to order their lives. They bitterly resented the literary sophistication and cold institutional practices of churches traditionally dominated by the elite and led by high-toned, college-educated ministers who interpreted the Bible for them. They wanted no such intermediaries between themselves and their God. They demanded instead the visceral personal experience provided by an egalitarian religion. In the absence of gentry leadership, simple folk gathered wherever they could—in an open field, an unused barn, or a brother's home—to express themselves physically and emotionally and to create fresh self-initiated bonds of fellowship. Led by half-educated men recruited from their own ranks, these people responded to a type of religious appeal that mixed emotionalism, plain language, and the Scriptures.

Evangelicals, whether Methodists, Baptists, or Shaker, shared a common bond: a deep and abiding enmity toward orthodox authorities. Most evangelical leaders incorporated the language of the Revolution in their attacks on existing authority; in the process their Christianity became republicanized. Just as the people were sovereign in government, so too should they be their own theologians in religion. They must no longer depend upon others to interpret Scripture for them and to instruct them how to behave. Evangelicals urged believers to dispense with established churches, presbyters, institutional doctrines, and priests. The people themselves were competent to run their own churches and to assume control over them. More important, many evangelical leaders suggested that the people might be capable of gaining their own salvation. Their revivalistic methods suggested that sin no longer stemmed from innate human depravity but instead represented a weakness of will that could be purged through individual effort. As a result men and women felt free to accept or reject a preacher or a church based on personal, subjective criteria. Evangelical churches became voluntary associations of like-minded individuals attempting to make sense of their disordered lives.

The religious enthusiasm generated by evangelicals released passions among ordinary folk that were difficult to keep in check. Itinerant preachers mocked pretentious clergymen, exalted the common man, and depicted a polarized American society pitting ordinary people against an array of political, legal, military, and religious elites. Christian newspapers translated into print the resentment that had permeated a popular oral culture for decades. The familiar Revolutionary themes of liberty, slavery, tyranny, and the Antichrist now described the machinations of American gentlemen rather than British ministers. Elites of all kinds, but particularly the clergy, described as "tyrannical oppressors," "hireling priests," and "an *aristocratic body of uniform nobility*," now threatened liberty in America. Any people who would endure such tyranny were "slavishly dependent" or "passively obedient" but certainly not independent republican citizens.[7]

Ordinary folk eagerly embraced religious groups that treated them as equals, spurned social distinctions, and rested on voluntarism. The religious thrust of the 1790s and early 1800s that countenanced the right of each individual to seek his own salvation closely paralleled a secular impulse building within the nation that impelled individual citizens to break free of all artificial social and political restraints. Thus the evangelical Christianity that drew nearly twenty thousand eager souls to the great revival at Cane Ridge, Kentucky, in August 1801 and the democratic impulse that impelled thousands of Americans to question Federalist control of government throughout the previous decade comprised separate manifestations of a common cultural force gathering strength in the late eighteenth century that moved ordinary, obscure individuals to seek control over their own lives and to create a society responsive to their needs and aspirations. Such attitudes remained pervasive, yet unformed, elements of the American environment until they gained ideological force and clarity in the political turmoil that developed in the 1790s.

Political Divisiveness

Once the Constitution had been ratified, life had to be breathed into the national government created by that document. This process prompted deep and bitter divisions to surface within the federal government and throughout the larger society as Americans battled to define their social and political institutions. This struggle did not create new divisions among Americans nearly so much as it reflected preexisting ones. At issue was the fundamental question that had divided Americans for decades: What form of government and type of society were to develop within the new nation? Would the principles of hierarchy or localism prevail throughout the nation?

When Congress convened in April 1789, there was little, if any, sign of controversy. The fall elections of 1788 had resulted in a large Federalist majority in both the House and the Senate, and the electoral college unanimously elected George Washington to the presidency. The new government rested firmly in the hands of men who had supported the Constitution. These same men fully intended to exploit the opportunities presented by that document to create a consolidated commercial nation under the auspices of a strong government in the hands of the nation's natural elite. They envisioned a classical heroic state—an Augustan society—for America.

Leadership in achieving such promise for American society fell to Alexander Hamilton, the thirty-five-year-old secretary of the treasury. Hamilton, an admirer of the hierarchical culture of England as well as its elitist ministerial style of government, intended as best he could to develop similar institutions in America. Toward that end he submitted separate reports to Congress in 1790–91 dealing with credit, revenue, a national bank, and manufactures. To establish the credit of the United States Hamilton proposed to fund the national debt and to assume the debts of the states. This would be accomplished by calling in all federal and state bonds and loan certificates and paying them at par value with newly issued federal securities. In this way Hamilton created a refunded, consolidated, permanent national debt that would serve in the same manner that England's national debt had for decades: to tie moneyed interests to the national government. In order to meet the regular interest payments due on the national debt, Hamilton secured passage of customs duties and excise taxes. Such interest payments not only established the credit of the United States throughout the world but provided additional investment opportunities for American speculators.

All that was needed now was an adequate circulating medium of currency and a centralized banking institution to oversee the economic affairs of the nation. Hamilton achieved this with the creation of the Bank of the United States, which, patterned upon the Bank of England, forged an alliance between government and private individuals. The bank and its branches became the depository for the government, as well as its fiscal agent, and served as a regulatory agent over state banks. Most important, however, notes issued by the bank—payable on demand in gold and silver and receivable in payment for debts owed the federal government—would provide the nation with a much-needed circulating medium. The government held one-fourth of the bank's stock and appointed one-fifth of its directors. Ownership of the remaining stock and the appointment of the majority of directors fell to the investing public. Once again wealthy elements within the country were drawn ever closer to the federal government. Hamilton's fourth and final report, dealing with manufactures, offered complex proposals for industrializing America patterned on Great Britain's system of tariffs, bounties, and incentives for improved techniques of production. Intended by Hamilton as the capstone of his grand design to centralize governmental authority and to industrialize the United States through government aid to business and to businessmen, the final report, unlike his previous ones, received only scattered support.

While Hamilton's reports dealt entirely with economic matters, both he and his Federalist colleagues intended for them to serve political and social ends as well. Although concerned for the commerical prosperity of the nation, these men also viewed issues such as funding, assumption, and the bank as means to a greater end: the achievement of a hierarchical order patterned upon that of the British. They meant to further the Anglicization process interrupted by the war and simultaneously to blunt the egalitarianism spawned by the Revolution.

By re-creating the dependent relationships that characterized the eighteenth-century hierarchical world, Federalists assumed they could accomplish these goals. Their new fiscal measures, by providing the dominant social and commercial elements with lucrative economic returns, not only established lines of dependency between the federal government and these social orders but gave them the means to create links of economic dependency with those below them. Gradually, aided by appointments to the federal judiciary and other federal offices, shrewd management of the bank, and related economic measures, a web of mutually reinforcing support grew between local notables and the Federalist leaders in Congress. Those bonds gained greater strength as a result of displays of strength by the federal government (the smashing of Indian resistance in the Old Northwest and the crushing of the Whiskey Rebellion in 1794) that encouraged the local elites' natural affinity for power and authority.

Opposition to Hamilton's program developed slowly. Leadership of dissenting members of Congress gradually began to coalesce around James Madison, who worried about the direction that Hamilton seemed to be taking the new government. He and others feared that the consolidating tendencies of Hamilton's financial measures concentrated power in the national government to such an extent that it corrupted that government and threatened liberty throughout the nation. Thomas Jefferson believed that Hamilton and his fiscal policies would bring about a transition "from the present republican form of government, to that of a monarchy of which the English constitution is to be the model."[8] John Taylor of Caroline, senator from Virginia, claimed that "a design for erecting aristocracy and monarchy, is subsisting—that a *money impulse*, and not a *public good*, is operating on Congress."[9] As early as December 1790 the Virginia legislature had attacked Hamilton's fiscal measures on the grounds that the legislators "discern[ed] a striking resemblance between this system and that which was introduced into England at the Revolution—a system which has perpetuated upon that nation an enormous debt . . . and daily threatens the destruction of everything that appertains to English liberty."[10] A "republican interest" emerged in Congress and throughout the nation. Individuals began to refer to themselves as Republicans in opposition to the Federalists and to express fears that Federalist domination meant corrupt, self-serving political leaders.[11]

These beliefs gained legitimacy in the eyes of Hamilton's opponents in the summer of 1791 when there was a wild scramble for bank stock on the part of speculators. The fact that many of these men were also members of Congress greatly alarmed Madison and others. Hamilton's fiscal manipulations were corrupting the republican legislature and polluting the larger society by means of a fiscal system that encouraged restless speculation and immorality. Understood in these terms, the Federalist emphasis on a large standing army in time of peace, excise taxes, a perpetual public debt, the "court" manners affected by so many Federalists, and the economic measures supported by the secretary of the treasury became part of a clear pattern. A Republican critic drew the only conclusion possible: "After having wrested the scepter from the hand of a British tyrant, they have suffered it to be assumed by a monied aristocracy, where it will be found more oppressive and injurious to the people."[12] Hamilton and his Federalist colleagues threatened the very soul of American republicanism.

Such fears became increasingly passionate following the outbreak of war in 1792 between monarchical Britain and republican France. In the minds of many Republicans the success or failure of their own republican experiment remained inextricably linked to the fate of their French compatriots. Republican editors viciously attacked Federalist officeholders as tools of monarchy. For their part Federalist editors, influenced by Edmund Burke's *Reflections on the Revolution in France* (1790), saw Jacobin schemes in every Republican action. Each side remained convinced that the other was part of a worldwide conspiracy against law, authority, right, and republicanism. Inflamed by such rhetoric, all areas of domestic life—social clubs, business meetings, and religious ceremonies—became highly politicized and polarized. Passions ran high; long-time friends refused to acknowledge one another on the street, violence erupted in the streets, fights broke out in state legislatures and even disrupted meetings of Congress.

The partisan associations of Federalists and Republicans represented ideological persuasions that emerged from long-standing cultural tensions. They existed as ways of looking at the world—modes of thought—long before they were modes of politics. The political issues of the 1790s gave public expression to deeply ingrained although long unexamined cultural beliefs. Their searching criticism of one another required Federalists and Republicans to present an explicit articulation of their own philosophies of government and society. The polemics of the 1790s forced the opposing sides to translate into political language their understanding of the changes that had taken place over the previous decades.

Federalist Ideology

Federalism rested on a social ideal that stressed stability, harmony, dependence, and the common good.[13] More than anything else an identity with established authority and customary ways of life attracted individuals to it. Whether economically dependent upon an established member of the community, psychologically wedded to a deferential society, or members of the elite themselves, those who became Federalists identified with a hierarchical social and political order. They esteemed their "betters" and felt obliged to guide and direct those inferior to themselves. They found a stable, structured society to be a source of real security and identity in a rapidly changing, chaotic world.

Adherents of Federalism articulated the hierarchical attitudes of an earlier era. George Cabot, perhaps the wealthiest man in New England, spoke in terms of society as a "well regulated family"—an organic whole whose harmony resulted from "each one learning his proper place and keeping to it." For Cabot there was no equality of condition. The "better sort" "ruled" rather than governed in a political system held together by a deferential spirit that imbued the "multitude" from birth to "submit to the subordination necessary in the free'est state" and accustomed the "natural rulers of society" to expect such behavior.[14] A prominent import merchant, Stephen Higginson, declared: "The people must be *taught* to confide in and reverence their rulers."[15] Jonathan Jackson, a leading import merchant and banker, concurred. Young people must be taught "their just rights, at the same time they are taught proper subordination." The militia took on great significance for Jackson because it could instill these lessons in adults. Indeed, it inculcated the single most basic lesson: "that discipline of the mind—*subordination*—for who can govern properly in any department that has not learned to obey?"[16] Nathaniel Chipman, chief justice of the Vermont Supreme Court, declared: "The greater part of his [man's] rights are not exclusively, and independently, in himself. They arise in society and are relative to it. . . . The rights of all have a reciprocal relation to the rights of each, and can never be rightly apprehended distinct from that relation."[17] Federalists remained very much aware of inequalities in society and intended to maintain a governing elite supported by the votes of the people by strengthening traditional habits and customs of deference through the family, church and government. They believed, above all else, in *"a speaking* aristocracy *in the face of a silent* democracy."[18]

From a Federalist perspective, though, something deeply disturbing was at work within American society. As a result of the economic and social changes wrought by the Revolution and the corrupting influence of the French Revolution, older standards of behavior were coming under attack and new ones arising in their stead. Instead of accepting their status in life, all sorts of people now struggled for material wealth and political prominence. Individuals who had always sought only the respect of their neighbors now clamorously appealed for the votes of the mob. Such degenerative sorts had banded together to form a political party—the very bane of a republican government's existence—that aimed at nothing less than the total transformation of society. Courting all men regardless of their status or worth, this new party intended to create the new man who would demand equality—social, political, and economic—with even the most genteel.

To Federalists, the Republican party appeared to be the means by which individuals advanced their selfish interests at the expense of the whole community. The party would place men of obscure origins in power by bypassing the established hierarchical structure. To the outrage of the Federalist elite, the Republican party was becoming the primary vehicle for entrepreneurship in and through politics; it created the very men to whom it appealed for support and became the means by which these men advanced in society. Unrestrained competition not only threatened the social harmony of a republican commonwealth but set into motion a dangerous proclivity on the part of Americans to disdain rank, status, and order—the foundations of a true republic.

From a Federalist viewpoint, Republicans masked their socially disruptive, self-seeking actions behind a rhetoric of public service. They flattered the public and gained positions not by serving the commonwealth but from boldly advancing their own selfish interests. Indignant Federalists viewed such men as "creatures who, under pretense of serving the people, are in fact serving themselves."[19] While Federalists attempted to safeguard principle, integrity, and traditional institutions, Republicans sought only "to obtain office, and change the customs and habits of the country." Republicans could only be considered "the enemies of order who are seeking their own emolument in the confusion of innovation & misrule."[20] In their scramble for personal advantage Republicans proposed measures that would prove dangerously unsound when put into practice. "Never," Noah Webster warned his countrymen in a Fourth of July oration, ". . . let us exchange our civil and religious institutions for the wild theories of crazy projectors; or the sober, industrious moral habits of our country, for experiments in atheism and lawless democracy. *Experience* is a safe pilot; but experiment is a dangerous ocean, full of rocks and shoals."[21] Taking the term from Jonathan Swift, Federalists considered Republicans "Laputans"—men who walked about with their heads in the clouds and through their abstract impracticability threatened the destruction of a harmonious, stable republic.

In the eyes of Federalists the worst trait of Republicans was their unscrupulous search for popular favor. Lacking the values that might serve as a compass in changing times, such men altered their course according to the opinions of the day, patterning their lives according to fashionable current tastes in a futile effort to gain status and recognition. Federalists were troubled by the knowledge that Republican efforts were futile only if judged by traditional criteria that recognized true merit working within customary hierarchical channels. The problem for Federalists was that such traditional standards themselves seemed to be passing out of existence. In the place of esteemed political figures who had risen slowly to positions of honor after years of dedicated public service, "mushroom politicians," who bypassed the traditional hierarchy and curried favor with the people, sprang up overnight. An angry Federalist warned of the dangers of "the novel doctrine of new-fashioned republicans, that the hasty opinions of the populace are infallible" and, even worse, *"that character should be tried at the bar of public opinion."* In exasperation he bemoaned: "What senseless jargon! The decision would frequently be against the truly meritorious, and in favor of the most worthless."[22]

For most Federalists the Republican party represented the culmination of troubling tendencies that had been at work within their society since the Revolution. Throughout the 1780s and 1790s Federalists became increasingly disillusioned. Instead of the ordered, Augustan society the Revolution was supposed to usher in, America seemed to be in danger of becoming a scrambling, commercial society dominated by the pecuniary needs and desires of ordinary citizens rather than the austere and rational guidance of its natural aristocrats. No longer were Americans knit together by simple virtue; a process John Adams described as "disaggregation" was taking place.[23] The irony was that Federalists themselves contributed to these troubling circumstances. Through their advocacy of capitalistic economic measures, they had helped to create a competitive, fiercely individualistic social environment; there was no way to restrict the new business practices to gentlemen.

The problem facing the Federalists consequently became how to maintain order and stability in a society rapidly splintering into competing interests. Most supported the creation of strong institutions of social control in which power and liberty would be mutually dependent and where true freedom and liberty could exist only within clearly circumscribed limits. Jonathan Jackson exclaimed that in "simple democracies" there was "no regularity; no one knows his place, or how to keep it." "Governments, in which the principles of all are combined, and which are properly limited by sufficient checks, are those only which can promise us permanency, at the same time they can afford us any real freedom."[24] In an oration presented to the Massachusetts Society of Cincinnati, a Federalist speaker stated that "a relaxation in the reins of government is as productive of anarchy and confusion as the despotick law of an eastern monarch is of tyranny and oppression."[25] Chief Justice John Jay articulated such Federalist beliefs in his first charge to grand juries (1790) in which he observed that "nothing but a strong government of laws, irresistibly bearing down arbitrary power and licentiousness can defend it [United States] against those two formidable enemies."[26]

Abandoning their reliance on the virtue of the people and the natural tendency toward subordination that emanated from that virtue, Federalists turned to energetic government to preserve order and stability. Under Hamilton's leadership they intended to move America ahead into a more complex stage of social development—to emulate the eighteenth-century English model where the nation's economic development was directed from the center through governmental fiscal and banking policies. The economic and moral health of the nation would be controlled by direct intervention from a centralized hierarchy. Federalists envisioned a centrally organized, economically activistic government overseeing a commercial order devoted to established social authority. The newly created national government provided a powerful vehicle through which the cosmopolitan urge to extend hierarchy over all areas of the nation could be actively promoted.

Jeffersonian Republicans

The Federalist actions of the 1790s had an unsettling effect on Americans bred upon an egalitarian localism; such people had an innate suspicion of distant governments and the men who wielded power within them. Yet localism itself was undergoing a crucial transformation. By the 1790s the forces of change spawned by the Revolution had begun to affect great portions of the American population previously isolated from the mainstream. As commerce and the market economy penetrated interior areas, localism's emphasis upon communal egalitarianism became transmuted into an emphasis upon individual success and popular control of government. The old fear that higher authority would erode local customs gradually gave way to a personal distrust of all social distinctions that would impede the ordinary individual's quest for profit and status. Throughout the post-Revolutionary period many Americans slowly, hesitantly, perhaps unconsciously, worked toward the creation of an ideology that would afford legitimacy to these feelings. This impulse surfaced in the scattered voices of William Thompson in South Carolina, John Dudley in New Hampshire, Benjamin Austin in Boston, and the itinerant preachers tending the fires of revivalism across the frontier. It found its strongest voice, its clearest articulation, though, in the political opposition to the Federalist attempt to shape American government and society in the last decade of the eighteenth century.

Those who became Republicans inherited the same Revolutionary ideology of so many other Americans. They integrated a strong belief in Locke's insistence on the protection of property and the good of the people as the only legitimate end of government with a libertarian fear of power and the enslavement of the people at the hands of corrupt officeholders. Along with these ideas, however, Republicans emphasized a peculiar perspective of a number of English writers—particularly James Burgh, John Cartwright, Richard Price, and Joseph Priestley—who claimed that humanity was capable of unbounded improvement. Such improvement would come about, however, only in the least constraining civil, political, and religious environment. Progress resulted not from the benevolent paternalism of an elite, they contended, but from the separate efforts of free and equal individuals. Their beliefs hinged on the related ideas that all people were by nature created free and equal and that whatever distinctions arise in society should result from merit, not status. Cartwright thundered out in *Take Your Choice* (London, 1776) that "All are by nature free; all are by nature equal: freedom implies choice; equality excludes degrees in freedom." James Burgh exclaimed: "All honours and powers ought to be personal only, and to be given to no individual, but such as upon scrutiny, were found to be men of such distinguished merit, as to deserve to be raised to distinguished places, though sprung of mean portents."[27] From such a perspective monarchy, aristocracy, and other civil or religious establishments thwarted the natural proclivity of people of talent and ability to prosper and to change society for the better. A natural civil society rewarded talent and merit; artificial manipulations of the political economy by government created privileged elites and spawned corruption and degeneracy.

In the face of beliefs such as these, Hamiltonian fiscal measures created grave doubts among Americans about the effect such governmental actions would have on the future development of the young republic. These doubts prompted a searching critique of the role of government in the political economy of the nation and searing indictments of Federalism from individuals representing a wide variety of local perspectives. In the process of castigating their Federalist opponents, these men groped toward the articulation of a new political persuasion that would at last translate the realities of the American environment into a dynamic social and political ideology.

From the time debates began in Congress over Hamilton's financial program until the election of Thomas Jefferson to the presidency in 1800, individuals from all regions of the nation and from a wide diversity of callings attacked Federalists and their policies in the most vitriolic manner. In his *Letters Addressed to the Yeomanry of the United States* (Philadelphia, 1791) George Logan, wealthy Pennsylvania landowner and physician, wondered how long Americans would suffer themselves "to be duped by the low cunning and artifice of half-informed Lawyers and mercenary Merchants" who obtained the passage of legislation sacrificing the productive members of society to "indolent characters desirous of lucrative government offices supported by the labor of their fellow men."[28] John Taylor of Caroline, author of a number of widely circulated pamphlets, declared the national bank to be the "master key of that system that governs the [Federalist] administration."[29] Hamilton, "by administering gilded pills to influential characters," stimulated "exhorbitant wealth, to provide an aristocracy as the harbinger of monarchy."[30] In Taylor's mind, "the *natural interest* . . . ought exclusively to legislate" within a truly republican society.[31] This was not the case under the Federalists. By means of their program, "Government, though designed to produce national happiness, will be converted by a paper junto simply into a scheme of finance. Instead of dispensing *public welfare*, it will become a credit shop only, to dispense *unequal wealth.*"[32]

Taylor's charge that the Federalists perverted the natural republican order within America by means of self-serving legislation received ample support. In a pamphlet entitled *A Review of the Revenue System Adopted by the First Congress under the Federal Constitution* (Philadelphia, 1794) William Findley, a Republican congressman from western Pennsylvania, saw a "systematic plan for subverting the principles of government" that was creating "an aristocracy formerly unknown in the United States." He wondered if "changing the state of society by a rapid increase of wealth in the hands of a few individuals, to the impoverishing of others, by the artificial aid of the law; the instituting a bank, with an enormous paper capital, and connecting it in such a manner with the government as to be a center of influential, ministerial, and speculating influence; and to promote this influence, filling both Houses of Congress with bank directors or stockholders, [was] a national blessing?" All Findley could see was the creation of a "consolidated government" that would create a "wealthy aristocracy" by means of "the funding system without labor."

In the pages of his newspaper, *The Farmer's Letter,* and his magazine, *The*

Scourge of Aristocracy, William Lyon kept up a constant attack on Federalists and their policies. Lyon had arrived in America from Ireland as an indentured servant, fought with Ethan Allen's Green Mountain Boys, and risen to become a Republican congressman from Vermont. In his mind Federalists constituted "a set of gentry who are interested in keeping the government at a distance and out of the sight of the people who support it."[33] By means of a "phalanx of falsehood and corruption" they intended to foster an "aristocratic junto" bent upon "screw[ing] the hard earnings out of the poor people's pockets for the purpose of enabling the government to pay enormous salaries" and to "vie with European Courts in frivolous gaudy appearances."[34]

Republican leaders in urban areas hammered at these same themes. George Warner, a sailmaker in New York City, declared in a Fourth of July oration in 1797 that all citizens must acquaint themselves with political affairs and keep a vigilant eye on their leaders. He spoke particularly to "tradesmen, mechanics, and the industrious classes of society" who for too long had considered "themselves of TOO LITTLE CONSEQUENCE to the body politic." Far too often voters had been attracted to men of wealth. Instead voters needed to turn to "men of TALENTS and VIRTUE whatever their situation in life may be." If this were not done and the present administration was not altered, "the dividing line between the *rich* and the *poor* will be distinctly marked, and the *latter* will be found in a state of vassalage and dependence on the former."[35]

When Federalists mocked the sorts of ideas Warner expressed, Republican leaders responded with sharp newspaper essays tauntingly signed "one of the swinish multitude" or "only a mechanic and one of the rabble" that berated Federalists as men who "despise mechanics because they have not snored through four years at Princeton."[36] The most adept of the urban Republican authors, Benjamin Austin, articulated the egalitarian distrust of elites forming within the cities in a series of essays published under the title *Constitutional Republicanism in Opposition to Fallacious Federalism* (1803). In these essays Austin declared that governments were "organized for the happiness of the whole people; no exclusive privileges are the birth-right of particular individuals." But under the Federalists "the industrious part of the people" had fallen prey to an "aristocratical junto" and were forced to support "in idleness a set of stock jobbers."

The Republican cause in America gained two articulate spokesmen when the English radicals Thomas Cooper and Dr. Joseph Priestly settled in Northumberland, Pennsylvania, in 1794. Cooper's essays, *Political Arithmetic* (1798) and *Political Essays* (1800), and Priestley's *Letters to the Inhabitants of Northumberland* (1799) became Republican campaign literature in the election of 1800. Both men spoke out in the strongest terms in favor of social, political, and economic freedom.

The most violent attacks on Federalism appeared in the Republican news-papers and periodicals that flourished throughout the 1790s. From the time that Madison and Jefferson established Philip Freneau as the editor of the antiadministration *National Gazette* in 1791, a burgeoning number of Repub-lican editors bluntly attacked Federalist men and measures in direct language aimed at an ever-increasing political constituency.[37] One editor promised his readers to review the history of the United States in such a way as to reveal the "origins, progress and alarming influence of that system in iniquity, rob-bery, bribery, and oppression, hypocrisy and injustice, which may be traced from the attempt of Alexander Hamilton to palm off upon the [Constitu-tional] Convention a monarchical constitution, through the corrupted mazes of funding and banking, stock-jobbing, and speculating systems, down to the alien and sedition laws, standing army and navy of the present day." Another exhorted his fellow Americans to "keep up the cry against Judges, Lawyers, Generals, Colonels, and all other designing men, and the day will be our own." A fellow editor saw American society divided into those who worked and those who "live on the stock of the community, already pro-duced, not by *their labor,* but obtained by their *art* and *cunning.*" In his mind these were "for the most part merchants, speculators, priests, lawyers and men employed in the various departments of government."

How effective Republican rhetoric was in influencing the broader popu-lace is difficult to determine. That its primary themes permeated the thoughts of the untutored Massachusetts farmer, William Manning, is clear. In 1798 Manning addressed a lengthy essay, "The Key to Libberty," to "all the Republicans, Farmers, Mecanicks, and Labourers in America" under the signature of a "Labourer."[38] Claiming to be a "Constant Reader" of newspa-pers, Manning, in a simple, straightforward manner, articulated his percep-tion of the condition of the republic. For him good government meant the protection of life, liberty, and property—a society in which "the poor man's shilling aught to be as much the care of government as the rich man's pound." The failure of free states in the past had always resulted "from the unreason-able demands & desires of the few," who could not "bare to be on a leavel with their fellow creatures, or submit to the determinations of a Lejeslature whare (as they call it) the Swinish Multitude are fairly represented, but sicken at the eydea, & are ever hankerig & striving after Monerca or Aristoc-racy whare the people have nothing to do in maters of government but to seport the few in luxery & idleness."

The assault on Federalism that joined such men as John Taylor of Caro-line, the southern slaveholding planter, Matthew Lyon, the aggressive man on the make on the Vermont frontier, William Findley, the self-made political leader from western Pennsylvania, Benjamin Austin, the urban agitator, the radical British émigrés Joseph Priestley and Thomas Cooper, and the simple

Massachusetts farmer William Manning produced no quintessential Republican. Rather a variety of elements throughout the nation—agrarian and urban entrepreneurs resentful of the power and prestige of urban merchants who controlled the Atlantic trade; ambitious, unconnected individuals no longer willing to defer to entrenched elites; radical republicans innately suspicious of the tyranny of a centralized government; old republicans fearful lest the advent of widespread commercial development bring a loss of American virtue; groups caught up in the egalitarianism spawned by the Revolutionary attack on the corporatism of the old order; independent producers frustrated with the elite control and social restraints characteristic of an ordered, paternalistic hierarchy—joined to form Republican coalitions.

But if Republicanism incorporated a diverse constituency, its adherents spoke a uniform language. Whether urban radicals or southern gentry, they employed similar ideas, principles, and even rhetoric, for their Republicanism incorporated ideas long familiar to Americans into its perception of political and social development. Lockean liberalism and classical republicanism provided the essential underpinning for this political persuasion. For Republicans, though, Locke's concept of individual liberty promoted an affective individualism—a concern for one's fellow citizen and the larger community—rather than the possessive individualism associated with philosophers like Thomas Hobbes. Republicanism thus emphasized the individual but not as a figure freed from social restraints and set against one another and the community.

Such a perception of the individual blended nicely with the Republican belief in the classical republican tenets of virtue and citizenship. In order to protect an always fragile civic virtue, classical republicanism called for vigilant, well-informed, independent citizens to guard against corruption in government—particularly the executive branch—and to maintain private virtue. Individuals found meaning and identity in their lives through service that promoted the common good. Such republicanism saw a constant struggle by advocates of liberty to fend off the forces of power—standing armies, unnecessary and unfair taxes, ministerial influence, special privilege, and corrupt elites. In a word Republicanism instilled a fear of centralization, which came to stand for the corruption of a natural society by an avaricious, corrupt set of government officials intent upon subverting republican society in favor of a ministerial government or aristocracy.

The Republican fusion of liberalism (individual needs) and republicanism (communal values) into a well-integrated cultural system rested upon the insights of the Scottish philosopher Adam Smith. Indeed the Republican persuasion cannot be understood apart from the thought of Adam Smith, particularly his *Inquiry into the Nature and Causes of the Wealth of Nations* (1776).[39] In that book Smith elucidated a mysterious force—an "invisible hand"—working within a free market economy that could foster virtuous community life by transmuting the actions of the least virtuous individual into socially beneficial behavior. Throughout *The Wealth of Nations* Smith sought to establish the viability of a free market economy. He did this not to promote unrestrained self-interest in the ruthless pursuit of wealth but to encourage by means of rational methods man's natural magnanimity that he first posited in *The Theory of Moral Sentiments* (1759). For Smith man was, above all else, a passionate creature motivated principally by an inner drive for self-preservation. Individuals also possessed an innate sympathy for their fellows—an instinctive, irrational desire to share their pain and to feel genuine concern for their welfare. Passion, therefore, and not reason, created all that was beneficial in society. Consequently the good of society resulted not from rational instruction and guidance at the hands of an elite but instead from arranging public policy in such a way as to release every individual's instinctual drives so that they might develop in socially creative directions.

Such philosophic breadth underlay *The Wealth of Nations* and contributed to its popularity. The sharp tone with which Smith presented his message, however, and the conclusions he drew from his philosophic stance accounted for the book's broad appeal and influence. In a brilliant synthesis of economic ideas that were current in the middle of the eighteenth century, Smith provided penetrating observations on the transformations sweeping across the economic and social life of mid-eighteenth-century England. These changes had resulted in great fortunes for some and grinding poverty for many. *Wealth of Nations* offered a trenchant critique of the system that resulted in such maldistribution of wealth and such social disorder.

In Smith's mind British devotion to mercantilism stifled economic growth and created terrible inequities. All this stemmed from a "benevolent" system based on a belief that a wise, disinterested aristocracy knew best how to direct the government so as to produce a vibrant economy and society. In the ostensible interests of producing a greater Britain, those in power created navigation laws, privileged monopolies, bounties, tariffs, and a great variety of excise laws. From Smith's perspective this whole panoply of commercial regulations resulted from the greed and monopolizing impulses of British merchants and manufacturers. Under the guise of promoting national strength and prosperity these groups had gained vast governmental subsidies for commerce and industry. The entire system was not only ridiculous and corrupt but counterproductive as well. Only when Britain removed all commercial restrictions and stultifying mercantile shackles would true prosperity be possible. Trade should be allowed to follow its natural course and not be artificially diverted by subsidies, bounties, and tariffs into channels extremely profitable for a few but seriously damaging to the overall national economy.

A belief that legislators must know their limitations also formed a basic element in Smith's critique. Governments must base their decisions on natural facts and thus enable a "system of natural liberty" (Smith never employed the term *capitalism* or *laissez faire*) to emerge. Any economic system based on natural facts must, above all, take into consideration the human passion for self-preservation. If a national leadership was incapable of creating nation-wide economic programs, individuals in their own more limited environments would always know what policies best suited their interests. A productive society could not result from the government's trying to teach people virtue; it could, however, come to flourish if each citizen's desires could be freed to take whatever direction that individual felt necessary.

To achieve such a free and open society would require a profound change in the social order. Instead of benevolent rule by a "disinterested" elite of wealth, status and education, government would pass into the hands of a natural aristocracy of men who would inevitably emerge from the middle and lower orders once all artificial social and economic restrictions had been removed. Through talent and ability such men would rise to positions of leadership. These men would be peculiarly suited to govern not because of any natural virtues they possessed but because of their ambition, their drive to succeed, and their dogged determination to hang onto whatever they had gained. Each man's drive for achievement served as a counterweight to every other man's and resulted in a balance that prevented anarchy or tyranny. Thus *The Wealth of Nations* offered a clarion call for a pluralistic and entre-preneurial society and state.

Smith's book provided Republicans a grand design for creating a genuine republic in America. Federalist-inspired legislation was corrupting America in the exact manner Smith so graphically described in his analysis of the devastating effects of mercantilism upon English society. Unjust laws di-verted the natural course of trade and commerce in favor of a privileged few at the expense of the larger community. If they wished to preserve a natural order in America, Republicans had no alternative but to oppose the Bank of the United States, a funded debt, excise taxes, tariffs, bounties, and other commercial measures demanded by the Federalists in their effort to repro-duce an aristocratic European culture within the young republic.

More important Adam Smith allowed Republicans to express themselves with a confidence grounded in what they considered to be irrefutable au-thority. In *The Wealth of Nations* Smith articulated inchoate beliefs that had permeated American society for decades. Republican pamphleteers had long employed ideas drawn from Locke and the Commonwealthmen, but Smith harmonized these into a coherent social philosophy. Most of all, though, his ideas integrated the egalitarian and communal impulses of American localism just as they were breaking apart. Citizens could now find community through their own individual efforts. In many ways, then, individualism was becoming the ultimate localism.[40]

The Republican persuasion that evolved in the last decade of the eighteenth century emphasized individual rights as well as popular control of the government.[41] For Republicans the Revolution secured individual autonomy rather than individual freedom. Thus they stressed the affective individualism combining individual independence with moral responsibility to the community so prominent in the thought of John Locke and Adam Smith. At the same time they assumed that the Revolution established for all time that the ultimate decision-making process in government could safely rest with the people. In their minds Federalism threatened these assumptions. American republicanism suffered from the corrupt, aristocratic tendencies of Federalist measures. Rather than their society's being characterized by an open-endedness, where autonomous individuals remained free to change their society for the better, it seemed to be developing in a closed, elitist manner under Federalist control. Consequently Republicans felt they must effect two integrally related revolutions—one economic and one political—both premised on the idea of equality. The first could be accomplished only by expanding commercial opportunities for a larger number of people in such a way as to promote greater prosperity and equality of opportunity. The other demanded the destruction of an elitist, deferential politics in favor of one that fostered the active participation of all men. Within its broadest parameters, then, the Republican persuasion held out the promise to Americans of autonomy as economic individuals and the right to equal political participation as individual citizens.

Republicans worked to create a revolutionary theory of government integrating a program of economic development with a social policy for nation building. Believing that industrious, self-reliant citizens represented the natural economy of America, Republicans made the commercial prosperity of ordinary individuals the primary economic base for a democratic, progressive nation. In their minds a dynamic economy that incorporated the majority of Americans would nurture the release of human potential long held in check by artifical governmental restraints. This belief underlay the Republican conception of a democratic republic: a fusion of economic freedom and politicy democracy.

While most political leaders realized the vast economic potential of America, the critical and divisive issue of the late eighteenth century became how this potential could best be realized. Federalists and Republicans agreed on the need for an effective, unified national government but not on whether that government should become highly centralized through the manipulation by a few citizens of public credit and public funds or should remain open and responsive to the individual needs of ordinary people.

Republicans considered republicanism superior to all other forms of rule because it prevented governments from restraining the free acquisition of wealth. In a republic all citizens should enjoy an equal opportunity to acquire a comfortable livelihood. This would be the case, however, only so long as government did not acquire significant powers to control or influence the economic behavior of its citizens. Here many Republicans voiced the classical libertarian's fear that increasing governmental power inevitably meant encroachments on liberty. The more powerful was the government, the stronger were the exploiters and the weaker the producers. The best hope for a republic remained the constant free access of its citizens to their government and to the means of getting a living. Consequently Republicans firmly believed that republican government endured only so long as opportunities for the acquisition of property remained available to an ever-increasing population. By "property" they almost always meant land. Widespread landholding and the predominance of farming in the economy remained essential to republicanism; they created precisely the sort of individual industriousness that spawned the virtue upon which all republican states depended.

The worldwide demand for grain that emerged in the early national period provided a practical material base upon which to build this vision of America. Rising prices, resulting from an increasing world demand for staples, held out the promise of a flourishing trade in American foodstuffs that could easily be produced on family farms. Rather than stagnating in subsistence farming, the independent husbandman could partake in the spreading economic prosperity. Indeed the prosperity of the ordinary farmer could now become the basis for a democratic, progressive America. Free land, free trade, and scientific advances in agricultural methods spelled progress and prosperity for all Americans, rather than a special few.

In order to support a nation of independent farmers engaged in the commercial exploitation of agriculture, America needed to combine landed and commercial expansion; open markets as well as open space became essential. Commerce, if linked to agricultural surpluses, could become the handmaiden of agriculture and, as a consequence, be moderated by the nation's most virtuous class—its independent, economically secure farmers. To achieve such a political economy required wise political action. Over time Republicans would respond by making land in the national domain readily accessible to the individual farm owner and by dramatically increasing the amount of such land available to future generations. They would employ diplomatic initiatives to open world markets for farm products and commit public funds to internal improvements. At the same time Republicans vigorously opposed fiscal measures that bore unfairly on ordinary taxpayers and that created special privilege and class distinctions. They intended at all times to promote the free competition of individual citizens in an open, competitive marketplace. Their hope that ordinary people might free themselves from economic and political subservience to their social superiors rested on the bright promise of commercial agriculture. Republicans integrated the virtuous yeoman ideal of classical republicanism with Adam Smith's concept of the self-interested individual to form a radical new moral theory of government and society. Fragmenting society into its individual human components, they endowed each with a fundamental economic character and a natural capacity for personal autonomy. They invested the independent producer with the moral qualities long associated with the virtuous citizen extolled by classical republicanism. The purpose of government in such a society was to foster an environment that liberated the individual's self-actualizing capabilities.

Confrontation

The Republican perception of government and society that evolved throughout the 1790s inevitably brought its advocates into conflict with Federalists—thoroughly eighteenth-century-minded men who clung to a traditional belief in hierarchy. For their part Republicans believed that self-interest provided everyone with the capability of making rational decisions regarding individual personal needs; the traditional contention that a gentlemanly elite had a special capacity for governing lost all relevance. Thus, self-interest, as viewed by the Republicans, became a powerful leveling force; it placed all people—ordinary as well as genteel—on the same level of autonomy and competency.

In this regard the emergence of Democratic-Republican societies particularly offended the genteel.[42] One indignant Federalist wrote Alexander Hamilton in 1793 that bands of "banditti-like" people were organizing into societies to express their opposition to Federalist policies. Another characterized a local Democratic society as comprised of "butchers, tinkers, broken hucksters, and trans-Atlantic traitors." Convinced that these societies harbored "the lowest orders of mechanics, laborers and draymen," Federalists took great offense at the presumption of such people to declare it "the unalienable right of free and independent people to assemble together in a peaceable manner to discuss with firmness and freedom all subjects of public concern, and to publish their sentiments to their fellow citizens, when the same shall tend to the public good." An attitude seemed to pervade these societies that all people, no matter what their station in life, should "freely discuss and publish as we do or as they might choose, that the views of each might be made manifest and bear the proper weight with an enlightened and orderly people." Such groups even declared that they preferred such self-created societies "because in them every grade and capacity can furnish something to the general stock of improvement, and because they tend to fraternity, consistence, and due order." The activities of these societies, however, paled in comparison to the Republican newspapers that spewed their venom at will on the genteel.

Federalist gentlemen could accept vituperative attacks on themselves from men of their own social status; this had been an integral part of Anglo-American political life for over a century.[43] To endure such vitriol from social inferiors, however, created indignation and alarm. Under the control of ordinary individuals—Republican editors and members of Democratic societies—such abusive language seriously damaged the public character of governmental leaders and threatened to undermine the entire political order. Convinced of the malicious and traitorous intent of Republican editors, Federalists enacted the Sedition Law (1798) to enable the government to stifle dangerous elements within American society. This law empowered the national government to prosecute for seditious libel any person who criticized federal officals. In addition, the passage of the Alien Acts sought to undercut the support Republicans gained from immigrants by extending the naturalization period for citizenship.[44]

The Sedition Law inaugurated a struggle between Republicans and Federalists that went to the heart of their cultural conflict. Federalists held on to the traditional perception of the universal and constant nature of truth. Truth could always be determined by well-educated, rational men. Republicans argued that a great variety of opinions regarding both the principles of government and elected officials circulated at any time, and their truth or falsity could not be definitively determined by any judge or jury, regardless of how reasonable and intelligent. Thomas Jefferson declared that all opinions, true or false, malicious or benevolent, should be allowed to "stand undisturbed as monuments of the safety with which error of opinion may be tolerated where reason is left free to combat it."[45] Madison echoed these sentiments when he observed that "some degree of abuse is inseparable from the proper use of every thing"; consequently it was "better to leave a few of its noxious branches, to their luxuriant growth, than by pruning them away, to injure the vigor of those yielding the proper fruits."[46]

Such sentiments left Federalists incredulous. The notion that all free individuals should be allowed to voice their opinions, no matter how scandalous or abusive, remained beyond their ken. Republicans, who had come to believe that a gentlemanly elite no longer had an exclusive right to voice political opinions, not only believed that true and false statements should be tolerated equally but that all members of society should be equally free to articulate them. Instinctively Republican theorists viewed public opinion in the same manner as the free market economy; just as an invisible hand led a variety of competitors in the marketplace to promote an end that was not part of the conscious intent of any of those involved, so too might the efforts of a great variety of individual minds—intellectual competitors in a free market—create an end result, public opinion, that was not the conscious creation of any single group or individual but rather sprang spontaneously from the collective efforts of all.

By 1800 the cultural forces of the previous decades were becoming clearly delineated. Federalists staunchly defended the traditional past, and Republicans championed an optimistic, open-ended future. Federalists, in spite of their promotion of overseas commerce and a national banking structure, remained skeptical of the emergence of a liberal society, with its culture of self-restrained ambition. They adhered to a paternalistic world of hierarchy and social order that prompted them to view the emergence of the self-made man with a mixture of fear and disdain. Their encouragement of commercial growth remained entrenched within traditional channels as well. While playing a major role in the expansion of the Atlantic trade that took place in the 1790s, they remained inclined to justify their efforts in the customary and limited terms of mercantilism; expanding profits among merchant groups would revitalize and thereby perpetuate the existing social structure and thus strengthen the republic's chances in the international struggle for survival. Their progressive economic programs were meant to reinforce a conservative social world.

In opposition to Federalism the followers of Thomas Jefferson called on the egalitarian spirit of Revolutionary republicanism to protect society from dangers they perceived in Federalist control of government: the corruption of American society emanating from detestable Old World court politics, the social inequities resulting from a mercantilist political economy, and the artifical and unfair restraints imposed by an elitist, paternalistic society. Republicans held out the promise of a dynamic republic of independent producers, a nation in which hard-working individuals—farmers, artisans, mechanics, and entrepreneurs—would be able to attain economic independence and thereby strengthen their capacity to fulfill their role of virtuous political citizens. They offered the vision of a virtuous republic in which a limited government would respect the political integrity and influence of independent citizens, where social freedom would allow autonomous individuals the free exercise of their talents, and where a political economy based on increasing production and territorial expansion would reward the industry and energy of the independent producer. Against the paternalistic and centralized power represented by the Federalists, the Republicans pitted their image of individual opportunity and social mobility. They endowed their political economy of self-interest with the same moral force to bind the community together that they bestowed on a social order comprised of autonomous individuals. Independent producers would be the backbone of a virtuous nation. Their vision, grounded in the optimistic hope that the seemingly limitless resources of their young nation could support the prosperity of all citizens, promised an equal commitment to material and moral progress under a government where the ultimate authority for all decision making rested with the sovereign people. With the victory of Thomas Jefferson in 1800, Republicans committed the nation to support individual autonomy and popular sovereignty. In this dual commitment lay the roots of modern American democracy.

Epilogue

The kind of society that would emerge from the democratic roots being formed in the late eighteenth century was unclear in 1800. Even by that time the perception of personal autonomy and individual self-interest had become so inextricably intertwined that few Republicans had any clear comprehension of the entrepreneurial and capitalistic nature of the social forces shaping their lives.[1] Under the pressure of rapidly changing socioeconomic conditions the autonomous republican producer—integrally related to the welfare of the larger community—gradually underwent a subtle transmutation into the ambitious self-made man set against neighbors and community alike. Ironically eighteenth-century republican traditions formed a fertile seedbed within which nineteenth-century liberal commitments to possessive individualism, a competitive ethos, and economically self-interested politics would flourish.

By incorporating as its own the dynamic spirit of a market society and translating it into a political agenda, Republicanism had developed a temper and a momentum that would carry it beyond its original goals. Even by 1800 personal independence no longer constituted a means by which to ensure virtue; it had itself become the epitome of virtue. This transformation was invariably complex, quite often confused, and more often than not gave rise to unintended consequences. Its ultimate outcome resulted nonetheless in profound changes in American culture in the nineteenth century.

Republicanism created the social, political, and cultural framework within which the nineteenth-century liberal commitments to interest group politics, materialistic and utilitarian strivings, and unrestrained individualism emerged. Simultaneously, however, Republicanism also fostered a rhetoric of selfless virtue that obscured the direction in which society was moving.

By promoting the desire for unrestrained enterprise indirectly through an appeal to popular virtue, Republicanism helped produce a nation of capitalists blind to the spirit of their enterprise. Consequently the Republican movement enabled Americans to continue to define their purpose as the pursuit of traditional virtue while actually devoting themselves to the selfish pursuit of material wealth. Irresponsible individualism and erosive factionalism replaced the independent producer's commitment to the common good. Still, the free enterpriser, who by the 1850s would include publicly chartered business corporations, fell heir to the Republican belief that an independent means of production attached individual interests to the good of the commonwealth. Entrepreneurial fortunes became an investment in the general welfare, and the entrepreneur, freed by the American belief in virtuous independence, could proceed unencumbered by self-doubts, secure in the belief, attributed to Thomas Jefferson, that "the public good is best promoted by the exertion of each individual seeking his *own* good in his own way."

For a brief period—a "Jeffersonian moment"—following the Republican triumph in 1800, the virtues of republicanism and eighteenth-century liberalism were integrated into a cohesive political philosophy offering the bright promise of equal social and economic advancement for all in a land of abundance.[2] That the moment was brief stands less as a critique of the individuals who combined to bring Jefferson to the presidency than it is a comment on the forces that impelled them: forces over which they had little control and, perhaps, even less understanding. The ideology that had emerged finally translated the realities of the American environment into a coherent social philosophy. But those very realities would carry American society far beyond the original goals of the Jeffersonian movement as they transmuted eighteenth-century American republicanism into nineteenth-century American democracy.

Notes and References

Chapter One

1. Quoted in Harold James Perkin, *The Origins of Modern English Society, 1780–1880* (London: Routledge & Kegan Paul, 1969), 25.

2. Quoted in Henry F. May, *The Enlightenment in America* (New York: Oxford University Press, 1976), 27.

3. Quoted in Philip J. Greven, Jr., *The Protestant Temperament: Patterns of Child-Rearing, Religious Experience, and the Self in Early America* (New York: Alfred A. Knopf, 1977), 296.

4. Gordon Wood, "The Democratization of Mind in the American Revolution," in *Leadership in the American Revolution* (Washington, D.C.: Library of Congress, 1974), 63–88.

5. Quoted in ibid., 67.

6. May presents a provocative analysis of the "Moderate Enlightenment" in *Enlightenment in America*.

7. Gordon Wood, "Social Radicalism and Equality in the American Revolution," in *The B. K. Smith Lectures in History* (Houston: University of Houston Press, 1976), 5–14; Richard L. Bushman, "'This New Man': Dependence and Independence, 1776," in Richard Bushman et al., *Uprooted Americans: Essays to Honor Oscar Handlin* (Boston: Little, Brown, 1979), 79–93; Richard L. Bushman, *King and People in Provincial Massachusetts* (Chapel Hill: University of North Carolina Press, 1985); and May, *Enlightenment in America*.

8. Quoted in Gary B. Nash, *The Urban Crucible: Social Change, Political Consciousness, and the Origins of the American Revolution* (Cambridge, Mass.: Harvard University Press, 1979), 263.

9. My presentation of the localism of the outlivers rests on the insights of Kenneth Lockridge, *Settlement and Unsettlement: The Crisis of Political Legitimacy before the Revolution* (London: Cambridge University Press, 1981).

10. Quoted in ibid., 42.

11. Quoted in William G. McLoughlin, *New England Dissent, 1630–1833* (Cambridge, Mass.: Harvard University Press, 1971), 1:337.

12. Rhys Isaac, *The Transformation of Virginia, 1740–1790* (Chapel Hill: University of North Carolina Press, 1982).

13. Quoted in Kenneth Lockridge, *A New England Town: The First Hundred Years*, expanded ed. (New York: W. W. Norton, 1985), 187.

14. Quoted in Richard L. Bushman, *Puritan to Yankee: Character and the Social Order in Connecticut, 1690–1765* (Cambridge, Mass.: Harvard University Press, 1967), 252.

15. Quoted in ibid., 257.

16. No attempt is made to present a definitive treatment of social unrest in the mid-eighteenth century. Rather, these three phenomena are offered as representative examples of unrest spawned by localistic impulses within the colonies.

17. Quoted in James P. Whittenburg, "Planters, Merchants, and Lawyers: Social Change and the Origins of the North Carolina Regulators," *William and Mary Quarterly*, 3d series, 34 (1977):215–38. The quotation appears on 236.

18. Quoted in Charles Jellison, *Ethan Allen: Frontier Rebel* (Syracuse: Syracuse University Press, 1969), 34.

19. Lockridge, *Settlement and Unsettlement*, 104.

Chapter Two

1. Jack P. Greene, *The Quest for Power: The Lower Houses of Assembly in the Southern Royal Colonies, 1689–1776* (Chapel Hill: University of North Carolina Press, 1973).

2. Quoted in Wood, "The Democratization of Mind," 71.

3. My discussion of urban tensions rests on the insights of Nash, *Urban Crucible.*

4. Quoted in ibid., 297.

5. These quotations appear in ibid., 304–5.

6. My treatment of Concord rests on Robert A. Gross, *The Minutemen and Their World* (New York: Hill & Wang, 1976).

7. The following discussion draws from Rhys Isaac, "Evangelical Revolt: The Nature of the Baptists' Challenge to the Traditional Order in Virginia, 1765–1775," *William and Mary Quarterly*, 3d ser., 31 (1974):345–68.

8. Gordon Wood presents a provocative examination of the strains present in Virginia society in his "Rhetoric and Reality in the American Revolution," *William and Mary Quarterly*, 3d ser., 23 (1966):3–32. My discussion of the Virginia gentry incorporates Wood's insights.

9. These quotations appear in ibid., 28.

10. These quotations appear in ibid., 29.

11. Kenneth Lockridge, "Social Change and the Meaning of the American Revolution," *Journal of Social History* 6 (1973):403–39.

12. See Joyce Appleby, "Liberalism and the American Revolution," *New England Quarterly* 49 (1976):3–26, and Jack P. Greene, "The Social Origins of the American Revolution: An Evaluation and an Interpretation," *Political Science Quarterly* 88 (1973):1–22.

13. Bernard Bailyn offers a stimulating analysis of the sources of American Revolutionary thought, as well as its ideological implications, in *The Ideological Origins of the American Revolution* (Cambridge, Mass.: Harvard University Press, 1967). Bailyn's work informs my discussion of this thought.

14. These quotations appear in Pauline Maier, *From Resistance to Revolution: Colonial Radicals and the Development of American Opposition to Britain, 1765–1776* (New York: Alfred A. Knopf), 21–22.

15. Quoted in Bailyn, *Ideological Origins*, 50.

16. Gordon Wood presents a brilliant analysis of the development of American republicanism in *The Creation of the American Republic, 1776–1787* (Chapel Hill: University of North Carolina Press, 1969). My discussion draws upon this work, as well as Wood's introduction to *The Rising Glory of America* (New York: George Braziller, 1971).

17. These quotations appear in Wood, *Rising Glory*, 6–7.

18. Lockridge presents an excellent analysis of these "needs" in "Social Change and the Meaning of the American Revolution." This essay informs my discussion of the manner in which various elements within American society viewed the Revolution.

19. My discussion of these isolated, localistic people draws upon Lockridge, *Settlement and Unsettlement*.

20. Isaac Kramnick offers an insightful analysis of this middle-class impetus in his "Republican Revisionism Revisited," *American Historical Review* 87 (1982):629–64. Kramnick's work informs my discussion of this literature.

21. Charles Royster, *A Revolutionary People at War* (Chapel Hill: University of North Carolina Press, 1979).

Chapter Three

1. Quoted in Joseph J. Ellis, *After the Revolution: Profiles of Early American Culture* (New York: W. W. Norton, 1979), 5.

2. Quoted in ibid., 7.

3. Quoted in ibid., 25.

4. Quoted in Kenneth Silverman, *A Cultural History of the American Revolution* (New York: Columbia University Press, 1976), 454–55, 460.

5. Quoted in Neil Harris, *The Artist in American Society: The Formative Years, 1790–1860* (New York: George Braziller, 1966), 33.

6. Quoted in ibid., 34.

7. Quoted in ibid., 37.

8. My discussion of John Trumbull rests on the analysis of Irma Jaffe, *John Trumbull, Patriot-Artist of the American Revolution* (New York: New York Graphic Society, 1975).

9. Quoted in ibid., 59.

10. Quoted in ibid., 66.

11. Quoted in Silverman, *Cultural History*, 462.

12. Quoted in Jaffe, *John Trumbull*, 88.

13. My discussion of Peale draws on Ellis's excellent analysis in *After the Revolution*.

14. Quoted in ibid., 70.

15. The following discussion of Billings depends upon the insights of Silverman in his *Cultural History.*

16. Quoted in ibid., 203.

17. Quoted in ibid., 398.

18. Quoted in ibid., 400.

19. Quoted in ibid., 229.

20. Quoted in ibid., 230.

21. Quoted in May, *Enlightenment in America*, 187. May's work provides excellent insight into the life and work of the Wits.

22. Quoted in Alexander Cowie, *John Trumbull, Connecticut Wit* (Chapel Hill: University of North Carolina Press, 1936), 174–75.

23. Quoted in Silverman, *Cultural History*, 514.

24. Quoted in ibid., 515.

25. Quoted in Arthur L. Ford, *Joel Barlow* (New York: Twayne Publishers, 1971), 109.

26. Quoted in Silverman, *Cultural History*, 565.

27. My analysis of Brackenridge draws on Ellis's perceptive evaluation in *After the Revolution.*

28. Quoted in ibid., 88.

29. Quoted in ibid., 98.

30. Hugh Henry Brackenridge, *Modern Chivalry*, ed. Claude M. Newlin (New York: American Book Co., 1937), 21.

31. Quoted in Ellis, *After the Revolution*, 100.

32. Quoted in Silverman, *Cultural History*, 549.

33. Royall Tyler, *The Contrast* (New York: Dunlap Society, 1887), 35–36.

34. Quoted in Silverman, *Cultural History*, 562.

35. My discussion of Dunlap rests on Ellis's insights in *After the Revolution.*

36. Quoted in ibid., 116.

37. Quoted in David Grimsted, *Melodrama Unveiled: American Theatre and Culture, 1800–1850* (Chicago: University of Chicago Press, 1968), 3.

38. Quoted in Ellis, *After the Revolution*, 143.

39. Neil Harris employs this phrase in his description of American Culture in "The Making of an American Culture: 1750–1800," in Charles Montgomery and Patricia Kane, eds., *American Art: 1750–1800 Towards Independence* (Boston: New York Graphic Society, 1976), 22–31.

Chapter Four

1. Quoted in Willi Paul Adams, *The First American Constitutions: Republican Ideology and the Making of the State Constitutions in the Revolutionary Era* (Chapel Hill: University of North Carolina Press, 1980), 61.

2. Quoted in Merrill Jensen, *The Articles of Confederation: An Interpretation of the Social-Constitutional History of the American Revolution, 1774–1781* (Madison: University of Wisconsin Press, 1940), 61.

3. Quoted in John R. Howe, Jr., *The Changing Political Thought of John Adams*

(Princeton: Princeton University Press, 1966), 65, 66.

4. Quoted in Wood, *Creation of the American Republic* 355.

5. Quoted in ibid., 355.

6. Quoted in Jackson Turner Main, *The Anti-Federalists: Critics of the Constitution, 1781–1788* (Chapel Hill: University of North Carolina Press, 1961), 15–16.

7. Quoted in Jensen, *Articles of Confederation*, 216.

8. Quoted in Adams, *First American Constitutions*, 287.

9. Quoted in Wood, *Creation of the American Republic*, 359.

10. Gordon Wood presents a brilliant discussion of the changes taking place in American attitudes toward government in his *Creation of the American Republic*. The following discussion draws on his insights.

11. Quoted in ibid., 281.

12. Quoted in Howe, *John Adams*, 84.

13. Quoted in Lockridge, *Settlement and Unsettlement*, 111.

14. Gordon Wood analyzes the effects of these developments upon late eighteenth-century American society in "Interests and Disinterestedness in the Making of the Constitution," in Richard Beeman et al., *Beyond the Confederation: Origins of the Constitution and American National Identity* (Chapel Hill: University of North Carolina Press, 1987), 69–109. His insights illuminate the following discussion.

15. Jackson Turner Main, *The Sovereign States, 1775–1783* (New York: Franklin Watts, 1973).

16. My analysis of divisions within the states depends on the insights of Jackson Turner Main's *Political Parties before the Constitution* (Chapel Hill: University of North Carolina Press, 1973).

17. The terms *cosmopolitan* and *localist* were not employed at the time. They are the creation of Jackson Turner Main in ibid.

18. Quoted in ibid., 401–2.

19. The following discussion draws on Wood, *Creation of the American Republic*. The quotations appear on 482–83.

20. Quoted in Wood, "Interests and Disinterestedness," 75. Wood's essay informs my discussion of the fears of gentlemen.

21. Quoted in ibid., 76.

22. Quoted in Wood, *Creation of the American Republic*, 410, 413.

23. Quoted in ibid., 429.

24. Quoted in ibid., 467.

25. James Madison, "Vices of the Political System of the United States," in William T. Hutchinson et al., eds., *The Papers of James Madison* (Chicago: University of Chicago Press, 1962–), 9:348–57. The quotation appears on 357.

26. Quoted in Lance Banning, "The Practicable Sphere of a Republic: James Madison, the Constitutional Convention, and the Emergence of Revolutionary Federalism," in Beeman, *Beyond the Confederation*, 162–87. The quotations appear on 186.

27. *Federalist* No. 10 printed in Marvin Meyers, ed., *The Mind of the Founder: Sources of the Political Thought of James Madison* (Indianapolis: Bobbs-Merrill, 1973), 122–31. The quotation appears on 124.

28. Ibid., 126.

29. Ibid., 130–31.

30. Quoted in Wood, *Creation of the American Republic*, 477.

31. Wood employs these terms to describe the conflict between Federalists and Anti-federalists in his *Creation of the American Republic*. His insights inform my discussion of the conflict over the Constitution.

32. Quoted in Main, *Antifederalists*, 131, 132–33, 134.

33. Quoted in ibid., 132.

34. The above quotations appear in Cecilia M. Kenyon, *The Antifederalists* (Indianapolis: Bobbs-Merrill, 1966), 48, 55–56, 383.

35. Quoted in ibid., 1.

36. Quoted in Wood, "Interests and Disinterestedness," 100. Wood's analysis underlies my discussion of Findley and Anti-federalism.

37. Quoted in ibid., 100, 101–2.

Chapter Five

1. Rush to Richard Price, 25 May 1786, in Lyman H. Butterfield, ed., *Letters of Benjamin Rush* (Princeton: Princeton University Press, 1951), 1:388.

2. Quoted in Brooke Hindle, *The Pursuit of Science in Revolutionary America* (Chapel Hill: University of North Carolina Press, 1956), 253.

3. "On the Education of Youth in America," in Noah Webster, *A Collection of Essays and Fugitive Writings* (Boston, 1790), 36.

4. Quoted in May, *Enlightenment in America*, 193.

5. Quoted in Carl Kaestle, *Pillars of the Republic: Common Schools and American Society, 1780–1860* (New York: Hill & Wang, 1983), 6.

6. Webster, Essays, 24.

7. Ibid.

8. Ibid., 17–18.

9. Ibid., 25–26.

10. Quoted in Kaestle, *Pillars of the Republic*, 9.

11. Manning's *The Key to Libberty* is reprinted in Samuel Eliot Morrison, "William Manning's *The Key to Libberty*," *William and Mary Quarterly*, 3d series, 13 (1956):202–54. The following quotations appear on 221, 231, 232.

12. Quoted in Kaestle, *Pillars of the Republic*, 7.

13. Webster, *Essays*, 16.

14. Quoted in Wood, *Rising Glory of America*, (1971), 22.

15. Quoted in Ellis, *After the Revolution*, 211–12, 161.

16. Quoted in David J. Rothman, *The Discovery of the Asylum: Social Order and Disorder in the New Republic* (Boston: Little, Brown, 1971), 59. Rothman's work informs my discussion of American perceptions of crime.

17. Quoted in ibid., 61.

18. These quotations appear in William E. Nelson, *Americanization of the Common Law: The Impact of Legal Change on Massachusetts Society, 1760–1830* (Cambridge, Mass.: Harvard University Press, 1975), 68, 145. The following discussion of law in America draws on this book, as well as Morton J. Horwitz, *The Transformation of American Law, 1780–1860* (Cambridge, Mass.: Harvard University Press, 1977).

19. Quoted in Horwitz, *Transformation of American Law*, 2.

20. Quoted in ibid., 3.

21. Quoted in ibid., 28.

22. The following discussion draws primarily on Linda K. Kerber, *Women of the Republic: Intellect and Ideology in Revolutionary America* (Chapel Hill: University of North Carolina Press, 1980); Mary Beth Norton, *Liberty's Daughters: The Revolutionary Experience of American Women, 1750–1800* (Boston: Little, Brown, 1980); and Jan Lewis, "The Republican Wife: Virtue and Seduction in the Early Republic," *William and Mary Quarterly* 3d series, 44 (1987):689–721.

23. Webster, *Essays*, 16.

24. My analysis of American attitudes toward Indians depends primarily on Bernard W. Sheehan, *Seeds of Extinction: Jeffersonian Philanthropy and the American Indian* (Chapel Hill: University of North Carolina Press, 1973).

25. Quoted in ibid., 171.

26. My observations regarding the impact of liberal society upon the Indian and the theme of regeneration through violence rest on the insights of Michael P. Rogin, *Fathers and Children: Andrew Jackson and the Subjugation of the American Indian* (New York: Alfred A. Knopf, 1975), and Richard Slotkin, *Regeneration Through Violence: The Mythology of the American Frontier, 1600–1860* (Middleton, Conn.: Wesleyan University Press, 1973).

27. Quoted in Robert E. Shalhope, "The Armed Citizen in the Early Republic," *Law and Contemporary Problems* 49 (1986):140.

28. Sheehan, *Seeds of Extinction*, 277.

29. My analysis of slavery and the black man within American society draws primarily on Winthrop D. Jordon, *White over Black: American Attitudes toward the Negro, 1550–1812* (Chapel Hill: University of North Carolina Press, 1968), and David B. Davis, *The Problem of Slavery in the Age of Revolution, 1770–1823* (Ithaca: Cornell University Press, 1975).

30. Quoted in Davis, *Problem of Slavery*, 264.

31. My discussion of the emergence of republican thought in Virginia and its relationship to slavery incorporates the insights of Edmund S. Morgan, *American Slavery American Freedom: The Ordeal of Colonial Virginia* (New York: W. W. Norton, 1975).

32. Quoted in ibid., 384.

33. Jordan, *White over Black*, 581–82.

34. For an analysis of the influence of ideology and the manner in which it affects thought and action, see Robert E. Shalhope, "Thomas Jefferson's Republicanism and Antebellum Southern Thought," *Journal of Southern History* 42 (1976):529–56.

Chapter Six

1. Quoted in Nathan O. Hatch, "The Christian Movement and the Demand for a Theology of the People," *Journal of American History* 67 (1980):545–67. The quotations appear on 563–64.

2. Quoted in Maxwell Bloomfield, *American Lawyers in a Changing Society, 1776–1876* (Cambridge, Mass.: Harvard University Press, 1976), 42.

3. Quoted in ibid., 57.

4. Sean Wilentz employs this term to describe the emerging ideology of workers in the late eighteenth century. Wilentz, *Chants Democratic: New York City and the*

Rise of the Working Class, 1788–1850 (New York: Oxford University Press, 1984). The following discussion draws on Wilentz's perceptive insights.

5. Quoted in ibid., 70.

6. My discussion of religious thought draws on the provocative analyses of Gordon Wood, "Evangelical America and Early Mormonism," *New York History* 41 (1980):360–86, and Hatch, "Christian Movement."

7. Quoted in Hatch, "Christian Movement," 554n.

8. Quoted in Robert E. Shalhope, *John Taylor of Caroline: Pastoral Republican* (Columbia: University of South Carolina Press, 1980), 72.

9. John Taylor, *An Inquiry into the Principles and Tendency of Certain Public Measures* (Philadelphia, 1794), 7.

10. Quoted in Lance Banning, *The Jeffersonian Persuasion: Evolution of a Party Ideology* (Ithaca, N.Y.: Cornell University Press, 1978), 150.

11. Henceforth *Republican* denotes the political party forming in opposition to the Federalists, while *republican* refers to the political philosophy shared by most Americans.

12. Quoted in Banning, *Jeffersonian Persuasion*, 192.

13. My discussion of Federalism draws principally on David H. Fischer, *The Revolution of American Conservatism: The Federalist Party in the Era of Jeffersonian Democracy* (New York: Harper & Row, 1965), and James M. Banner, Jr., *To the Hartford Convention: The Federalists and the Origins of Party Politics in Massachusetts, 1789–1815* (New York: Alfred A. Knopf, 1970).

14. Quoted in Fischer, *Revolution*, 3–5.

15. Quoted in ibid., 5.

16. Jonathan Jackson, *Thoughts upon the Political Situation* (Worcester, Mass., 1788), 27, 58.

17. Nathaniel Chipman, *Sketches of the Principles of Government* (Rutland, Vt., 1793), 42.

18. Quoted in Fischer, *Revolution*, 17.

19. Quoted in Banner, *To the Hartford Convention*, 77.

20. Quoted in ibid., 77.

21. Quoted in Linda Kerber, *Federalists in Dissent: Imagery and Ideology in Jeffersonian America* (Ithaca, N. Y.: Cornell University Press, 1970), 21.

22. Quoted in Banner, *To the Hartford Convention*, 78.

23. John R. Howe, Jr., discusses Adams's thought in his *The Changing Political Thought of John Adams* (Princeton: Princeton University Press, 1966). See particularly 133–55.

24. Jackson, *Thoughts*, 164–65.

25. Quoted in John Zvesper, *Political Philosophy and Rhetoric: A Study of the Origins of American Party Politics* (New York: Cambridge University Press, 1977), 49.

26. Quoted in ibid., 49–50.

27. John Cartwright, *Take Your Choice! Representation and Respect: Imposition and Contempt* (London, 1776), 21; James Burgh, *Political Disquisitions* (London, 1774), 2:89–90.

28. George Logan, *Letters Addressed to the Yeomanry of the United States* (Philadelphia, 1791). The quotations appear on 32, 11.

29. Taylor, *An Enquiry*, 7.

30. "Franklin" essay printed in the *Philadelphia National Gazette*, 2 March 1793.

31. Taylor, *Enquiry*, 56.

32. John Taylor, *Definition of Parties, or the Political Effects of the Paper System Considered* (Philadelphia, 1794), 10.

33. Quoted in Aleine Austin, *Matthew Lyon: "New Man" of the Democratic Revolution, 1749–1822* (University Park: Pennsylvania State University Press, 1981), 80.

34. *Scourge of Aristocracy* 1 (1798):21; 2 (1798):46–47.

35. George Warner, *Means for the Preservation of Political Liberty* (New York, 1797), 13–14.

36. Quoted in Alfred Young, "The Mechanics and the Jeffersonians: New York, 1789–1801," *Labor History* 5 (1964), 247–76. The quotation appears on 274.

37. The following quotations appear in Donald H. Stewart, *The Opposition Press of the Federalist Period* (Albany: State University of New York Press, 1969), 103, 389, 390.

38. This essay, which was sent to the *Independent Chronicle* in Boston, was never published by that paper. It is printed in its entirety in Morison, "William Manning's *The Key to Libberty*," 202–54. The quotations appear on 211, 217, 220.

39. The following discussion of Adam Smith rests principally on Joseph Cropsey, *Polity and Economy: An Interpretation of the Principles of Adam Smith* (The Hague: Nijhoff, 1957), and Robert Kelley, *The Transatlantic Persuasion: The Liberal-Democratic Mind in the Age of Gladstone* (New York: Alfred A. Knopf, 1969).

40. Lockridge argues this in *Settlement and Unsettlement*.

41. My analysis of the Jeffersonian movement draws on the work of Joyce Appleby, *Capitalism and a New Social Order: The Republican Vision of the 1790s* (New York: New York University Press, 1984); Drew McCoy, *The Elusive Republic: Political Economy in Jeffersonian America* (Chapel Hill: University of North Carolina Press, 1978); and Zvesper, *Political Philosophy*.

42. The following quotations appear in Philip S. Foner, ed., *The Democratic-Republican Societies, 1790–1800* (Westport, Conn.: Greenwood Press, 1970), 3, 7, 8, 11, 26.

43. The following discussion of the struggle between Federalists and Republicans over the Alien and Sedition Laws draws on Wood, "Democratization of Mind," 63–88.

44. John C. Miller, *Crisis in Freedom: The Alien and Sedition Acts* (Boston: Little, Brown, 1951); James M. Smith, *Freedom's Fetters: The Alien and Sedition Laws and American Civil Liberties* (Ithaca: Cornell University Press, 1956).

45. Quoted in Wood, "Democratization," 81.

46. *The Kentucky-Virginia Resolutions and Mr. Madison's Report of 1799* (Richmond, 1960), 63.

Epilogue

1. Steven Watts offers provocative insights into the dynamic nature of early nineteenth-century American culture in *The Republic Reborn: War and the Making of Liberal America, 1790–1820* (Baltimore: Johns Hopkins University Press, 1987). I have

drawn upon Watts's work in my analysis of nineteenth-century republicanism.

2. James Kloppenberg presents a brilliant analysis of this moment in his "The Virtues of Liberalism: Christianity, Republicanism, and Ethics in Early American Political Discourse," *Journal of American History* 74 (1987):9–33. I am indebted to Kloppenberg for my understanding of late eighteenth-century republicanism and liberalism.

Bibliographic Essay

This bibliography is not intended to be a comprehensive or a definitive treatment of late eighteenth-century American culture and thought. Rather, it is meant to offer suggestions to those interested in reading further. I have included books and essays that helped shape my own analysis and that I believe will provide helpful insights to readers seeking greater depth in particular subjects.

A number of books and essays deal with the cultural and intellectual transformations taking place throughout the last half of the eighteenth century. Particularly helpful are Gordon S. Wood's "The Democratization of Mind in the American Revolution," in *Leadership in the American Revolution* (Washington, D.C.: Library of Congress, 1974), 63–88; "Social Radicalism and Equality in the American Revolution," in *The B. K. Smith Lectures in History* (Houston: University of Houston, 1976), 5–14; "Rhetoric and Reality in the American Revolution," *William and Mary Quarterly*, 3d ser. 23 (1966):3–32; and his introduction to *The Rising Glory of America, 1760–1820* (New York: George Braziller, 1971). Other essays that offer provocative analytic insights include Kenneth Lockridge, "Social Change and the Meaning of the American Revolution," *Journal of Social History* 6 (Summer 1973):403–39; Joyce Appleby, "Liberalism and the American Revolution," *New England Quarterly* 49 (March 1976):3–26; Richard Bushman, "'This New Man': Dependence and Independence, 1776," in Richard Bushman et al., *Uprooted Americans: Essays to Honor Oscar Handlin* (Boston: Little, Brown, 1979), 79–95; Jack P. Greene, "Search for Identity: An Interpretation of Selected Patterns of Social Response in Eighteenth-Century America," *Journal of Social History* 3 (Spring 1970):189–224; Jack P. Greene, "The Social Origins of the American Revolution: An Evaluation and an Interpretation," *Political Science Quarterly* 87 (1973):1–22; and John M. Murrin, "The Great Inversion, or Court versus Country: A Comparison of the Revolution Settlements in England (1688–1721) and America (1776–1816)," in J. G. A. Pocock, ed., *Three British Revolutions: 1641, 1688, 1776* (Princeton: Princeton University Press, 1980), 368–453. Richard Bushman presents an excellent analysis of how a monarchical culture rested upon a republican society in his *King and People in Provincial Massachusetts* (Chapel Hill: University of North Carolina, 1985).

Works dealing with republicanism have multiplied greatly over the past several decades. Caroline Robbins, *The Eighteenth-Century Commonwealthman: Studies in the Transmission, Development and Circumstances of English Liberal Thought from the Restoration of Charles II until the War with the Thirteen Colonies* (Cambridge: Harvard University Press, 1959) and J. G. A. Pocock, *The Machiavellian Moment: Florentine Political Thought and the Atlantic Republican Tradition* (Princeton: Princeton University Press, 1975), present an outstanding picture of the evolution of republican ideas. Two books that provide the sharpest insight into the form that republican ideas assumed in America are Bernard Bailyn's *The Ideological Origins of the American Revolution* (Cambridge: Harvard University Press, 1967), and Gordon S. Wood's magisterial accomplishment, *The Creation of the American Republic, 1776–1787* (Chapel Hill: University of North Carolina Press, 1969). Several essays furnish additional insights into republicanism's impact within America. These include Joyce Appleby, "Republicanism and Ideology," *American Quarterly* 37 (Fall 1985):461–73; Linda Kerber, "The Republican Ideology of the Revolutionary Generation," *American Quarterly* 37 (Fall 1985):474–95; and Robert Kelley, "Ideology and Political Culture from Jefferson to Nixon," *American Historical Review* 80 (June 1977):531–62. For comprehensive surveys of the literature on republicanism as well as analysis of its impact within American society, see Robert E. Shalhope, "Toward a Republican Synthesis: The Emergence of an Understanding of Republicanism in American Historiography," *William and Mary Quarterly*, 3d series, 29 (January 1972):49–80 and "Republicanism and Early American Historiography," *William and Mary Quarterly*, 3d series, 39 (April 1982):334–56. Isaac Kramnick, "Republican Revisionism Revisited," *American Historical Review* 87 (June 1982):629–64, and John P. Diggins, *The Lost Soul of American Politics: Virtue, Self-Interest, and the Foundations of Liberalism* (New York: Basic Books, 1984), question the centrality of republicanism in favor of a far more liberal intellectual and cultural milieu in the period, while James Kloppenberg presents a brilliant analysis of liberal and republican thought in his "The Virtues of Liberalism: Christianity, Republicanism, and Ethics in Early American Political Discourse," *Journal of American History* 74 (1987):9–33. The work of Henry F. May, *The Enlightenment in America* (New York: Oxford University Press, 1976), and Donald H. Meyer, *The Democratic Enlightenment* (New York: G. P. Putnam's Sons, 1976), provides excellent discussions of the broader intellectual framework within which republicanism developed.

The clearest discussion of the tension between localism and hierarchy within colonial America appears in Kenneth Lockridge, *Settlement and Unsettlement: The Crisis of Political Legitimacy before the Revolution* (New York: Cambridge University Press, 1981). Jackson Turner Main provides a provocative analysis of the struggle between localists and cosmopolitans in his *Political Parties before the Constitution* (Chapel Hill: University of North Carolina Press, 1973). For insights into this tension in specific locales, see David Szatmary, *Shays' Rebellion: The Making of an Agrarian Insurrection* (Amherst: University of Massachusetts Press, 1980); Thomas P. Slaughter, *The Whiskey Rebellion: Frontier Epilogue to the American Revolution* (New York: Oxford University Press, 1986); and James P. Whittenburg, "Planters, Merchants and Lawyers: Social Change and the Origins of the North Carolina Regulators," *William and Mary Quarterly*, 3d ser., 34 (1977):215–38.

Works dealing with religion in the late eighteenth century are legion. Those that I have found most helpful in delineating the cultural tensions of the period include Nathan O. Hatch, *The Sacred Cause of Liberty: Republican Thought and the Millennium in Revolutionary New England* (New Haven: Yale University Press, 1977); Richard L. Bushman, *From Puritan to Yankee: Character and the Social Order in Connecticut, 1690–1765* (Cambridge: Harvard University Press, 1967); Rhys Isaac, "Evangelical Revolt: The Nature of the Baptists' Challenge to the Traditional Order in Virginia, 1765–1775," *William and Mary Quarterly*, 3d series, 31 (1974):345–68; Isaac, "Preachers and Patriots: Popular Culture and the Revolution in Virginia," in Alfred Young, ed., *The American Revolution: Explorations in the History of American Radicalism* (DeKalb: Northern Illinois University Press, 1971), 125–56; Isaac, *The Transformation of Virginia, 1740–1790* (Chapel Hill: University of North Carolina Press, 1982); William G. McLoughlin, *New England Dissent, 1630–1833*, 2 vol. (Cambridge: Harvard University Press, 1971). Essays that are particularly helpful in understanding the religious changes taking place in the late eighteenth century and the early nineteenth century include Harry Stout, "Religion, Communications, and the Ideological Origins of the American Revolution," *William and Mary Quarterly*, 3d ser., 34 (1977):519–41; Gordon Wood, "Evangelical America and Early Mormonism," *New York History* 61 (1980):360–86; Nathan Hatch, "The Christian Movement and the Demand for a Theology of the People," *Journal of American History* 67 (1980):545–67; and Hatch, "New Lights and Revolution in Rural New England," *Reviews in American History* 8 (1980):323–28.

Research dealing with urban culture in the Revolutionary and early national periods is also growing enormously. The work that I have found most useful includes Gary Nash, *The Urban Crucible: Social Change, Political Consciousness, and the Origins and the American Revolution* (Cambridge: Harvard

University Press, 1979); Robert A. Gross, *The Minutemen and Their World* (New York: Hill and Wang, 1976); Eric Foner, *Tom Paine and Revolutionary America* (New York: Oxford University Press, 1976); and Sean Wilentz, *Chants Democratic: New York City and the Rise of the American Working Class, 1788–1850* (New York: Oxford University Press, 1984).

The sharpest insight into the arts in this era comes from Kenneth Silverman, *A Cultural History of the American Revolution* (New York: Columbia University Press, 1987), and Joseph J. Ellis, *After the Revolution: Profiles of Early American Culture* (New York: W. W. Norton, 1979). Also helpful are Neil Harris, *The Artist in American Society: The Formative Years, 1790–1860* (New York: George Braziller, 1966), and Irma B. Jaffe, *John Trumbull: Patriot-Artist of the American Revolution* (Boston: New York Graphic Society, 1975).

With respect to the development of republican governments, scholars are deeply indebted to Gordon Wood's brilliant *The Creation of the American Republic, 1776–1787*. Wood establishes the frame of reference that provides the clearest insight into American thought about government in this era. J. R. Pole, *Political Representation in England and the Origins of the American Republic* (New York: St. Martin's Press, 1966) and *The Pursuit of Equality in American History* (Berkeley: University of California Press, 1978); Willi Paul Adams, *The First American Constitutions: Republican Ideology and the Making of the State Constitutions in the Revolutionary Era* (Chapel Hill: University of North Carolina Press, 1980); and Jackson Turner Main's *Political Parties before the Constitution* and *The Anti-Federalists: Critics of the Constitution, 1781–1788* (Chapel Hill: University of North Carolina Press, 1961) provide important analyses of political development in the late eighteenth century. An outstanding collection of essays published in Richard Beeman et al., *Beyond Confederation: Origins of the Constitution and American National Identity* (Chapel Hill: University of North Carolina Press, 1987), offers provocative insights into thought about government and society.

The emergence of a multifaceted "republican culture" provides fascinating reading. The best introduction to American attitudes about crime and punishment may be found in David J. Rothman, *The Discovery of the Asylum: Social Order and Disorder in the New Republic* (Boston: Little, Brown, 1971). The changing nature of the law is the focus of three provocative books: Maxwell Bloomfield, *American Lawyers in a Changing Society, 1776–1876* (Cambridge: Harvard University Press, 1976); William E. Nelson, *Americanization of the Common Law: The Impact of Legal Change on Massachusetts Society, 1760–1830* (Cambridge: Harvard University Press, 1975); and Morton J. Horwitz, *The Transformation of American Law, 1780–1860* (Cambridge: Harvard University Press, 1977). The best insight into the role of education in a republican culture may be found in Lawrence A. Cremin, *American Education: The National Experience* (New York: Harper & Row, 1980), and Carl Kaestle, *Pillars of the Republic: Common Schools and American Society, 1780–1860* (New York:

Hill and Wang, 1983). Linda Kerber's *Women of the Republic: Intellect and Ideology in Revolutionary America* (Chapel Hill: University of North Carolina Press, 1980) and Mary Beth Norton's *Liberty's Daughters: The Revolutionary Experience of American Women, 1750–1800* (Boston: Little, Brown, 1980) are outstanding studies of the role of women in this era. My analysis of American attitudes toward Indians draws upon Bernard W. Sheehan, *Seeds of Extinction: Jeffersonian Philanthropy and the American Indian* (Chapel Hill: University of North Carolina Press, 1973); Michael Paul Rogin, *Fathers and Children: Andrew Jackson and the Subjugation of the American Indian* (New York: Alfred A. Knopf, 1975); and Richard Slotkin, *Regeneration through Violence: The Mythology of the American Frontier, 1600–1860* (Middletown: Wesleyan University Press, 1973). For American attitudes towards blacks and slavery, I have relied primarily upon three outstanding books: David B. Davis, *The Problem of Slavery in the Age of Revolution, 1770–1823* (Ithaca: Cornell University Press, 1975); Winthrop D. Jordan, *White over Black: American Attitudes toward the Negro, 1550–1812* (Chapel Hill: University of North Carolina Press, 1968); and Edmund S. Morgan, *American Slavery and American Freedom: The Ordeal of Colonial Virginia* (New York: W. W. Norton, 1975).

My approach to the political unrest of the 1790s as a manifestation of the larger cultural tensions of the era rests on two essays: Ronald P. Formisano, "Deferential-Participant Politics: The Early Republic's Political Culture, 1789–1840," *American Political Science Review* 68 (1974):473–87, and Robert E. Shalhope, "Southern Federalists and the First Party Syndrome," *Reviews in American History* 8 (March 1980):45–51. Two books provide an excellent introduction to the cultural and ideological tensions of the era. They are John Zvesper's *Political Philosophy and Rhetoric: A Study of the Origins of American Party Politics* (New York: Cambridge University Press, 1977) and Richard Buell, Jr., *Securing the Revolution: Ideology and American Politics, 1789–1815* (Ithaca: Cornell University Press, 1972). The best understanding of the cultural milieu of the Federalists emerges from a reading of David H. Fischer, *The Revolution of American Conservatism: The Federalist Party in the Era of Jeffersonian Democracy* (New York: Harper & Row, 1965); James M. Banner, Jr., *To the Hartford Convention: The Federalists and the Origins of Party Politics in Massachusetts, 1789–1815* (New York: Alfred A. Knopf, 1970); and Linda Kerber, *Federalists in Dissent: Imagery and Ideology in Jeffersonian America* (Ithaca: Cornell University Press, 1970). For insights into the Jeffersonians as a cultural movement, see Drew R. McCoy, *The Elusive Republic: Political Economy in Jeffersonian America* (Chapel Hill: University of North Carolina Press, 1980); Lance Banning, *The Jeffersonian Persuasion: Evolution of a Party Ideology* (Ithaca: Cornell University Press, 1978); and Joyce Appleby, *Capitalism and a New Social Order: The Republican Vision of the 1790s* (New York: New York University Press, 1984).

Historians are just beginning to focus on the transformations that republicanism underwent in the first decade of the nineteenth century. Several authors do, however, offer outstanding analyses of this period. Steven Watts presents a brilliant treatment of the manner in which republican and liberal attitudes intertwined in the years 1790–1820 in his *The Republic Reborn: War and the Making of Liberal America, 1790–1820* (Baltimore: Johns Hopkins University Press, 1987). Rowland Berthoff offers a provocative analysis of the transmutation of republican attitudes throughout the early nineteenth century in two insightful essays: "Independence and Attachment, Virtue and Interest: From Republican Citizen to Free Enterpriser, 1787–1837," in Bushman et al., *Uprooted Americans*, 99–124, and "Peasants and Artisans, Puritans and Republicans: Personal Liberty and Communal Equality in American History," *Journal of American History* 69 (1982):579–598. These authors provide excellent starting points for the study of American thought and culture in the nineteenth century.

Index